RODALE'S
SUCCESSFUL ORGANIC GARDENING™
LANDSCAPING
WITH PERENNIALS

RODALE'S
SUCCESSFUL ORGANIC GARDENING™
LANDSCAPING
WITH PERENNIALS

TEXT BY ELIZABETH STELL

"PERENNIALS FOR EVERY PURPOSE" BY C. COLSTON BURRELL

Rodale Press, Emmaus, Pennsylvania

Copyright © 1995 by Weldon Russell Pty Ltd

If you have any questions or comments concerning this book, please write to:

Rodale Press
Book Readers' Service
33 East Minor Street
Emmaus, PA 18098

Library of Congress Cataloging-in-Publication Data

Stell, Elizabeth.
 Landscaping with perennials / text by Elizabeth Stell ; perennials for every purpose by C. Colston Burrell.
  p.   cm. — (Rodale's successful organic gardening)
 Includes index.
  ISBN 0–87596–663–2 hardcover — ISBN 0–87596–664–0 paperback
  1. Perennials. 2. Landscape gardening. 3. Organic gardening.
  I. Burrell, C. Colston. II. Title. III. Series.
SB434.S77 1995
635.9'3284—dc20   94–34274
                                                      CIP

Produced by Mandarin Offset, Hong Kong
Printed in Hong Kong on acid-free ⊗ paper

Rodale Press Staff:
 Executive Editor, Home and Garden Books: Margaret Lydic Balitas
 Editor: Nancy J. Ondra
 Copy Editor: Carolyn R. Mandarano
 Editor-in-Chief: William Gottlieb

Produced for Rodale Press by Weldon Russell Pty Ltd
107 Union Street, North Sydney NSW 2060, Australia
a member of the Weldon International Group of Companies

 President: Elaine Russell
 Publisher: Karen Hammial
 Managing Editor: Ariana Klepac
 Editorial Assistant: Cassandra Sheridan
 Horticultural Consultant: Cheryl Maddocks
 Copy Editor: Yani Silvana
 Designer: Rowena Sheppard
 Finished Artists: Trevor Hood, Rachel Smith
 Picture Researcher: Elizabeth Connolly
 Illustrators: Tony Brit-Lewis, Barbara Rodanska
 Indexer: Michael Wyatt
 Production Manager: Dianne Leddy

A KEVIN WELDON PRODUCTION

Distributed in the book trade by St. Martin's Press

2 4 6 8 10 9 7 5 3 1 hardcover
2 4 6 8 10 9 7 5 3 1 paperback

Opposite: *Salvia farinacea* and *Rudbeckia* sp.
Half title: *Aurinia saxatilis* and *Muscari* sp.
Opposite title page: *Stachys byzantina* and *Veronica* sp.
Title page: *Veronica* sp. and *Paeonia officinalis* 'Rubra'
Opposite contents: *Monarda didyma* cultivar
Contents: *Aster* sp. (left) and *Hemerocallis* 'Black Magic' (right)
Back cover: *Echinacea purpurea* (bottom)

CONTENTS

INTRODUCTION

Growing perennials is a fun and easy way to add color and beauty to any landscape. From the bright hues of early bulbs to fall's purple asters, these plants provide an endless variety of flowers and forms in an ever-changing display throughout the growing season. Some evergreen perennials can even provide interest in winter.

Unlike annuals, you don't have to replant perennials every year; these beauties come back on their own. They are cheaper than most trees and shrubs, and they're simple to move or replace if you want to change the look of your yard. Perennials are dependable and easy choices for beginners, and they come in enough variety to satisfy the most experienced gardeners.

Perennials look grand grouped into individual beds and borders, but they're also wonderfully flexible tools for decorating all parts of your landscape. Small perennials can decorate a deck or patio; others are large enough to screen your view of unsightly objects such as trash cans that you don't want to see from the patio. Depending on where you place your perennials, you can make a small yard seem bigger or divide a large yard into intimate, comfortable spaces. A winding path lined with foliage plants or flowers can create a bit of mystery and lead people to a seat in the shade or a wonderful view. By landscaping with perennials, you'll increase the value of the house and yard to yourself and those living with you; this also translates into a real increase in property value.

From planning your landscape through planting and maintenance, *Rodale's Successful Organic Gardening: Landscaping with Perennials* tells you what you need to know to create a beautiful yard. You'll learn how to develop perennial plantings that thrive with minimal care. You'll discover great ways to use perennials to turn difficult sites—including slopes, wet spots, and shady areas—into eye-catching landscape features. And you'll find out how to organize your perennials into unique themes—perhaps a cottage garden, a butterfly garden, or a fragrant garden—to provide loads of colorful flowers and foliage you can enjoy indoors and out. Once you start adding perennials to your yard, you'll immediately begin to enjoy the beauty and versatility of these easy-care plants.

Whether you want year-round color, flowers for cutting, meadows for wildlife, cottage gardens for casual beauty, or low-maintenance plants for easy care, there's a variety of wonderful perennials for you to choose from.

HOW TO USE THIS BOOK

Whether you are starting your first garden or redoing an existing one, *Rodale's Successful Organic Gardening: Landscaping with Perennials* will guide you through the entire process of creating a great-looking perennial landscape. You'll find lots of ideas and inspiring photos to help you decide what you want from your property and which perennials will meet your particular needs.

For your plants to look their best, you must put them in the right place. In "Learning about Your Landscape," starting on page 12, you'll learn to understand the different growing conditions your yard has to offer: the amounts of sun and shade, the kind of soil you have, and the different kinds of topography. You'll also find out how your climate can affect your perennial choices.

Turn to "Planning Your Perennial Landscape," starting on page 22, and you'll discover how to turn your dreams into actual designs. The little time you spend on planning will save you from spending more time rearranging plants and moving entire flower beds. This chapter also gets you thinking about your particular gardening goals—the easiest way to focus your decisions and assure that you get what you want. Plus you'll get tips on how to combine plants, new ideas for how to use perennials in your yard, and several ways to add interest to your landscape in every season.

Once you know what you want, you're ready for the nitty-gritty of "Growing Your Perennial Landscape," starting on page 36. This chapter tells you how to buy vigorous plants and bulbs and how to prepare the planting site for good future growth. You'll learn the simple maintenance tasks—from pinching to pruning to staking—that keep your garden looking good after you plant. With this chapter's quick review of common

pests and diseases, you'll be able to identify and safely control most common problems that can pop up.

If you know or discover that your growing conditions are less than ideal, turn to "Solving Landscape Problems with Perennials," starting on page 54. You'll find out why perennials make smart solutions for spots that are too steep, too shady, or too wet for lawns. Tired of those boring clipped evergreens in front of your house? Learn how to replace or accent them with colorful, easy-care perennials. This chapter also includes tips on planning any perennial planting for low maintenance.

When you're ready to get beyond the basics and look for new ideas, turn to "Perennial Gardens for Every Site," starting on page 68. Expand your horizons with these pictures and descriptions of fun garden themes you may never have seen or considered. Whether your passion is herbs or scented flowers, meadows or butterflies, cut flowers or container gardens, you'll find out which of the plants described in this volume are best for each type of garden.

Plant-by-Plant Guide

The second half of this book, "Perennials for Every Purpose," is an encyclopedia of great plants you can grow. This section, starting on page 86, lists 130 reliable, easy-to-grow perennials that don't require a lot of fussing. Many are great for all-around use—others are especially good for particular sites and purposes, such as bog gardens and cut flowers. Use this section to discover new plants you'd like to try or to help you narrow down your plant choices.

Each entry gives the specific information you need to decide if a particular plant will be happy in your yard. The "Season of Interest" information will help you plan for a continuous display of flowers. The descriptions of landscape uses and compatible companions will also prove invaluable for your garden planning.

These individual plant entries are alphabetized by botanical names. If you're looking for a particular plant and aren't sure of its botanical name, look up the common name in the index; the cross-reference will tell you just where to turn. The diagram below will show you where to look for important information on these handy encyclopedia pages.

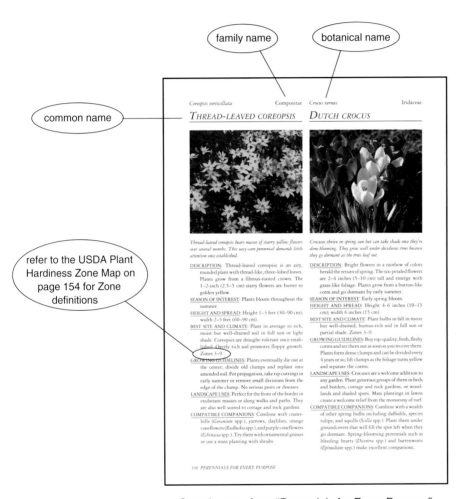

Sample page from "Perennials for Every Purpose"

LEARNING ABOUT YOUR LANDSCAPE

To have a great-looking landscape, you need to choose perennials that are naturally well adapted to your growing conditions. And the key to selecting the right plants is spending some time to get to know your yard. Even if you've lived in the same house for years, you may never have thought about what kind of soil you have or about how and when sunlight reaches different parts of the yard. These two factors will have a large effect on which plants will thrive for you. You'll also need to take into account whether your yard is sloping or flat and what kind of temperatures and rainfall your area normally receives.

This chapter will guide you through the steps to learning about your site and summarizing what you've learned into a permanent plot plan. You can start at any time of year (although you won't be able to study your soil when the ground is frozen).

Good soil is the backbone of any garden. Perennials growing in hard, nutrient-poor soil simply won't grow to their potential. Fortunately, soil isn't too difficult to understand. A simple squeeze test will tell you a lot about your soil's texture, and a professional soil test (or a complete home test kit) can tell you what you need to know about nutrient levels. "Study Your Soil" on page 14 will tell you just what you need to know about your soil to grow great-looking perennials.

Your climate also has a great effect on which perennials will thrive in your garden year after year. Since part of the benefit of growing perennials is not having to replant each year, you want to make sure that your plants can survive the winter conditions of your area. Few things are as disappointing as carefully tended perennials that don't make it through the winter! Cold tolerance isn't the only factor you'll have to consider, however. Some plants need cool or humid summers to thrive; others may rot away in the humidity of the deep South. "Consider Your Climate" on page 16 will help you learn as much as you can about the climate in your area, so you won't be struggling with weak, sickly plants that can't take your conditions.

The exposure (shade and sun) of your yard will influence which perennials can thrive in a particular spot. Most plants are somewhat flexible in the light levels they can tolerate, but some have very particular needs. Plants that don't get enough light grow tall and spindly and don't bloom well; shade-lovers growing in too much sun may turn brown and crispy. "Examine Your Exposure" on page 18 will help you determine how much sun and shade you have in different parts of your yard, so you can choose plants that grow well in the amount of light available.

As you investigate the different features of your yard, also notice its shape, or topography. A flat site is easy to work on, but it may not drain well if it is surrounded by higher ground. Slopes can be more challenging to plant, but they do tend to be well drained. "Think about Topography" on page 20 will help you locate possible drainage problems and find which spots are most sheltered from frost.

Once you've learned all of these things about your yard, it's a good idea to record your observations, as explained in "Create a Site Map" on page 21. That way, you'll be able to see at a glance what conditions you're dealing with in each part of the property. Then you'll be able to plan a practical, easy-care landscape and choose the best possible perennials for your particular site.

The secret to growing perennials and bulbs successfully is choosing plants that can take the growing conditions you have to offer. Many bulbs, for instance, thrive in sun and average soil but languish in dark or wet sites.

Study Your Soil

Before you start planning and planting, invest a little time in learning about your soil. Once you know what soil conditions your yard has to offer, you can choose perennials that will grow and thrive there for years to come. Your hands, a trowel to dig up a little soil, and a simple soil test kit are all you need to get a basic picture of what's going on in the earth beneath your feet.

What's Up Down Below

Up until now, you may have thought that all soil was pretty much the same. But when you start looking at it more closely, you'll find that even soils that look the same can have very different traits. These traits will determine which perennials will thrive on a particular site.

Professional Tests for Professional Results

While you can buy complete soil test kits at most garden centers, it's easier and less expensive, as well as more precise, to have your soil tested by a laboratory. Contact your local Cooperative Extension Service or nearest state agricultural college to find out how to collect and send the sample and how much it will cost for the test. Allow at least 1 month for processing time in spring, when the labs are busiest. Fall is a great time to get your soil tested, as you'll get the results more quickly. Retest every 5 years.

Soil Texture Almost all soils are made up of three basic mineral components: sand grains, somewhat smaller silt particles, and extremely fine clay particles. The relative amounts of these three mineral particles determine the texture of your soil.

You can get a very basic idea of your soil's texture by doing a simple test: Just take a handful of moist soil, squeeze it, and match the results you get with one of the points below.

- If the soil won't stay in a clump in your open hand, it's on the sandy side.

Thrift will tolerate poor sandy soil that drains quickly.

Once you know the soil conditions your site has to offer, you can choose perennials and bulbs that thrive there.

- If the soil forms a loose clump that breaks apart when you tap it lightly with your finger, it's a loam—a balanced mixture of sand, silt, and clay that's ideal for many garden plants.
- If the soil forms a sticky lump that you can mold into various shapes, it's high in clay.

Soils that have lots of sand are said to be light or sandy. Light soils lose water and dissolved nutrients quickly, so they tend to be dry and infertile. Loamy soils usually drain well but hold enough water and nutrients for good plant growth. Heavy (clayey) soils tend to hold a lot of water and nutrients, but they can be waterlogged when wet and hard when dry.

There isn't any practical way to change the texture of your soil. You can, however, improve the soil's structure to make it more suitable for the perennials you want to grow.

Soil Structure Structure refers to how the sand, silt, and clay particles in your soil stick together. Many small, crumb-like clumps create ample space for the air and water that roots need to grow well. Tight, compacted soils have

Cardinal flower thrives in rich, evenly moist soil.

Adding organic matter helps sandy soil to hold water and fertilizer and improves drainage in clayey soil.

little or no structure, making them hard for you to dig and hard for the roots of your perennials to grow through. Loose sandy soils with little structure lose water and nutrients quickly.

Organic matter provides the basic materials that help to clump the soil particles together. To improve and maintain good soil structure, work in generous amounts of compost before planting, and use organic mulches like chopped leaves to keep the soil well stocked with organic matter.

Understanding Organic Matter

Organic matter and humus are essential parts of healthy soil. Organic matter is the "fresh" dead material that gets added to the soil, such as fallen leaves and grass clippings. As soil organisms feed on the organic matter, they break it down into nutrients, which your plants can use, and humus. Humus forms loose connections between soil particles and gives the soil a good crumbly structure. It acts like a sponge to hold water and nutrients where roots can absorb them.

Adding ample quantities of organic matter—in the form of compost, chopped leaves, or similar materials—will help to improve just about any kind of soil.

Knowing about Nutrients

Soil with lots of organic matter is called "rich" because it holds ample reservoirs of nutrients. The big three plant nutrients are nitrogen (N), phosphorus (P), and potassium (K). (The 5-10-5 or 5-10-10 listed on bags of fertilizer is the percentage of these three chemical elements [N-P-K].)

Plants need nitrogen to grow healthy green leaves and to regulate the use of other nutrients. Phosphorus helps form healthy roots and flowers; it also strengthens resistance to pests. Potassium also promotes strong roots and general resistance, but it's important in photosynthesis as well.

Plants need several other nutrients, such as iron and calcium, in smaller quantities. Soils with ample amounts of organic matter usually contain enough nutrients to keep many kinds of perennials thriving. But you'll also need to make sure your soil is at the right pH so those nutrients will be available to your plants.

A soil test can tell you whether your soil is acid or alkaline and if the supply of different nutrients is adequate for growing perennials. The results of a professional soil test will also tell you exactly what to add to correct any nutrient deficiencies.

Peonies grow best in soil that's enriched with organic matter.

Puzzling Out pH

Plant nutrients tend to be most available to roots when the soil pH is near neutral (around 6.5 to 7.0). When the soil is either very acid (with a lower pH) or alkaline (with a higher pH), some nutrients form chemical compounds that make them unavailable to your plants. A home test kit (which you can buy at a garden center) or a professional soil test can tell you what pH your soil has. Balance acid soils by adding lime and alkaline soils by adding sulfur. Your test kit or results sheet should tell you how much to apply.

Sandy soil is usually dry and infertile.

Clay is nutrient-rich but drains poorly.

Loamy soil tends to be moist and fertile.

Consider Your Climate

To have healthy, vigorous perennials that will grow and thrive year after year with minimal care, you need to choose plants that are well adapted to your climate.

If you've lived in the same area for many years, you already know a lot about your climate, even if you've never applied it to gardening. If you're new to an area, you'll have to ask local gardeners or do a bit of research to find out about the conditions in your region. It's worth a little effort, since you'll save yourself the time, money, and aggravation of coping with poorly adapted perennials that don't make it through more than one or two seasons.

Understanding Hardiness Zones

Start learning about your climate by finding out what hardiness zone you live in. You'll find a copy of the USDA Plant Hardiness Zone Map on page 154. This map divides the country into many different zones, based on average minimum yearly temperatures.

If you buy plants that are reportedly hardy in your zone, you can be fairly confident that those plants will survive an average winter in your area. To really be on the safe side, you may want to stick with plants that are hardy to at least one zone colder than yours. If you live in Zone 6, for instance, you can depend on perennials that are hardy to Zones 4 or 5.

Hostas are durable, dependable perennials that can adjust to either warm- or cold-climate gardens.

You'll find that the plant entries in this book and in many other books and catalogs give a range of hardiness zones—such as "Zones 5 to 8"—for a particular plant. That's because cold temperatures aren't the only factor that determines if a plant will grow well in an area; heat can have a great effect, too. The upper limit of a plant's hardiness range will give you an idea of what kind of summer temperatures that plant can tolerate. If a plant is listed as hardy in Zones 5 to 8, for example, you could grow it in Zones 5, 6, 7, and 8; Zones 4 and lower would probably be too cold, and Zones 9 and 10 could be too hot.

Learning about Local Weather

Hardiness zones are helpful for narrowing down your plant choices, but they aren't foolproof guidelines. If you live in a large town or city, for instance, your area may be significantly warmer than the hardiness map would predict. Higher elevations and open, exposed areas may get a little colder than other properties in the same zone. In cold areas, consistent snow cover provides fabulous insulation and may allow you to grow plants from warmer zones.

Knowing when and how much it rains in your area is very important if you want to choose plants that won't demand regular watering. As a broad rule of thumb, most perennials need about 1 inch (25 mm) of rain each week during the growing season. If your area doesn't get enough rain during the crucial growing months, you'll lose plants unless you spend a lot of time watering or switch to water-wise landscaping (as explained in "Tough Perennials for Hot, Dry Sites" on page 65).

Wind can make your climate more severe than you

Evergreen perennials, such as bergenias, offer winter interest in climates that don't have heavy snow cover.

Sedums and other late-blooming perennials can still look good through the first few frosts of fall.

walls, solid fences, or hedges. In exposed areas with cold winter winds and no consistent snow cover, choose plants that are rated for at least one zone colder than yours to be on the safe side. Or, if you're willing to go to the extra trouble, you could cover plants that are normally adapted to your zone with a generous layer of branches (or chopped leaves) for winter protection.

Managing Microclimates

Now that you understand your local climate, look at your yard to see what different microclimates it contains. A microclimate is simply a relatively uniform climate in a small area. For instance, the microclimate beneath a large, old oak tree is significantly cooler (as well as much shadier) than a sunny patch of ground on the other side of the same yard. Slightly sunken areas can catch water that has drained off higher parts of the yard, allowing you to grow

Long-stemmed flowers like delphiniums are prone to wind damage.

moisture-loving perennials such as astilbes and primroses without extra watering.

think. As you spend time in your yard, observe which direction the wind usually comes from. Is your yard exposed to strong winds, or is it fairly sheltered by trees, buildings, or hills? Strong winds may quickly dry out plants and erode bare soil. When it's cold, winds can draw water out of exposed plant tops and roots faster than it can be replaced, leading to severe damage or death. Wind can be an asset in very humid climates, where good air circulation becomes more important to prevent the development of plant diseases.

Where winds are strong or frequent, protect your gardens by locating them on the sheltered side of

You'll find more tips on identifying microclimates under "Examine Your Exposure" on page 18 and "Think about Topography" on page 20. Keep notes on your observations about different sites in your yard. Each year, as you learn more and more about the different areas of your garden, you'll be able to fine-tune your planting schemes to take even greater advantage of these special microclimates.

Cool-loving primroses will thrive and spread in a shady microclimate, such as this one at the base of a tree.

A fence can block or reduce the force of strong winds, so your plants are less likely to be blown over.

The amount of sun your yard receives can vary through the day. Consider this factor as you plan your plantings.

Examine Your Exposure

Exposure refers to the amount of sun and shade your yard receives throughout the day. The exposure of different places on your property can vary widely, depending on where each garden is in relation to the house and to other shade-casting features such as trees and fences.

South-facing Sites

Locating a garden on the south side of your house (or a wall or fence) provides the maximum amount of light in the Northern Hemisphere. In cool Northern summers, many sun-loving perennials thrive against a south wall. But where summers are hot, all but the most heat- and drought-tolerant perennials may bake against south walls because of the high temperatures there.

Eastern Exposures

Many perennials thrive with an eastern exposure, such as that along the eastern edge of woods, on the east side of a steep hill, or against an east-facing wall. Plants on these sites receive up to a half day of direct light, and they're sheltered from the hot afternoon sun. This protection from strong afternoon rays prolongs bloom time where summers are hot. When you read a description that suggests afternoon shade for a particular plant—such as lady's-mantle (*Alchemilla mollis*), cranesbills (*Geranium* spp.), or Japanese anemone (*Anemone* x *hybrida*)—try an eastern exposure.

West-facing Sites

Western exposures are a challenge for plants. The site is generally cool and shady in the morning, but the temperature can change dramatically when strong sun hits it during the warmest part of the day. Shade-loving perennials generally don't handle such extremes well; their leaves may turn brown or off-color.

In the North, the temperature differences between morning and afternoon may be moderate enough not to harm plants, especially if a tree, fence, or outbuilding casts a little shade there in the afternoon.

In Southern gardens, try tough, drought-tolerant perennials that can take sun or partial shade, including blue false indigo (*Baptisia australis*), boltonia (*Boltonia asteroides*), Cupid's dart (*Catananche caerulea*), cushion spurge (*Euphorbia epithymoides*), daylilies (*Hemerocallis* spp.), common sundrops (*Oenothera tetragona*), patrinia (*Patrinia scabiosifolia*), and violet sage (*Salvia* x *superba*).

Northern Exposures

A garden set against a north-facing wall or fence or on the north side of a steep hill receives much less light and remains cool throughout the day. If the site is open (without large trees or buildings to the east or west), it will probably still be bright. A bright,

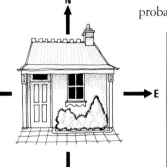

evenly cool spot is ideal for most shade-loving plants; even those preferring full shade should grow well here. Try flowering and foliage perennials such as hostas, ferns, and lungworts (*Pulmonaria* spp.).

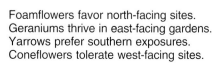

Foamflowers favor north-facing sites. Geraniums thrive in east-facing gardens. Yarrows prefer southern exposures. Coneflowers tolerate west-facing sites.

Lady's-mantle thrives in a spot with morning sun and afternoon shade; an eastern exposure is ideal.

Spots under deciduous trees are sunny until late spring, providing ideal conditions for early bulbs and wildflowers.

Understanding Sun and Shade

Identifying the direction that your property faces will give you a general idea of the growing conditions you have to offer. But unless you have a flat, featureless lot, you'll also have to consider the shade cast by trees, shrubs, fences, hedges, trellises, buildings, and other structures.

How do you tell if a particular spot has full sun, partial shade, or full shade? Watch the spot regularly over the course of a day (check on it every hour or so), and note each time you look whether the spot is sunny or shady. Any site with less than 6 hours of direct sunlight is shady. Perennials that prefer full sun need 6 hours or more of direct sunlight to grow well. A site that receives a few hours of morning or late afternoon sun, but no direct midday sun, is described as having partial shade. Many perennials that prefer full sun will tolerate partial shade.

A generally bright site that receives little direct sun but lots of filtered or reflected light is said to have light or dappled shade. Typically, this kind of shade occurs beneath high-branched deciduous trees (such as honey locusts [*Robinia pseudoacacia*]) that don't cast solid shadows. Full, dense, or deep shade is darker, and fewer plants grow well in it. The area under hemlocks or other evergreens is in deep shade all year long. Plants growing under maples, beeches, and other densely branched deciduous trees are in full shade most of the summer.

Keep in mind that shade changes during the year, both because the angle of the sun changes in the sky and because deciduous trees grow and shed their leaves. A site that appears sunny on July 1 may be shaded by a nearby tree or building in April or October when the sun is much lower in the sky.

The deep shade under a maple or oak disappears when the tree loses its leaves, and the ground below stays bright until mid- to late-spring. Many spring wildflowers, including bluebells (*Mertensia virginica*) and foamflowers (*Tiarella* spp.), have adapted to take advantage of this temporary sun and bloom before the overhead trees leaf out. Spring-blooming bulbs such as daffodils, which go dormant by the time the trees are fully leafed out, are also a good choice. Even if your yard is deeply shaded the rest of the season, you can probably enjoy masses of color in the spring and beautiful green and patterned foliage the rest of the year. For more specific advice on landscaping shady sites, turn to "Succeeding in Shade" on page 60.

Japanese anemones usually thrive in sun, but they appreciate some afternoon shade in hot climates.

Think about Topography

Is your yard flat or on the side of a hill? Or does it contain gradual ups and downs that you only notice when you're pushing a lawn mower? The shape of your land will effect your growing conditions and landscaping options.

Gardening on Flat Sites

If your yard is completely flat or at the bottom of a slope, check for drainage problems. After a heavy rain, do puddles always form in the same spot? Puddles indicate poor drainage that you'll need to correct (by adding lots of organic matter or building raised beds) in order to grow most perennials well. Or you may choose to turn those sites into moist meadows or bog gardens designed around perennials that like wet feet, including cardinal flowers (*Lobelia cardinalis*), ligularias (*Ligularia* spp.), rodgersias (*Rodgersia* spp.), and marsh marigolds (*Caltha palustris*).

Even if puddles don't form, check the soil after several days with no rain. Squeeze a handful; if the soil is still sticky and wet, you'll know it doesn't drain well. The same low spots that often don't drain well tend to be the first hit by frost and the last to warm up in the spring.

Coping with Slopes

Sloping sites rarely have the drainage problems that can plague flat sites, but they present their own challenges. Note which direction your slope faces; as explained under "Examine Your Exposure" on page 18, slopes facing different directions have different microclimates. Hilltops may be exposed to winds, so their microclimate is often more severe than protected areas on the sheltered side of the same hill.

Marsh marigolds demand constantly moist or wet soil, so they're perfect along streams or in soggy sites.

Gentle slopes are an asset in planting and maintaining an attractive landscape. They drain well, add visual interest, and are generally easy to mow or to garden on. Steep slopes are hard to plant, weed, or mow, and bare soil tends to wash off them in heavy rains.

If you want to (or have to) garden on a slope, you can do it—it just takes some planning. Consider building terraces to create a stepped series of level areas for easy planting and maintenance. See "Handling Hillsides" on page 58 for landscaping solutions that convert steep slopes from headaches to lovely, low-maintenance features.

If you have a steep slope, build terraces or a retaining wall to reduce the grade and make a usable planting area.

Ligularias look their best with steady soil moisture, so plant them in low spots where water tends to collect.

Create a Site Map

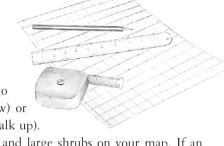

The easiest way to record everything you've learned about your site—the soil conditions, drainage, exposure, slope, and microclimates—is by making a site plan. It will show you the factors you'll need to consider when planning which perennials you can grow and where you can put them. The more accurate your plan, the more useful it will be.

You'll need just a few simple tools: a 50- or 100-foot (15 or 30 m) tape measure, graph paper, a pencil, and a ruler. A second person is a big help. If you're by yourself, you may find measuring easier with a long (100 foot [30 m]) length of string tied to a short, pointed stake at each end.

Start with a survey map of your property. If you don't have one, draw a rough outline of the yard to scale; 1 inch (2.5 cm) on paper for each foot (30 cm) of garden space is a good scale for most gardens. Locate north with a compass or from a local street map, and indicate it on your map. Draw outlines of your house, driveway, paths, and patios. Also sketch in sheds or garages, plus fences, hedges, and existing gardens.

Mark significant topographical features on your map, too. Include low areas (and whether or not they are wet) and hilltops as well as large boulders. Note which direction slopes face and whether slopes are gentle (easy to walk up or mow) or steep (hard to walk up).

Include trees and large shrubs on your map. If an area contains many trees and shrubs, outline it and mark it as woods. Note any other areas that get less than 6 hours of direct sun and whether they have light, partial, or dense shade. Also note areas that may be sunny in spring and shady once the trees leaf out.

Finally, look for good views that you'd like to preserve and bad views that you might want to screen out. Mark nice views with an arrow so you'll remember not to block them with tall perennials. Also indicate which windows you look out of to see your yard. Mark anything you'd like to screen, such as trash cans, and areas you don't want to mow, such as around posts and trees.

Make several photocopies of your finished map, so you'll be able to sketch in different landscaping ideas and see how they look. Now you're ready to move on to "Planning Your Perennial Landscape," starting on page 23, to assess your garden goals and plan your plantings.

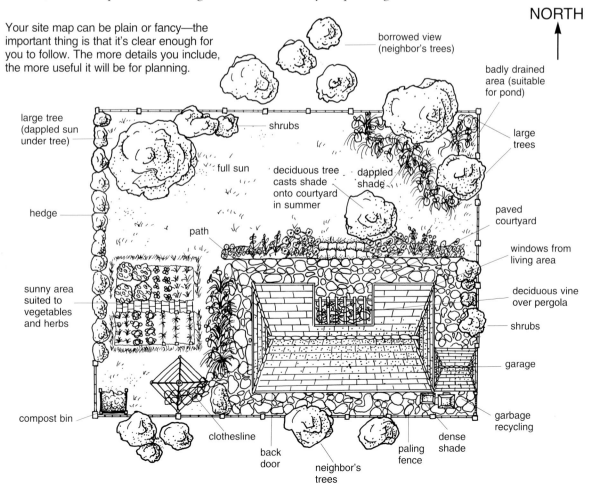

Your site map can be plain or fancy—the important thing is that it's clear enough for you to follow. The more details you include, the more useful it will be for planning.

NORTH

borrowed view (neighbor's trees)

badly drained area (suitable for pond)

large tree (dappled sun under tree)

shrubs

large trees

full sun

deciduous tree casts shade onto courtyard in summer

dappled shade

hedge

paved courtyard

path

windows from living area

sunny area suited to vegetables and herbs

deciduous vine over pergola

shrubs

garage

compost bin

clothesline

back door

neighbor's trees

paling fence

dense shade

garbage recycling

PLANNING YOUR
PERENNIAL LANDSCAPE

With so many wonderful perennials to choose from, it's hard to resist planting one of each. But if you buy them one by one and plop them in the ground wherever there's room, your garden will look like a plant collection—interesting, perhaps, but not beautiful.

Before you dig your garden, buy plants, or start rearranging an existing planting, you need to figure out what you want to grow and where you want to grow it. Garden design is basically the process of refining your plant choices, placement, and combinations to get the best effect. It's what transforms a bunch of individual plants into a pleasing composition.

Part of the fun of landscaping with perennials is creating an ever-changing display. Working with living material that changes from week to week and season to season makes designing a garden different from redecorating a room, even though it builds on the same principles of contrast, balance, texture, and color.

For a garden design to be effective, it has to match your site conditions, your style, the amount of time you have for gardening, and the results you want from the garden. Ideally it should also blend in with the topography and complement your house so everything looks like it belongs right where it is. You'll find design decisions easier and get the best results if you start with a good site map, as explained in "Create a Site Map" on page 21.

Once you know what conditions you're starting with, it's time to start figuring out what perennials you can and want to grow and where you can put them. This chapter summarizes some of the basic landscape design principles that have proven useful for generations of gardeners. It's intended to save you years of trials and errors and to speed the process of developing your own sense of design. But don't feel that you have to follow any of these guidelines exactly. What really matters is what you like and don't like.

In this chapter, you'll learn what to look for in combining plants and how to design a garden that looks good throughout the year. One of the secrets to creating great multiseason plant combinations is including perennials that have beautiful leaves as well as flowers. Once you decide which plants will give you the flowers and foliage effects you want, when you want them, you're ready to take pencil and paper in hand and turn that list into a landscape design.

Pull all of your different design ideas together with a planting plan. Sketching ideas on paper is the easiest way to tell whether your design will provide interest in different seasons. Drawing out plans is a fun way to work on your garden when pouring rain, blistering heat, or frozen ground deters you from being outside.

If there's one thing that all gardeners have in common, it's that they love to experiment. New garden designs that break the old "rules" (from color combinations to plant combinations) appear all the time. So take some time to learn about these design basics, then use the ideas that appeal to you as you plan and plant your own perennial landscape.

One of the best parts of landscaping with perennials is creating exciting combinations. The spiky flower heads of sea holly (*Eryngium* sp.), for instance, form a dramatic contrast to the satiny blooms of bellflower (*Campanula* sp.).

Deciding How and Where to Plant Perennials

The time you spend thinking about what you want from your new perennial landscape is probably the most important time you'll ever spend on it. In order to have a garden that suits your needs and looks good in your yard, you need to decide why you want to grow perennials, how big you want the garden to be, and what sort of style you are most comfortable with. Knowing your personal goals will guide you through the planning process and ensure that you end up with the garden you want.

Grow fragrant perennials such as lavender and lemon balm along paths, where you can enjoy the scents as you pass by.

Why Grow Perennials?

Take a few minutes to jot down why you want to add perennials to your yard. Do you want a parade of flowers all season long or just a bit of color to liven up a drab, shady spot? Do you want to attract butterflies, or do you want a wide selection of fresh flowers for arrangements? Do you want to plant perennials to fix an eroding hillside or camouflage the compost bin?

Identifying what you want your perennials to do will help you narrow down your planting options. If you're trying to grow perennials to solve a landscaping problem, you'll need to stick with plants that can adapt to those conditions. If you want perennials for cutting or for attracting butterflies, you'll want to choose plants that have proven themselves to be good

for those purposes. Either way, you'll find this kind of information in the individual plant entries in "Perennials for Every Purpose," starting on page 86.

Where Can You Plant?

Use the information you gathered for your site map (as explained in "Create a Site Map" on page 21) to decide where you want to grow your perennials. If you have a fairly flat site with moist but well-drained soil, you can plant a wide variety of perennials almost anywhere. But chances are good that you'll have at least one area in the yard with more challenging conditions, such as slopes or wet spots.

Choosing a Garden Style

Formal gardens are laid out with straight lines and symmetrical plantings.

Informal gardens tend to have curved lines and a wider variety of casual plantings.

Even small plantings—like a patch of pinks (*Dianthus* spp.) and lamb's-ears (*Stachys byzantina*)—add color.

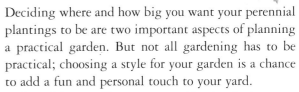

If you have a difficult spot, you might decide to ignore it and limit your perennial plantings to the most hospitable areas of the yard. Or you may choose to take up the challenge and plan a garden of perennials that are naturally adapted to those tough conditions. You may be pleasantly surprised to see how well-chosen perennial plantings can turn a problem site into a pleasing garden spot. You'll find specific suggestions for dealing with slopes, wet spots, and other difficult sites in "Solving Landscape Problems with Perennials," starting on page 54.

How Big Should Your Garden Be?

A key part of planning a great-looking landscape is being realistic about how much time you have to spend on it. Digging up and planting the area is the most obvious chunk of time you'll spend on the garden. But you'll also need to allow for the aftercare—the mulching, weeding, watering, fertilizing, staking, and pest control that your chosen plants will need to look their best.

For example, you'll probably need to spend a few hours each month to maintain a 200-square-foot (18.6 sq m) flower garden once it's established. That doesn't include any planning or preparation time. It also assumes you keep it mulched to discourage weeds and reduce the need for watering.

Your own garden may take more or less time, depending on the plants you choose, how perfect you want them to look, and how carefully you've planned it. It's always safe to start small, so plan your first garden a bit smaller than you think you want. Live with your first garden for a few years, and see how comfortable you are with the time you spend on it. As the plants become established, you'll have less watering and weeding to do, and you'll get a good idea of how much maintenance your garden really needs. Then, if you want to expand, you'll have a more realistic feel for how much garden you can actually handle.

What's Your Style?

Deciding where and how big you want your perennial plantings to be are two important aspects of planning a practical garden. But not all gardening has to be practical; choosing a style for your garden is a chance to add a fun and personal touch to your yard.

One thing you'll want to consider is whether your landscape will have a formal or informal feel. Formal landscaping uses straight lines, sharp angles, and symmetrical plantings with a limited number of different plants. These kinds of landscapes often include features such as clipped hedges or brick walls to define different spaces in the garden. Formal designs tend to have a restful feel. But they may not be as restful for the gardener, since you'll need to clip, stake, and weed frequently to keep the plants looking perfect.

Informal landscapes use curving lines to create a more natural feeling. They tend to have few permanent features such as walls, although elements such as rustic split-rail fences and wood-chip paths add greatly to the informal feel. These kinds of gardens generally include many different kinds of plants—trees, shrubs, annuals, herbs, and vines as well as perennials. Informal designs are relaxed and lively. Since the plants are free to spread, sprawl, and lean on each other, they tend to need less regular maintenance to still look well tended. You won't need to keep sharp edges on the beds, and the few weeds that pop up won't immediately be obvious and ruin the look of the garden.

Whether you choose a formal or informal landscape may depend on your personal style or on the style of your house. It's hard to mix informal and formal areas effectively outdoors, so choose one for harmonious landscaping.

Low, spreading perennials are charming cascading over walls or out of planters.

Fleeceflowers (*Polygonum* spp.) and other spiky plants look wonderful contrasted with mounded plants, such as hostas.

Designing Beds and Borders

Once you know what you want from your perennial landscape, you're ready to start planning the layout. Two of the most common ways to group perennial plantings are beds and borders. In the sections that follow, you'll find out more about these two different types of gardens and how to use them in your landscape. For more ideas on grouping perennials for particular purposes, see "Solving Landscape Problems with Perennials," starting on page 54, and "Perennial Gardens for Every Site," starting on page 68.

Perennial Borders

Perennial borders are long planting areas that create a visual edge to a lawn or other part of the landscape. They are usually sited so they're viewed from a distance. While they may stretch along a driveway, walkway, fence, or the edge of woods, they don't really have to "border" anything; borders may merely create the

illusion of a boundary to a "room" within the landscape.

Perennial borders are sometimes just that—only perennials. But more and more gardeners are enjoying the benefits of mixing their perennials with other plants, including shrubs, small trees, hardy bulbs, annuals, and ornamental grasses. These plants complement perennials by adding extra height, texture, and color to the border. Shrubs, trees, grasses, and bulbs also add year-round interest, with early spring flowers, attractive fall colors, and showy fruits or foliage that may last well into winter.

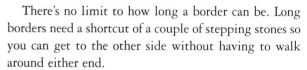

Shapes and Sizes Borders are often rectangular, but you can also design them with gentle curves for a more informal look. Because they're usually seen from one side, borders generally have a distinct front and back, with taller plants located to the rear.

There's no limit to how long a border can be. Long borders need a shortcut of a couple of stepping stones so you can get to the other side without having to walk around either end.

The width of the border will take some thought. Four to 5 feet (1.2 to 1.5 m) is enough room to include a good mix of plant heights. Long borders deeper than 5 or 6 feet (1.5 or 1.8 m) are a challenge to maintain because it's hard to reach more than 2 or 3 feet (60 to 90 cm) in from either side to weed, trim, or dig.

If you want a border more than 3 feet (90 cm) wide

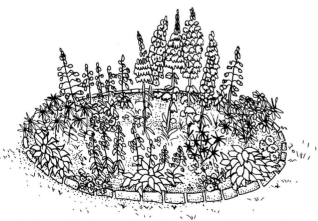

In island beds, set the tallest perennials toward the center and the shorter ones along the outside.

Mixing annuals, bulbs, and grasses with your perennial plantings adds height, color, and season-long interest.

allow you to reach all the plants from outside the bed, or place stepping stones in it for easy access.

Island Beds Beds surrounded by lawn are called islands; often these are oval or kidney shaped. They are a great way to add color and height to new property while you're waiting for the trees and shrubs to mature. Island beds are also useful for replacing the grass under trees, reducing the need for trimming and making mowing easier.

Like perennial borders, island beds are usually designed to be seen from a distance. As islands are often viewed from all sides, the design needs to look attractive all around, like a table centerpiece. Since there's no "back," put tallest plants toward the middle and surround them with lower plants.

in front of a hedge or wall, leave space behind it for a grassy or mulched access path so you can get to all parts of your border. If you plan to make your border longer than about 15 feet (4.5 m), make the access path as wide as your garden cart or wheelbarrow so you can easily haul in manure or compost and cart out trimmings.

Perennial Beds

Beds are often located closer to the house than borders, perhaps along the foundation or edging a patio. If you're going to put a bed where you'll see it all the time, choose your plants carefully for all-season interest. High-visibility beds will also need either some extra work or carefully chosen, low-maintenance plants to look their best all the time.

Shapes and Sizes Perennial beds come in many shapes and sizes. Choose a shape and style (formal or informal) that matches or balances nearby features. The front can curve even if the side up against the house is straight. Keep the bed narrow enough to

Include bergenias and other evergreen perennials for winter color. Bergenias also offer pink spring flowers.

Bed and Border Planning Pointers

Perennial borders and beds can be designed to feature one big seasonal show or to showcase long, overlapping seasons of bloom. If you have room for several different beds or borders, it can be fun to arrange each one with a different bloom season. That way you will always have at least one bed that is loaded with lovely flowers.

In small gardens or in plantings that you see every day, it's worth planning for long bloom times, attractive foliage, and year-round interest. Here are some planning tips you can try.

- Include some spring, summer, and fall-flowering perennials in each planting area.
- Look for perennials that have great-looking foliage all season, such as hostas, artemisias, lady's-mantle (*Alchemilla* spp.), and amsonias (*Amsonia* spp.).
- Pick long-blooming species and cultivars, like wild bleeding heart (*Dicentra eximia*) and 'Moonbeam' coreopsis (*Coreopsis verticillata* 'Moonbeam'); these can bloom for 8 weeks or longer.
- Include a few perennials with good-looking evergreen foliage for interest during the colder months. Bergenias (*Bergenia* spp.) and some alumroots (including *Heuchera americana* 'Dale's Strain' and 'Garnet') often turn a lovely reddish color in the cool temperatures of fall and winter.

Creating Great Plant Combinations

Great-looking gardens are basically sequences of many individual plant combinations. The best aren't just based on flower color and season of bloom; they consider the quality, color, and texture of each plant's leaves as well. Good combinations also feature different plant heights and forms: short, medium or tall; mat-like, spiky, or rounded. Equally important is overall texture—whether a plant is fine and delicate looking, like baby's-breath (*Gypsophila* spp.), or coarse and dramatic, like peonies and ligularias (*Ligularia* spp.).

As you decide which plants to grow and how you want to group them, keep these different factors in mind. A little thought at the planning stage can turn a collection of different perennials into a harmonious, pleasing landscape.

Contrasts and Complements

Well-planned gardens balance contrast and similarity. Contrasting colors, sizes, or other design elements are bold and stimulating. Use contrast to draw attention to a particular location and to add a lively feel. Overusing contrast—too many different textures or too many strong colors—can give your garden a jumbled, chaotic look.

Similarity—the absence of contrasts—increases the sense of harmony. Use subtle variations of closely related colors and gradual height transitions to create soothing garden designs. Too much similarity risks being uninteresting, so add a touch of contrast—a few perennials of different height, color, or texture—for balance.

Repetition acts as a bridge between similarity and contrast. Repeating similar elements will unify even the boldest designs. Exact, evenly spaced repetitions of particular plants or combinations create a formal look. Combine different plants with similar flower colors or leaf shapes to give an informal garden a cohesive but casual look.

Color Combinations

Different colors have different personalities. Warm colors—those related to red, orange, or yellow—are bold. They are stimulating and appear closer to the viewer. Cool colors—those related to violet, blue, or green—are more tranquil and appear to recede from the viewer. Pure hues—like true yellow, blue, and red—are more vibrant than lighter or darker versions of the same color. Mixing warm and cool colors will add depth and interest to your plantings.

Combining colors in gardens is as easy as combining colors in clothes—possibly even easier! The green background of the foliage harmonizes strong colors—such as reds and oranges—that you probably wouldn't think to combine in an outfit. Pastel colors like soft pinks, blues, and yellows may look washed out against a light-colored shirt, but they never get lost against dark green leaves.

Purple grape hyacinths are stunning with the yellow-green spring blooms of myrtle euphorbia (*Euphorbia myrsinites*).

Mixing a variety of reds, yellows, and oranges can produce exciting and dramatic plant combinations.

Color combinations are very personal creations. While certain types and combinations of colors tend to create specific effects, only you can decide whether you like that particular effect. Some gardeners enjoy the lively result of mixing orange and yellow with purple or blue; others prefer the crisp look of whites or the restful feel of pale yellows, soft pinks, and silvers.

Combining similar flower colors in the garden creates a harmonious effect. Try grouping reds with oranges and yellows, yellows with greens and blues, or blues with purples and reds. Colors sharing the same degree of lightness or darkness are also similar; for instance, several different pastels—like pale blues, yellows, and pinks—blend more harmoniously than several pure hues.

If contrast and excitement are what you're after, choose complementary hues like yellow and violet, red and green, or blue and orange. Or place a light tint next to a very bright or dark shade of the same hue (try pale blue with intense blue or dark blue or pale pink next to fuchsia or burgundy).

White and gray don't appear on the color wheel, but they play an important role in the garden. White has a split personality: it can be exciting or soothing. Bright white is surprisingly bold; it stands out among bright and dark colors, even in a group of soft pastels. A dash of pure white in a spread of harmonious colors is as dramatic as a dash of a bright complementary color. Cream and similar muted whites are softer; they blend well with everything.

Gray is the great unifier. Silvery or gray foliage works even better than green to soften the transition between two complementary or bold colors. Gray adds a certain drama of its own by contrasting with neighboring green foliage.

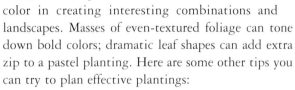

Texture and Form Factors

Two other plant characteristics, like texture and form, are as important as color in creating interesting combinations and landscapes. Masses of even-textured foliage can tone down bold colors; dramatic leaf shapes can add extra zip to a pastel planting. Here are some other tips you can try to plan effective plantings:

- Balance rounded clump-formers, such as shasta daisies (*Chrysanthemum* x *superbum*) and coreopsis, with spiky plants such as mulleins (*Verbascum* spp.), foxgloves (*Digitalis* spp.), and spike gayfeather (*Liatris spicata*).
- Contrast shiny leaves—like those of bear's-breech (*Acanthus mollis*) and European ginger (*Asarum europaeum*)—with velvety or fuzzy leaves, such as those of lamb's-ears (*Stachys byzantina*) or lungworts (*Pulmonaria* spp.).
- Contrast fine foliage, such as lacy fern fronds, with the smooth, broad leaves of hostas and similar plants.

Create an elegant effect by combining silvery artemisia and lamb's-ears with blue-leaved pinks (*Dianthus* spp.).

Persian onion (*Allium aflatunense*) and golden-chain tree (*Laburnum* x *watereri*) form a splendid spring spectacle.

Orchestrating All-season Interest

You see your yard every day of the year, so make sure it's worth looking at. A good selection of spring-, summer-, and fall-blooming perennials, plus a few plants with evergreen leaves for winter interest, will give you a landscape that is truly attractive all year long.

All-season interest starts with flower displays that spread beyond one season. Choosing perennials for different seasons is relatively easy: Just look under "Season of Interest" in the individual plant entries in "Perennials for Every Purpose," starting on page 86.

Foliage and plant form are other features you can use to keep your garden looking beautiful as flowers come and go. From spring through fall, many perennials have leaves in attractive colors—like the maroon leaves of 'Palace Purple' heuchera *Heuchera* 'Palace Purple')—or interesting shapes, such as the starry leaves of blood-red cranesbill (*Geranium sanguineum*). Unusual plant forms—such as the spiky leaves and flowers of yuccas, blackberry lily (*Belamcanda chinensis*), and spike gayfeather (*Liatris spicata*)—add drama, especially next to mounds such as cushion spurge (*Euphorbia epithymoides*). Use different types of foliage and forms to add contrast, or repeat similar leaves and shapes to unify a planting scheme.

Your Spring Landscape

After a long, dreary winter, few things are more welcome than colorful spring flowers. In spring, Lenten rose (*Helleborus orientalis*) and crocuses bloom before most of the garden shrugs off winter. Plant early bulbs where you'll see them from windows or as you enter the house so you can enjoy their bright colors when it's cold outside. Many wildflowers and shade-loving perennials bloom as trees leaf out, so spring is a good season to draw attention to areas that will be shady and green later on. Supplement early-blooming perennials with flowering shrubs and trees such as forsythias, azaleas, magnolias, dogwoods, flowering cherries, and crab apples.

A Wealth of Summer Color

As spring turns into summer, many old-fashioned perennials—including peonies, irises, and columbines (*Aquilegia* spp.)—reach their peak, making it an easy time to feature flowers. Supplement these with early summer shrubs and vines such as rhododendrons, roses, clematis, wisteria, and honeysuckle (*Lonicera* spp.).

As summer progresses, daisy-like perennials and annuals—including blanket flower (*Gaillardia* x *grandiflora*) and coreopsis (*Coreopsis* spp.)—take center stage. Good-looking foliage keeps up appearances

You can depend on asters to produce loads of colorful blooms for your late-summer and fall garden.

Plants that have variegated leaves—such as hostas (*left*) and some kinds of lemon balm (*right*)—provide all-season interest.

Liven up the area under a spring-blooming tree with late-flowering plants, such as autumn crocus (*Colchicum* spp.).

where early perennials have finished blooming. Silver leaves make dramatic partners for hot- or cool-hued flowers; yellow, purple, or variegated foliage also attracts attention. Flowering shrubs for July and August include abelia (*Abelia* x *grandiflora*), butterfly bush (*Buddleia davidii*), and hydrangeas. Sourwood (*Oxydendrum arboreum*) and Japanese pagoda tree (*Sophora japonica*) are large trees that bloom prolifically in late summer, as does the large trumpet creeper vine (*Campsis* spp).

Combinations for Fall

Asters, boltonia, and Joe-Pye weeds (*Eupatorium* spp.) keep blooming after fall frosts nip most annuals. As flowers fade, foliage brightens—and not just on trees

or shrubs such as burning bush (*Euonymus alata*). Leaves of peonies and common sundrops (*Oenothera tetragona*) turn beautiful shades of red, amsonias (*Amsonia* spp.) and balloon flower (*Platycodon grandiflorus*) leaves turn bright yellow, and many ornamental grasses bleach to gold. White baneberry (*Actea pachypoda*) and Jack-in-the-pulpit (*Arisaema triphyllum*) are perennials with dramatic berries that may last into fall.

Perennials for Winter Interest

After the leaves drop, attention turns to evergreen plants and those with interesting seedpods or fruits. Perennials with showy winter seedpods include blue false indigo (*Baptisia australis*), coneflowers (*Rudbeckia* and *Echinacea* spp.), blackberry lily (*Belamcanda chinensis*), and astilbes.

Many crab apples and shrubs such as viburnums, cotoneasters, and deciduous and evergreen hollies (*Ilex* spp.) display fruits well into winter. Ornamental grasses remain attractive for months; cut them to the ground when they look tattered to make way for spring's new growth.

The graceful spring flowers of columbines (*Aquilegia* spp.) are a traditional favorite in borders and cottage gardens.

Bulbs Belong Everywhere

Planting a variety of bulbs is a fast and easy way to add color to your yard from early spring through fall. Bulbs belong everywhere: in perennial beds, under deciduous shrubs and trees, by hedges or fences, among shady wildflowers or sunny meadows, in containers on a deck, among groundcovers—even in the cutting garden.

Basic Bulb Culture

Bulbs are perfect plants for beginners and busy people because they are almost foolproof if you meet their few basic needs.

Plant Properly Hardy bulbs need almost no maintenance in moderately fertile, well-drained soil. Where drainage is a problem, plant in raised beds; bulbs rot in soggy soils. Follow the planting depths and spacing recommended on the package or in the individual plant entries in "Perennials for Every Purpose," starting on page 86. Don't be tempted to skimp and dig a shallower hole; deep planting can encourage stronger bulbs and prevent damage from squirrels and other pests.

For the best blooms, mix in a balanced organic fertilizer at planting time. To keep bulbs going strong, sprinkle compost or more fertilizer (follow the application rate on the package label) over the bulb plantings each spring after shoots emerge.

Leave the Leaves The trick to having your bulbs come back year after year is letting the leaves ripen fully before you cut them off. The leaves allow the bulbs to build up enough food reserves to bloom the following spring. Removing spent flowers does no harm, but cutting off leaves while they're still green essentially starves the plant.

In flower beds and manicured areas, you'll need to camouflage the foliage after bulbs bloom because their yellowing leaves aren't much to look at. Locate bulbs behind perennials that fill out after the bulbs bloom: try daylilies, hostas, boltonia (*Boltonia asteroides*), or baby's-breath (*Gypsophila paniculata*). Or plant annuals there each year for season-long color as well as camouflage. Among groundcovers, plant shorter bulbs—crocus, grape hyacinths (*Muscari* spp.), and the like. The short leaves of these bulbs will disappear under the groundcover as they mature.

Grape hyacinths are excellent for naturalizing in lawns, groundcovers, and low-maintenance areas.

Landscaping with Bulbs

Versatile bulbs are easy to tuck into many parts of your yard. Try them in formal groupings in a flower bed or border, or naturalize them in a casual woodland garden or unmowed lawn.

Bulbs in Beds and Borders For the best effect, plant groups of a single color of the same bulb. Individual bulbs scattered here and there throughout a large bed just won't stand out for a good show. Daffodils and other large bulbs look great in groups

Unlike many of the short-lived hybrid tulips, Kaufmanniana tulips can bloom for many years without replanting.

In a small garden, you can enjoy growing bulbs in a planter.

of 12 or more. Plant smaller, less-expensive bulbs in even larger groups or drifts so you can see them without getting down on your hands and knees.

For a single, spectacular display, cluster groups of two or three different colors of bulbs that bloom at the same time. For a longer display, choose species and hybrids that bloom at different times. If you enjoy tulips, for instance, you could plant early-flowering Kauffmaniana tulip (*Tulipa kauffmanniana*) with mid-spring Darwin hybrids and late-spring parrot tulips for 2 months or more of bloom.

To get the most out of each planting area, try a technique called overplanting. This involves planting several kinds of bulbs together in one planting hole. Many small, early bloomers such as crocuses and grape hyacinths grow at shallower depths than large, later-blooming daffodils, hyacinths, and tulips. After planting the larger bulbs, cover them with just enough soil to make the hole the recommended depth for the smaller bulbs. Plant the smaller bulbs in the same area (try not to set them directly over the lower bulbs) before filling in the rest of the soil.

Add a unique touch to your garden with autumn crocuses. They bloom in fall, but the leaves don't appear until spring.

Blooming Bulbs through the Year

With some planning, you can have bulbs blooming with your perennials from spring through fall. Below is an approximate bloom schedule for gardens in Zone 6. Zone 3 gardens are usually a good 2 weeks later; gardens in Zone 8 and warmer parts of Zone 7 are about 1 week earlier. (If you're not sure which zone you live in, see the USDA Plant Hardiness Zone Map on page 154.)

Species crocus (including *Crocus tommasinianus*): early March
Snowdrops (*Galanthus* spp.): early March
Reticulated iris (*Iris reticulata*): early March
Dutch crocus (*Crocus vernus* hybrids): late March
Early daffodils: late March to early April
Species tulips: April
Grape hyacinths (*Muscari* spp.): mid-April
Siberian squill (*Scilla sibirica*): mid-April
Daffodils and narcissus: late April
Hyacinths: late April
Crown imperial (*Fritillaria imperalis*): late April
Hybrid tulips: late April to May
Giant onion (*Allium giganteum*): early summer
Lilies: early to late summer
Autumn crocuses (*Colchicum* and *Crocus* spp.): early fall to midfall
Hardy cyclamen (*Cyclamen* spp.): fall or early spring

Bulbs in Lawns and Woodlands Naturalizing—planting bulbs in lawns, meadows, or unmanicured woodsy areas—is another fun way to add bulbs to your yard. Look for species and selections that are described as good for naturalizing; almost all daffodils and crocuses qualify, as do grape hyacinths (*Muscari* spp.), Siberian squill (*Scilla sibirica*), and Spanish bluebells (*Hyacinthoides hispanicus*). Space bulbs in irregular patterns for the most natural look, and plant lots of them so you'll see them from a distance.

Putting It All Together

By now you probably have lots of thoughts and ideas swirling around in your head. You know where and how big you want the garden to be and which plants you want to grow. But before you start digging up the lawn or heading off to the garden center, it's smart to take a few minutes to jot down your ideas on paper.

In this section, you'll learn about the different techniques you can use to organize your gardening ideas. If you're really organized or if you're feeling a little nervous about the whole project, follow all of these steps and you'll end up with a clear plan of action for planting your landscape. Or perhaps you don't want to bother with formal maps and plans—you just want to get out there and start planting! You may prefer to stick with a shopping list and rough sketch, so you know what you want to buy and where you want it to go.

Plan Your Plant List

If your focus is on growing specific plants, making a list may be as simple as jotting down the names of species and cultivars that you want to try. This list will remind you what you're looking for as you browse through catalogs and shop at your local nursery. Check off the plants as you buy or order them, so you won't forget and purchase the same plant twice by mistake!

If you are trying to match the plants with a particular site, you'll need to look for perennials that can

Include asters, sedums, and other late-flowering perennials to extend the bloom season in beds and borders.

take the conditions you have to offer. Look through the individual plant entries in "Perennials for Every Purpose," starting on page 86, to find possibilities. Jot down a list of about 5 to 10 different plants, indicating their heights, spreads, and bloom times.

Try Out Your Ideas

Now, head outside with a copy of your plant list and your site plan (the one you drew up with the help of "Create a Site Map" on page 21). Outline the shape of the planting area with flexible hose or rope.

Step back and walk around the yard to see how the dimensions look from several viewpoints (including the view through your windows). If you have trouble visualizing how the filled bed will look, use trash cans,

Limiting your choices to a color theme can make shopping easier, and it creates an elegant-looking garden.

If you enjoy a casual cottage-garden style, you may decide to skip the paper-plan stage and just start planting.

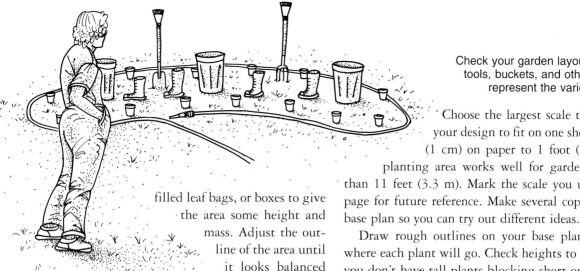

Check your garden layout by using tools, buckets, and other items to represent the various plants.

filled leaf bags, or boxes to give the area some height and mass. Adjust the outline of the area until it looks balanced from all viewpoints.

Put Your Plan on Paper

Sketching garden designs allows you to try out many different ideas, however unrealistic, without the hassle of physically digging up and moving existing plants. Your plan may simply be the outline of the bed with scrawled notes as to roughly where the plants will go. Or you may want to invest the time in drawing up a formal scale plan of the bed so you can make sure the garden will have just the right blend of colors, heights, and textures and so you'll know just what you need to buy.

To make a scale plan, measure the final outline of the bed decided on in "Try Out Your Ideas," and transfer the dimensions to paper.

If your garden is small, you could draw the area right onto your site map. In most cases, though, it's easier to draw each planting area on a separate piece of graph paper; that will give you more room to write.

Choose the largest scale that allows your design to fit on one sheet: 1 inch (1 cm) on paper to 1 foot (15 cm) of planting area works well for gardens shorter than 11 feet (3.3 m). Mark the scale you use on the page for future reference. Make several copies of this base plan so you can try out different ideas.

Draw rough outlines on your base plan to show where each plant will go. Check heights to make sure you don't have tall plants blocking short ones, unless the short plants bloom before the tall plants fill out. If you have room, allow space for three or five plants of each type—a few different plants in large masses can have a more dramatic effect than many single plants. Mark dots (or small xs) within outlines to show locations of individual plants.

As you plan the layout, check the spread of each plant; it's listed in the individual plant entries in "Perennials for Every Purpose," starting on page 86. Leave enough room between plants so that each can mature to its full spread and overlap by no more than a few inches. If your budget is tight, space plants farther apart; increase them by division the following year, or fill the gaps with annuals and bulbs. Allow for some unplanted (mulched) space at the front of the bed so the plants can sprawl out a bit without flopping into the lawn and creating a mowing headache.

Fine-tune Your Plan

If you really want to make sure your design is just right, you can make colored maps or overlays to help you visualize color combinations and different seasons. Make several copies of your scale plan, or use several sheets of tracing paper as overlays.

Use a different copy or overlay sheet for early spring, late spring/early summer, late summer, and fall; you may also want one for winter interest. Color the plants that bloom at each time. If you have old plant catalogs with color pictures, clip swatches of particular flowers and glue them inside the outline instead of coloring. If foliage color is important, add the color as a thick outline surrounding the area of flower color. When you're satisfied that your design meets your needs, make a clean copy that includes plant names.

Don't forget to consider the features of existing trees and shrubs when you plan your perennial plantings.

GROWING YOUR PERENNIAL LANDSCAPE

Careful planning and plant selection will take you a long way toward a great-looking landscape. The next step is to follow through with good soil preparation and aftercare to get those plants off and growing. This chapter will guide you through the process of preparing the site, planting, and caring for your perennials to keep them healthy and beautiful all season long.

Making a place for your perennials takes more care than it does for a plot of vegetables or annuals. Perennials will grow in the same spot for years, so you won't have the chance to correct any soil problems once you plant. If the soil conditions aren't right, your perennials will be weak, less attractive, and more prone to pest and disease problems. But when you choose plants that are naturally adapted to your soil's characteristics, loosen the soil well, and dig in plenty of organic matter, you're providing the right conditions for lush, vigorous growth and generous flower production.

Starting with healthy plants is a key step in having a naturally healthy garden. In this chapter, you'll learn how to buy strong, problem-free plants and bulbs and how to handle bareroot plants that arrive in the mail. You'll also find the best ways to plant container-grown perennials, bareroot perennials, and bulbs.

Once your beds are planted, you need to know how to keep them looking their best. Maintenance tasks are easiest if you do them regularly, as this will keep little tasks from mushrooming into overwhelming ones.

Weeding and watering are common chores, particularly with new gardens, but you'll learn how mulching can reduce the time you spend on both. Pinching, pruning, and staking take less time, but they can yield big rewards in promoting good looks. And you'll learn how to divide plants when they get too big or when you want to give some to friends.

With good soil and good care, your plants will naturally be more resistant to pests of all kinds. Organic gardeners often notice that after several years of building up the soil, keeping the garden clean, and encouraging natural predators, insect and disease problems diminish from a constant battle to the occasional flare-up. In this chapter, you'll learn the basics of identifying and handling any problems that do arise.

To help you keep up with your landscape throughout the year, the chapter ends with a monthly almanac. Use it as a reminder so you stay one step ahead in your garden instead of running to catch up. Since conditions vary widely from one area to another, calendars like this work best if you supplement them with your own garden journal. Keep track of plant combinations that worked well and record ideas that you'd like to try. Jot down the names of plants that need to be moved or divided later in the season. Gradually, you'll fine-tune your color display and gain the confidence you need to feel like a seasoned gardener.

Like any other plants, perennials do need some care to keep them looking super all through the season. Good soil preparation and regular mulching will go a long way toward keeping maintenance to a minimum, however.

Preparing for Planting

Healthy landscapes start with healthy soil. The effort you put into working the soil and preparing a good planting site will be more than repaid by the strong, vigorous growth of your perennials.

When to Start

If you can, prepare planting areas at least a month before you plant to give soil time to settle. Ideally, start in the fall for spring planting or in spring for fall planting. It's also ideal to have your soil tested before planting; for more details on soil testing, see "Professional Tests for Professional Results" on page 14.

Start digging when the soil is moist, but not wet. Digging moist soil is relatively easy, but dry soil requires extra effort, and working soil that's soggy can turn it into rock-like lumps. After 2 or 3 days without rain, dig up a shovelful in a couple of different spots and test for moisture by squeezing a handful of soil. If the soil oozes through your fingers or forms a sticky lump, it's too wet; wait a few days and repeat the test before digging. If the soil is dry and powdery or hard, water the area thoroughly and wait a day or two to dig.

What to Do

First lay out the area you want to dig, as you determined when you drew up your garden plan. Use stakes and string for marking the straight sides; lay out curves with a rope or garden hose. Step back and double-check your layout from several viewpoints, including indoors.

Next, remove existing grass and weeds. Slice off manageable pieces of sod by cutting small squares, then sliding your spade just under the roots. Toss the sod into the compost pile or use it to repair bare spots in your lawn.

Double-digging—removing the top layer of ground and loosening the soil underneath—will provide ideal conditions for good root growth. Your perennials will thrive.

Double-digging for Deep Rooting

Double-digging takes some time and lots of energy, but you'll know it's worth the effort when you see the results: strong, healthy, free-blooming plants.

To deeply loosen the soil, dig a trench along the long side of your bed, dumping soil on a plastic tarp or in a cart. Use a garden fork to loosen the soil at the bottom of the trench to a depth of 8 to 10 inches (20 to 25 cm); you don't need to turn this bottom layer. Dig another trench alongside the first, turning each shovelful into the first trench. Repeat the process across your bed, filling the final trench with the soil you removed from the first trench.

Loose, well-drained soil is the secret to success with lavender, rose campion (*Lychnis coronaria*), and many other perennials, especially in areas with cold, wet winters.

Next, loosen the soil over the entire planting area. Dig down as far as your spade or shovel will reach and turn over this top layer of the soil, or use a rotary tiller. For even better results, double dig the bed. Double-digging loosens the soil to twice the depth of single digging, providing ideal conditions for great root growth and helping to correct heavy or poorly drained soil. For details on this technique, see "Double-digging for Deep Rooting."

Once your soil is loose, mix in fertilizer to feed the plants and organic matter to condition the soil. Any balanced organic fertilizer will do. Scatter the fertilizer over the planting area at the application rate listed on the label.

Now spread organic matter about 4 inches (10 cm) deep over the entire area (you'll need about 2 cubic yards for every 50 square feet). If your soil feels as loose as a kid's sandbox (indicating drainage that's too fast) or if puddles always remain after a rain (indicating poor drainage), add even more organic matter.

Compost is the best source of organic matter; if you don't have enough, you may be able to buy more at your local garden center. Leaves are excellent, too; run the lawn mower over piles to chop them first or mix them with grass clippings. Sawdust and straw are good if you also add a source of nitrogen (in the form of manure or bloodmeal) to help them decompose. Manure alone is fine but can contain many weed seeds. Whichever material you choose, mix it well into the top 8 inches (20 cm) of soil.

After digging in the fertilizer and organic matter, water the area thoroughly. Remember to let the soil sit for a month before planting to give the organic matter time to break down (unless you used well-decomposed compost, in which case you could plant right away). Rake just before planting to level the bed.

Work some compost into the soil before planting to provide a supply of nutrients for healthy, steady growth.

Preparing a Bed

Set out stakes and string to mark the area you're going to dig.

Remove the sod by skimming it off the soil with a spade.

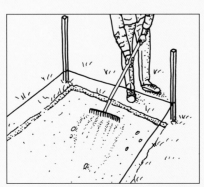

If a soil test indicates your soil is acid, apply lime and rake it in.

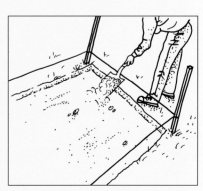

Scatter a layer of compost over the area, and dig it into the soil.

Buying Healthy Perennials and Bulbs

Starting out with healthy plants is a key part of developing a naturally problem-free landscape. In this section, you'll find out how to buy the best possible perennials from your local garden centers and nurseries and from mail-order sources.

Buying from Local Retailers

A good local nursery or garden center—one that offers a variety of plants and takes good care of them—is a real treasure. Usually its staff members are good sources of information specific to your area, such as which plants grow well there. The nursery may even have a demonstration garden where you can see how plants look when full grown and compare different cultivars.

Advantages and Disadvantages One advantage of buying locally is that you can inspect plants and bulbs before buying them. Also, your plants won't have to suffer through shipping. Most nurseries and garden centers offer container-grown plants, which are easiest to handle. On the down side, your selection may be limited, and the plants may be more expensive.

Buying Tips Inspect container-grown plants carefully before you buy. Plants should look healthy, with an even color and unblemished leaves. Look closely at the stems and leaves (check the undersides, too!) for signs of pests or their damage. Avoid purchasing plants that show any of these problems:

- Clouds of tiny white insects (whiteflies) that fly up when you move or brush the plant.
- Distorted and/or sticky leaves, with tiny green, pink, gray, or black insects (aphids) clustered along stems, on buds, and under leaves.
- Leaves that look bleached or stippled, sometimes with tiny webs on stems and leaves.

Don't forget to check the soil, too. It should be evenly moist, or at least moist just below the surface. Plants that are allowed to dry out frequently are stressed and weak, and their growth may be stunted.

When you have a choice, select small, vigorous-looking plants; they'll grow faster and soon outpace larger, already-blooming plants. While it's fun to see what flowers you're getting (and sometimes you'll want to make sure you get just the right color), it's

Lenten roses (*Helleborus orientalis*) are usually sold as small plants, but they make large clumps in a few years.

generally better to buy and plant perennials before they bloom. That way, they can settle into the garden and establish new roots before the stress of flowering.

If you buy larger container-grown plants, check to see if roots are growing out the bottom. Or gently slip the plant out of its pot to see if many roots are circling around the outside of the root ball. By the time several roots are escaping from the pot or encircling the root ball, a plant has probably suffered water stress from growing in a pot that's too small, so it may not adapt well to your garden.

With bulbs, purchase the largest size you can afford for flower beds and borders. Smaller-sized bulbs are great for naturalizing in lawns and low-maintenance areas, and you can sometimes buy quantities of 50 or 100 at a reduced price. Choose bulbs that are plump and firm with no soft spots or mold.

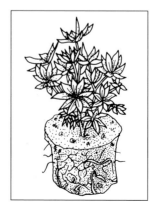

Good-quality perennials have healthy top growth and some visible roots.

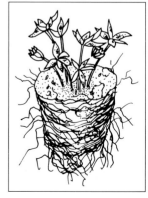

Avoid plants with spindly top growth and matted, circling roots.

Unless you need a particular flower color, it's best to buy perennials that aren't yet in bloom.

Buying by Mail

If you want unusual perennials, don't have access to a local nursery, or want to get the best possible prices, mail-order sources provide limitless possibilities. Write for catalogs several months before you want to plant so you'll have time to compare selections and prices. Some catalogs are great sources of information on the virtues of specific plants and cultivars; a few even have color photos and useful growing information.

Advantages and Disadvantages Catalog shopping is a fun way to while away dreary winter evenings, and it's convenient, too. You can learn about exciting new plants and often find good prices when you compare several catalogs. On the down side, you don't really know what you're paying for until you get it. Shipping stress can weaken even the strongest plants. If you get bareroot perennials (with roots that are wrapped in packing material), they'll need to be planted or potted up immediately.

Buying Tips The best approach to ordering by mail is to ask gardening friends which catalogs they've ordered from and which they would buy from again. If you don't know anyone who gets perennial catalogs, visit a library and get addresses and phone numbers from advertisements in recent gardening magazines.

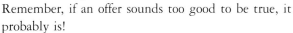

When you order from a source for the first time, just buy a few plants and see how they look. If you're happy with the quality for the price, order more; otherwise, shop elsewhere. Remember, if an offer sounds too good to be true, it probably is!

Inspect mail-order plants as soon as they arrive. If they are damaged, you should return them; contact the source right away to find out how to do so. Mail-order perennials are often shipped when they are dormant (not actively growing) and may look dead. Plant them anyway and water them well. If they don't produce any buds or new growth in a few weeks, contact the source.

If your plants were shipped in pots, water as needed and keep them out of bright sunlight for the first few days. Mail-order plants may also arrive bareroot—without any pot or soil. If they're bulbs, they're happy that way; keep them cool and in the dark until you're ready to plant. Other bareroot plants need more attention; for best results, plant them within a day or two after they arrive. If you can't plant right away, keep the packing material moist—not soggy—and store the plants in a cool, shaded place. If there isn't any packing material, soak the roots in room-temperature water for an hour or two, then wrap with damp paper towels or cover with compost.

Starting with vigorous, pest-free perennials is a key part of planting a healthy, beautiful, easy-care landscape that's filled with flowers.

Careful soil preparation and planting will get all of your perennials off to a good start.

Mulch bareroot and container-grown perennials after planting to keep the soil moist and to promote root growth.

Planting Is the Fun Part

Once the site is prepared and your perennials are by your side, you're ready to turn your dream garden into reality. In this section, you'll learn the right way to plant to get your landscape off to a good start.

When to Plant

Your perennials will grow best if you wait for an overcast afternoon to plant. If you must plant on a sunny day, leave the perennials in the shade while you dig all of the holes. Space the holes according to the spacings you worked out on your planting plan.

How to Plant Container-Grown Perennials

Container-grown perennials are easy to plant; just follow these simple steps:

1. Dig a hole as deep as the soil level in the pot.
2. Gently remove the plant from its pot. To do this, place one hand over the soil, with the plant stems between your fingers. Invert the pot so it's resting on this hand, then use the other hand to pull off the pot. Don't yank; if the pot refuses to come off, cut it off to avoid damaging roots.

3. If you find a mass of crowded roots, gently loosen them with your fingers. If the roots have formed a tight mat, take a sharp knife and cut a slit 1/4 inch (6 mm) deep from top to bottom in three or four places. This encourages the production of new roots that will grow into the surrounding soil.

4. Set the plant in the hole, and backfill with the soil you took out until the soil level is even with the rest of the bed. Be sure you don't pile extra soil around the base of the stems (the crown).

5. Water thoroughly and mulch, leaving a zone about 2 inches (5 cm) around the crown free of mulch.

6. If it's sunny out, shade the plants by inverting paper grocery bags over them as soon as they're in the ground. (Weight down the edges of the bags with rocks to keep them from blowing away.) Remove the bags after 2 days. Water if needed to keep the soil moist.

How to Plant Bareroot Perennials

Bareroot perennials aren't difficult to plant, but they need a little extra care to get settled.

1. Remove any packing material and prune off any damaged or broken roots. Cover the rest with room-temperature water for an hour or two before planting to make sure the roots are moist.

To get your perennials off to the best start, plant when the temperatures are moderate and rainfall is abundant.

Planting Bulbs

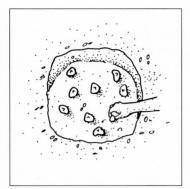

Dig a wide hole so you can space the bulbs as you wish.

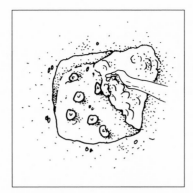

Cover the bulbs with the soil you removed from the hole.

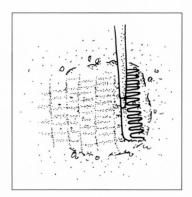

Tamp down the soil with a rake to firm it over the bulbs.

2. Check to see whether roots grow from one large central root (a taproot) or as a mass of many smaller fibrous roots. Taprooted plants need a narrow, deep hole, while fibrous-rooted plants need a wide, shallow hole. Dig the hole accordingly.

3. If you are planting a taprooted species, hold the crown (where the stems meet the roots) even with the soil surface, and backfill with the soil you removed.

4. If you're planting a fibrous-rooted perennial, form a mound of soil in the center of the hole, then gently spread the roots out over the mound. Check that the crown is even with the soil surface; if not, add or take away some of the soil in the mound. Once the level is correct, fill in the soil.

5. Gently tamp down the soil around the base of the plant with your hand or foot. Water the soil thoroughly and mulch, leaving a zone about 2 inches (5 cm) around the crown free of mulch.

How to Plant Bulbs

Planting hardy bulbs is easy. Plant them when you receive them, about the time your other perennials are starting to go dormant. You can either dig individual holes or one wide hole large enough for several bulbs. For the prettiest effect, plant your bulbs in clumps (try at least 15 small bulbs or a dozen large bulbs). Set the bulbs so that the depth of soil above their tops is about three times the height of the bulb. (You would, for instance, dig a 4-inch [10 cm] hole for a 1-inch [2.5 cm] high bulb.)

Loosen the soil at the bottom of the hole. Place bulbs in the hole—pointed ends up, if they have them, and sideways if you're not sure which end is up—and firm the soil around them as you fill in the hole.

Naturalizing You don't need to have any already-prepared planting areas for your bulbs. For an informal look, you can plant them in random patterns in a lawn or lightly shaded woods; this technique is called naturalizing.

For daffodils and other larger bulbs, dig a hole for each bulb, loosen the soil a bit, set the bulb firmly in its hole, and replace the soil. To naturalize smaller bulbs, it's easier to dig up an area large enough for several and plant them in groups. Use irregular spacing between bulbs for a more natural effect.

Create a breathtaking spring scene by naturalizing daffodils and other early bulbs under flowering trees.

Hoe or hand weed around newly planted perennials to allow them to get established without competition from weeds.

Maintaining a Healthy Garden

Taking regular walks through your perennial landscape is a great way to enjoy your flowers and appreciate the progress you've made. As you stroll through the garden, you'll also be helping to keep it healthy. You'll soon recognize when your plants look thirsty, so you can water before they get severely wilted and stressed. You can see and pull any weeds that pop up before they get big and start crowding out the perennials. And you'll have the chance to pinch off a spent flower or a lanky stem to keep your plants looking their best. Spending a few minutes on your garden every few days can keep these little jobs from piling up and getting out of hand.

Weeding

Weeding isn't just for looks. Underground, weeds compete with your perennials for water and nutrients; aboveground, they compete for space and light. If left to rampage, weeds could smother or strangle your perennials in as little as a year or two.

Weeding is easiest and most enjoyable if you do it regularly; you'll find young weeds easier to pull and you'll catch them before they go to seed. Weeding a day or two after a good rain makes the job even simpler, since the weeds' roots will come out of the soft soil more easily.

If you weed thoroughly before planting and use a mulch, your weeding chores should be fairly minimal. Eventually, a bed that is weeded regularly produces fewer and fewer weeds.

Watering

Except for drought-tolerant types, most perennials need about 1 inch (25 mm) of rainfall a week during the growing season. This general guideline is handy to keep in mind, but it's not infallible; it's really best to see how much water is available to the roots of your plants.

To check soil moisture, pull aside the mulch and dig a small hole with a trowel. If the top inch or two (2.5 to 5 cm) is dry, it's time to water. Avoid sprinklers; they waste water

Perennials growing in containers may need watering every day.

and encourage disease by wetting plant leaves. Instead, use a soaker hose or a drip irrigation system to water the roots and not the leaves. Watering the soil thoroughly encourages roots to grow deep, so they'll be better able to withstand dry spells. Each time you irrigate, make sure the water has moistened the top 4 to 6 inches (10 to 15 cm) of soil before you stop.

You can use leaves as an effective and natural-looking mulch in woodland gardens and other low-maintenance areas.

Mulching prevents soil from splashing onto flowers during heavy rains, so blooms stay clean and healthy.

Mulching and Fertilizing

A couple of inches of mulch greatly reduces your weeding and watering, shields your soil from hard rains, and protects your plants from frost heaving. Organic mulches are best because they add organic matter to the soil as they break down, helping to keep the soil healthy. Plants generally thrive with mulch over their roots because it keeps them cool and moist. (Don't pile mulch around the bases of plants stems, though; mulch can hold too much moisture around the stems and encourage disease problems.)

Aged bark chips make great mulch for perennial plantings. (Let freshly chipped material sit for a year and turn the pile every month or two before putting it on the garden.) Shredded leaves and compost are also good. Grass clippings are okay, too, if you're sure they

A yearly application of compost will supply all of the nutrients most perennials need to thrive.

came from a lawn that wasn't treated with herbicides. Pine needles look great but make the soil more acid, so use them only around plants that prefer acid soil, such as ferns, lilies, and woodland wildflowers. Avoid mulching with peat moss or fresh sawdust; both form crusts that shed water rather than soaking it up.

After the first hard frost, give your beds a generous layer of mulch to protect plants from frost heaving and dramatic temperature changes. Use about 1 inch (2.5 cm) of heavy materials, like bark chips, or about 3 inches (7.5 cm) of light mulches, such as pine needles or chopped leaves. In par-

ticularly cold or exposed sites without dependable snow cover, also add an extra cover of light branches (those from pine or fir work well), pine needles, or (after the holidays) boughs from a discarded Christmas tree. Remove any covering and pull the mulch back from around the base of the plants in early spring to let the soil warm up.

In mid- to late-spring, spread about 1 inch (2.5 cm) of compost over the bed; this will provide most of the nutrients your perennials need to thrive. For perennials that benefit from extra nutrients, including delphiniums, peonies, and phlox, scatter some balanced organic fertilizer around the base of the plant (following the label directions), and scratch it into the soil. It's important to feed in the spring rather than in the fall so your plants will use the nutrients for flowers instead of making lots of new growth right before frost.

After adding compost and any fertilizer, replace the mulch, leaving a 2-inch (5 cm) mulch-free zone around the base of each plant. Add more mulch as needed over the summer to keep it the right depth.

Pinching and Pruning

Judicious pruning keeps perennials looking their best. Remove flowers after they've faded, a process called deadheading. Doing this will keep plants from putting all their energy into producing seeds and will prevent unwanted seedlings from popping up all over. If plants like phlox and bee balm tend to get gray patches on their leaves (a sign of powdery mildew), thin the clumps in spring by cutting out the weakest stems; by improving air circulation, you'll discourage mildew.

Leggy, late-blooming perennials benefit from pinching back; these include daisy-like plants—asters, boltonia (*Boltonia asteroides*), and chrysanthemums—as well as obedient plant (*Physostegia virginiana*), garden phlox (*Phlox paniculata*), and turtleheads (*Chelone* spp.). In late spring, prune out the growing tips with your fingers (literally pinch them off). You'll be rewarded with more flower stems and shorter plants that are less likely to need staking.

Staking

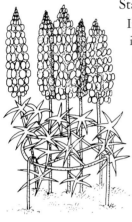

Hoop stakes are great for bushy perennials.

If you grow only short perennials, or if you don't mind your flowers sprawling or leaning on each other, you won't have to worry about staking. But anyone who has seen peonies flattened by rain or has watched a perfect giant delphinium toppled in a strong wind knows that a few minutes spent placing a few stakes is time well spent.

Slender green bamboo or plastic stakes will blend in well behind tall flower stalks. It's best to put the stakes out in early spring as new growth begins. Push each stake as deeply into the ground as you can so it won't fall over. As the flower stalk grows, secure it to the stake with string. Green yarn or twine is less conspicuous than white string; loop it around the stem once before tying it loosely to the stake.

Astilbe seed heads can look attractive even after they turn brown; consider leaving them for extra interest.

Take a minute early in the season to stake delphiniums, foxgloves, and other tall perennials to keep them upright.

Peonies, asters, lupines, and other bushy, multi-stemmed plants with many or large flowers are better supported by a wire ring or linking metal stakes. Buy commercial wire stakes or make your own from wire coat hangers. Install the rings or stakes as soon as leaves emerge, being careful to push the legs into the soil outside of the crown.

Baby's-breath (*Gypsophila paniculata*), many hardy geraniums (*Geranium* spp.), and other light but floppy perennials don't need the rigid support of a wire ring. Instead, try a small dead branch with several branchlets as a support. Or set three small sticks or stakes in a 4-inch (10 cm) triangle around the stem, then surround the plant and stakes with string. As the plant grows, it will cover the support.

Fall Cleanup

The last outdoor maintenance task of the season is preparing your perennials for winter. Give beds a thorough watering before the ground freezes. Remove dead foliage and cut dead stems back to the ground. Compost garden debris, unless it's diseased or full of seeds; then bury or dispose of it. Add mulch, as explained in "Mulching and Fertilizing" on page 45.

If fall is always a busy time for you and you never quite finish your garden cleanup, don't worry. Some plants, such as ornamental grasses and plants with interesting seedpods (including astilbes and blue false indigo [*Baptisia australis*]), are beautiful well into winter. You can leave these standing until early spring.

Most of the garden won't look as tidy if not cut back, but it will get through the winter just as well. Standing stems actually help hold lightweight mulches in place through winter storms. Focus your cleanup time on any plants that showed signs of disease this year or in previous years; fall cleanup reduces the chance of future recurrence.

In spring, get into the garden early (when the soil dries out and no longer squishes underfoot) to cut remaining stems back before new spring growth starts. Otherwise, it will become a much more complicated and time-consuming task as you try to trim out the old growth without damaging the new shoots. If you've had problems in the past with certain perennials (such as mulleins [*Verbascum* spp.]) reseeding too prolifically, also cut off those seed heads in the fall.

Orange coneflowers (*Rudbeckia* spp.) may reseed prolifically if you don't cut off the spent flowers in fall.

Dividing and Multiplying

After your garden has been in place for a few years, some clumps may get too large for your design and others may bloom less vigorously. Or you may want to increase your supply of a particular plant. Dividing your perennials is the answer to all three.

Divide perennials when they're resting, not when they're blooming. Early spring is generally the best time, though many plants can be divided in fall's cooler temperatures. For spring bloomers, wait until they've finished their show. Divide bulbs after they bloom and the foliage has withered but before the foliage disappears. Check the individual plant entries in "Perennials for Every Purpose," starting on page 86, for specific timing advice.

Carefully dig up the plant and brush or hose off the dirt so you can see all the roots. Use your fingers or a sharp knife for small roots and a sharp spade for large clumps (or, better yet, two garden forks placed back to back).

Cut or pull the clump until it splits apart, then repeat the procedure to make four clumps. Prune off any broken roots and any dead, woody parts. If the plant already has leaves, cut the foliage back by half. Replant the clumps, water thoroughly, mulch the soil around the plant, and provide shade for the first couple of days. Water as needed to keep the soil evenly moist until you see new leaves sprouting.

Dig up overgrown perennials or remove them from their pot.

Use your hands or a knife to separate the clump into sections.

Replant the new sections into prepared soil.

Controlling Pests and Diseases

"A stitch in time saves nine" is an old saying that's particularly appropriate where perennial gardening is concerned. Spotting developing problems early and dealing with them as soon as they appear simplifies pest and disease control dramatically.

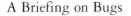

A Briefing on Bugs

Insect damage on your perennials can vary widely, depending on the pest causing the problem. If you figure out what's causing the damage, you'll be able to choose the best control.

If you use a commercial organic spray, always read the label first. Labels list important information on proper storage, target pests, and effective application. Even organic sprays and dusts can irritate skin or lungs, so wear gloves and protective clothing to be on the safe side.

Distorted or Discolored Leaves Small green, black, or pink insects called aphids cluster on young leaves and growing tips and may cause leaves to pucker or buds to drop. Tiny, light-colored specks on the tops of leaves, and often bits of webbing on the undersides and stems, are signs of spider mites. Stunted growth and streaked or withered flowers (especially on gladiolus, chrysanthemums, and daisies) are signs of thrips, small silvery pests that are usually too tiny to see. If clouds of white specks fly up from disturbed foliage, your plants have whiteflies.

If you suspect any of these problems, cut off and destroy severely infested shoots. For less-serious infestations, try dislodging the pests with a strong spray of water. If several days of such treatment isn't enough, spray with insecticidal soap; buy a commercial product or make your own by mixing 1 to 3 teaspoons of liquid dish soap (not laundry or dishwasher detergent) in 1 gallon (4 l) of water. Repeat every 2 or 3 days for 2 weeks until insects disappear.

Holes in Leaves When large holes appear in leaves, look for beetles or caterpillars. Handpicking pests and dropping them into a jar of soapy water controls most infestations. In extreme cases, spray or dust caterpillar-infested plants with BT (*Bacillus thuringiensis*), rotenone, or pyrethrin.

In humid climates, slugs and snails chew leaves and flowers in the dark of the night. They leave unmistakable evidence: a shiny trail. Both are easy to trap under boards or grapefruit halves or in shallow dishes of beer. Lift boards and fruit traps daily and dispose of the pests; empty beer traps as they get full.

Slugs and snails chew holes in flowers and leaves.

Tunnels in Leaves Leafminers disfigure the leaves of columbines, chrysanthemums, delphiniums, and other perennials with tan tunnels or splotches. Immediately remove and destroy infected leaves. If leafminers are a problem in your garden, remove garden debris in the fall (don't wait until spring); lightly scratch the soil around plants in fall and spring to expose overwintering pupae.

A Digest of Diseases

The best defense against diseases is strong, vigorous plants. Building healthy soil, keeping the garden clean, and planting disease-resistant species and cultivars will go a long way toward keeping your perennials problem-free. The individual plant entries in "Perennials for Every Purpose," starting on page 86, will tell you what conditions each plant needs to thrive

Toward the end of the season, it's normal for leaves to turn yellow.

Dusty white or gray spots are a sure sign of powdery mildew.

Aphids can cause distorted flowers and deformed leaves.

and what you can do to prevent special disease problems. Below, you'll learn about some of the most common diseases that can strike a variety of perennials.

Many Perennials with Stunted Growth or Discolored Foliage Diseases usually appear on particular species while ignoring others. If several types of plants growing together have similar symptoms, suspect a nutrient deficiency, not a disease. Pale or yellow leaves may indicate a lack of nitrogen or iron. Dark leaves with purple or red near the veins may lack phosphorus. Mottled leaves may need magnesium. Distorted growth and the death of young leaves and buds may indicate various micronutrient deficiencies.

The best approach to handling nutrient deficiencies is to take a soil test so you'll know what's missing and what you need to add. Sometimes, it's just a matter of adjusting the soil pH, so the nutrients that are already in your soil can become available to your perennials. For a quick but short-term solution, spray the leaves of plants with fish emulsion or liquid seaweed. Working compost into the soil before planting and using it as a mulch should keep your soil well stocked with a balanced supply of nutrients.

White Spots on Leaves In humid areas, powdery mildew is a common but not-too-serious disease. This fungus looks like grayish white powder dusted on leaves, especially on phlox and bee balm. Leaves may drop, but plants rarely die.

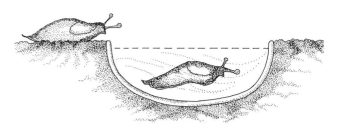
Trap slugs and snails in small pans of beer. Set the pan into the soil, so the edge is even with the soil surface.

In late spring, cut out weaker stems in dense clumps of phlox or bee balm to improve air circulation. Keep infections from spreading by picking off or picking up dropped, infected leaves. Treat the remaining foliage with baking soda spray (1 teaspoon in 1 quart {1 l} of water with a few drops of liquid dish soap), fungicidal soap, or sulfur. When you're shopping for new plants, look for resistant cultivars.

Spots on Leaves Rusts are named for the distinct orange color of their raised or powdery spots on leaves. These fungi appear most often on hollyhocks but may infect irises, pinks, and other perennials. Pick off and destroy infected leaves; treat remaining foliage with sulfur dust or fungicidal soap.

Other spots on leaves may be caused by several different factors, including fungi and bacteria. Pick off infected leaves and treat

Strong water sprays can discourage mites from feeding on hollyhocks.

the rest with baking soda spray or fungicidal soap. If symptoms reappear, insect pests may be at fault; control as explained in "A Briefing on Bugs."

Whole Plants Damaged or Dead When shoots or plants suddenly droop and die, suspect a blight or wilt. A common culprit is Botrytis blight, also known as gray mold. It produces a brownish gray mold that usually appears while plant parts wither, blacken, and rot. It can afflict peonies and bulbs, especially after long spells of damp weather or in soil that isn't well drained. Remove and destroy infected parts; try moving plants to a spot with better air circulation and drainage.

Fungal and bacterial leaf spots are common on many kinds of perennials.

Surround emerging shoots with sharp grit to deter slug and snail damage.

Month by Month
in the Perennial Garden

When is the best time to plant bulbs? When should you divide your perennials? What can you do in the garden on a cold November day? Even experienced gardeners sometimes forget what needs to be done in the garden and when to do it. In this section, you'll find a month-by-month calendar with handy reminders of the garden jobs that are appropriate for each month of the year.

This calendar is based on Zone 6, where the frost-free growing season is approximately late April to mid-October. If your garden is in a different zone, it's easy to adapt this calendar to fit your region. Not sure which zone you're in? Check out the USDA Plant Hardiness Zone Map on page 154.

In warmer climates (Zones 7 to 9), spring comes sooner, so do your March to May chores a month or two earlier (the warmer the climate, the sooner you can start); wait until frost for fall cleanup. In Zone 10 (you lucky gardeners), ignore the fall cleanup and mulching information; keep weeding, watering, and watching for pests throughout the year.

In colder zones and at high elevations (where the frost-free season is more like late May or early June to late August or early September), this calendar will be about a month ahead of you for much of the year. Wait a month to do your March to May chores, finish the

Winter is a great time to look in books and magazines for new ideas that you can use in your own garden.

September chores in August, and start your fall garden cleanup after the first frost.

January

- Review any notes that you made on last year's garden; transfer important reminders (such as plants that you want to move or divide) to a list or calender for the upcoming year.
  - Daydream about how you want to use your yard when warm weather returns. Start or revise your new or existing garden plans (even if you need snowshoes or an umbrella to inventory your yard).
- Take stock of seeds and stored summer bulbs; toss out any that aren't sound.
- Order summer bulbs and plants from mail-order catalogs soon to avoid the rush.
- During thaws, check beds for plant heaving; replace soil around any exposed roots.

February

- On warm days (or when snow melts), inventory the garden to list cleanup chores for next month.
- Plan a weeding session; warm days in February and March are great times for getting rid of winter annual weeds, such as chickweed.

March

- As weather permits, clean up stray leaves, winter debris, remaining stems, and anything left undone last fall. Cut back ornamental grasses. Try not to step in beds where the soil is still wet.
- When the forsythias begin to show their cheerful yellow flowers, pull some of the winter mulch off of your perennial beds so the soil can warm up.
- Check out garden shows in your area to get new garden design and planting ideas.
- Turn last year's compost pile so it will be ready to

spread when the ground warms up. Start a new pile with the debris from spring cleanup.

• Take soil tests.

April

• Finish garden cleanup; pull any weeds.
• Add nutrients recommended by your soil test results.
• Start scouting for pests.
• As you enjoy your spring bulbs, jot down some notes to remind you what you want to add in the fall for next year.
• Top-dress bulb plantings with compost or balanced organic fertilizer for good blooms next year. Remove spent flowers, but leave the foliage until it dies back so bulbs can store enough energy to bloom next year.
• Side-dress clumps of emerging perennials with compost or well-rotted manure. Give those that need rich soil—including delphiniums, bee balm (*Monarda* spp.), and phlox—a little organic fertilizer.
• Divide summer- and fall-blooming perennials when the new shoots are about 3 inches (7.5 cm) tall.
• In dry climates, set out drip irrigation systems for easy watering.

May

• Plant bareroot perennials and container-grown plants as you get them.
• Divide and replant spring-blooming perennials and crowded bulbs after they flower.
• Replace and replenish mulch.
• Pinch back perennials that tend to get leggy, such as chrysanthemums and New England asters (*Aster novae-angliae*).
• Thin out the weakest stems of clump-formers like garden phlox (*Phlox paniculata*) and bee balm (*Monarda* spp.).
• Pull or dig weed seedlings as soon as you spot them, or they'll quickly get out of hand.
• Place wire ring stakes around peonies and other perennials that tend to flop; stake any tall flower stalks individually.
• Plant tender perennials and tender bulbs (including dahlias and gladiolus) outside once danger of frost has passed.
• Plant annuals to hide dying foliage of hardy bulbs.
• If slugs are a problem in your garden, set out shallow pans of beer to trap them; empty traps regularly.

Divide crowded perennials and bulbs after flowering to promote better blooms in following years.

Put up stakes and supports early in the season so your plants can grow up through them.

Use garden shears to snip off the stalks of spent flowers if you want to prevent plants from reseeding.

June

- Walk through your garden regularly, both to enjoy it and to scout for problems.
- Remove and destroy diseased foliage.
- Watch the weather and water if rainfall is scarce. Wait until the top inch or two (2.5 to 5 cm) of soil is dry; then water thoroughly. Container plantings may need daily watering during hot spells.
- Stake perennials that need support, if you didn't do it last month.
- Remove spent blossoms to prevent plants from self-seeding.

July

- If you've kept up on your garden chores so far, you'll have earned a chance to relax just as the weather starts to heat up. Take some lemonade into the garden and make notes in your garden journal.

Bring the beauty of your garden indoors by snipping some leaves and blooms for arrangements.

- Water your perennials as needed. If the weather is very dry, consider watering the compost pile, too; it will break down faster when evenly moist.
- Cut flowers for indoor arrangements in the morning, before the heat of the day.
- Remove spent flowers.
- Order spring bulbs this month or next so they'll arrive in time for fall planting.

August

- Now is the best time to move or divide oriental poppies (*Papaver orientale*), bearded irises, and—at the end of the month—peonies.
- Keep up weeding, deadheading, pest patrol, and watering; remove tattered foliage.
- Cut flowers before they open fully for fresh arranging, drying, or pressing; cut leafy herbs for drying just when they start blooming.

September

- September is often a dry month; water as needed.
- Keep up weeding, deadheading, and pest patrol.
- This is a good time to divide many perennials that have finished flowering, to rearrange plants in beds, and to plant container-grown perennials and shrubs.

Daylilies are a wonderful addition to any perennial landscape for easy-care summer color.

Keep them well watered until winter to promote good root development.

- Start new beds. Plant a cover crop—such as winter rye—to protect the soil over winter (till it under before spring planting). Or dig in chopped leaves and garden wastes; they will decompose by spring.
- Now is a good time to get your soil tested and to correct pH imbalances.

October

- To extend your flower display a bit, cover tender plants on nights when frost is expected.
- Dig and store tender bulbs (such as tuberous begonias, dahlias, caladiums, and gladiolus) when their foliage turns yellow and withers.
- Pull annuals after frost and toss them in the compost pile, or leave them if they have interesting seed heads.
- Cut back dead stems and leaves or let them stand until spring for winter interest. Remove and destroy any diseased foliage.
- Rake leaves for the compost pile or till them into new beds. Chop leaves with the lawn mower for good winter mulch (but don't mulch yet!).
- Plant spring bulbs. Record where you planted them on your site map so you won't dig into them when you plant annuals in the spring.
- Water perennial beds (as well as new shrub and bulb plantings) thoroughly before they go dormant to help them survive through the winter.

Rake fallen leaves off your lawn and save them for mulching your perennials after the ground freezes.

November

- Mow wildflower meadows now or wait until late winter if you want to enjoy the seed heads and leave seeds for the birds.
- Retrieve stakes and replace missing plant labels.
- Drain and store hoses; shut off and drain outdoor water taps.
- Take stock of your gardening tools. Toss out what's beyond salvaging and note what needs replacing; mend, clean, and oil the rest.
- If you don't have a map of your garden, make one now or next month (before snow falls) for winter planning.
- After the ground freezes, add a thick layer of mulch. Cover plants needing extra protection with branches.

December

- Make a wish list of garden supplies for holiday presents or a shopping list for favorite gardeners.
- Catch up on garden reading. Look through all the books and magazines that piled up over the summer for new design ideas and new plants you'd like to try.
- Buy or make a new calendar for next year's garden.

Fall is a good time to look back on the season's triumphs and disappointments. Take notes now for winter planning.

SOLVING LANDSCAPE PROBLEMS

WITH PERENNIALS

It's a rare property that doesn't have at least one difficult spot. Maybe it's a steep, hard-to-mow slope between the yard and the street. Or a dry, shady area under mature maple trees on the side of the house. Or a low, soggy spot that never really dries out, even in the heat of the summer. Whatever the problem, some careful thought and plant selection can turn that difficult site into a beautiful landscape feature.

No matter what kind of site they have, most gardeners share a common problem: a lack of time. The solution is good planning, so your garden doesn't become just another series of chores and doesn't take more time than you have. No matter what kind of garden you want, "Planning for Low Maintenance" on page 56 will show you how a few hours of careful planning and site preparation will cut down amazingly on maintenance. You'll spend less time working on your yard and have more time to enjoy it!

Picking plants that are adapted to the conditions you have to offer is a key part of creating a healthy, beautiful, easy-care garden. Many perennials can adjust to a wide range of different light and soil conditions; others are particularly well suited to certain challenging growing conditions.

"Handling Hillsides" on page 58 shows you how to plan and plant a perennial garden that will turn an awkward slope into an attractive, easy-care asset. You'll also find a list of plants that can take the tough conditions that sloping sites usually offer.

Besides lack of time, shade is a common challenge that gardeners face. It could be the deep summer shade under deciduous trees, the moist, full-day shade on the north side of the house, or the afternoon shade cast by a neighbor's fence. No matter what kind of shade you have, "Succeeding in Shade" on page 60 will help you pick the best plants.

If a soggy site is your problem, check out "Turning Bogs into Beds" on page 62. Here you'll find tips for planning gardens in and around wet spots, along with a list of great-looking perennials that you can grow.

Hot, dry spots along driveways, sidewalks, and pools can be a real landscaping challenge. Fortunately, there are a number of plants that naturally thrive in these kinds of sites. In "Growing a Water-wise Landscape" on page 64, you'll find a list of suggested drought-tolerant perennials to choose from, along with tricks you can use to give those plants the best possible conditions to succeed.

Foundation plantings are typically one of the most visible and least interesting parts of any home landscape. You don't have to settle for the usual collection of cube-shaped shrubs, overgrown junipers, and spindly rhododendrons; add easy-care color with a mixture of great-looking perennials for year-round interest. You'll learn all the secrets in "Foundation Planting with Perennials" on page 66.

Perennials can be practical as well as pretty. Use them to cover steep slopes, fill in soggy areas, add color to shady sites, or create a lush look in a hot, dry spot. They also look great in foundation plantings.

Make mowing easier by using edgings or pathways to prevent perennials from sprawling into the lawn.

Easy-care perennials need less maintenance than a lawn, and they certainly provide a lot more color and interest.

Planning for Low Maintenance

With today's busy lifestyles, it is hard for many gardeners to find the time they want to keep their yard looking great all year long. Even if you have plenty of time to work in the garden, there are probably a number of chores—such as weeding or edging—that you tend to put off while you spend your time doing fun things, like planting. In this section, you'll learn how to tailor your landscape plans and plant choices to focus on maximum return for minimum effort.

What's the Most Work?

The key to landscaping for low maintenance is identifying your most bothersome gardening tasks. Which chores take the most time? Which do you like least? Landscape your yard to minimize the unpleasant chores so you can focus on the things you like most, whether it's fussing over a formal herb garden or sipping lemonade in the shade. Below are easy-care solutions to some of the most time-consuming landscape tasks.

Hand Trimming Reduce hand trimming around tree trunks, fences, posts, and bird baths by replacing the grass there with hostas, daylilies, or other groundcovers.

Plant perennials around trees and shrubs to minimize tedious trimming.

Mowing If you hate mowing, you can reduce the area of your lawn in favor of flowers, shrubs, or groundcovers. If the site is sunny, convert part or all of it into a wildflower meadow; you'll reduce mowing chores to once or twice a year. Landscape shady areas where grass grows poorly with shade-tolerant groundcovers or woodland plants; convert high-traffic areas into shady patios that are connected by paved or mulched pathways. In small yards, urban areas, and dry climates, consider eliminating the lawn altogether. Perennials look great next to paving stones, bricks, cement pavers, or gravel.

Edging If you hate edging flower beds and digging out the grass that invades from the lawn, install edging strips. Make sure the strips are level with or slightly below the top of the grass blades so you can mow over them.

Weeding Minimizing weeding starts at planting time. First, don't skimp on site preparation. Every weed you remove before you start means a whole bucketful of weeds you won't have to remove later. After planting, apply and maintain a good mulch cover. Check the mulch depth three or four times a year and add more if needed. You might have to remove a few occasional weeds that sprout in the mulch, but they'll be easy to pull.

One of the best things you can do to cut down on

weeding is to get in the habit of pulling weeds as soon as you see them. Otherwise, you give them a chance to spread or set seed and you'll end up with more work. Carry a basket, bag, or bucket with you every time you walk around the yard to collect pulled weeds. (They may reroot if you leave them on the soil.)

Watering If hauling hoses around the yard isn't your idea of fun, planning a water-wise garden will cut down on your watering chores. First, look for plants that thrive in your area without extra water. Fields, roadsides, graveyards, and abandoned lots are good places to get ideas of tough plants that can survive without supplemental watering.

Choose drought-tolerant perennials to reduce watering chores.

The mulch that you use on finished plantings to keep weeds down will also help to keep the soil moist and reduce watering chores. If you must water, consider laying soaker hoses or drip irrigation systems; then you'll only have to hook up the hose or turn on the system when you need to water, instead of standing there watering by hand.

Small bulbs like reticulated iris (*Iris reticulata*) are easy to plant, and they'll grow and thrive for years.

Dependable, Easy-care Perennials

Here's a list of some of the most trouble-free perennials you can grow. All of the plants below thrive in sun and average, well-drained soil with little fuss. (For suggestions of easy-care shade plants, see "Super Perennials for Shade" on page 60.) You'll find complete growing information on all of these plants in "Perennials for Every Purpose," starting on page 86.

Achillea filipendulina (fern-leaved yarrow)
Alchemilla mollis (lady's-mantle)
Anemone tomentosa 'Robustissima' (Japanese anemone)
Armeria maritima (common thrift)
Asclepias tuberosa (butterfly weed)
Aster novae-angliae (New England aster)
Baptisia australis (blue false indigo)
Boltonia asteroides (boltonia)
Centranthus ruber (red valerian)
Chrysanthemum x *superbum* (shasta daisy)
Coreopsis verticillata (thread-leaved coreopsis)
Echinacea purpurea (purple coneflower)
Echinops ritro (globe thistle)
Gaillardia x *grandiflora* (blanket flower)
Geranium sanguineum (blood-red cranesbill)
Hemerocallis hybrids (daylilies)
Iris sibirica (Siberian iris)
Liatris spicata (spike gayfeather)
Lilium hybrids (lilies)
Narcissus hybrids (daffodils)
Nepeta x *faassenii* (catmint)
Paeonia lactiflora (common garden peony, single-flowered cultivars)
Physostegia virginiana (obedient plant)
Platycodon grandiflorus (balloon flower)
Rudbeckia fulgida (orange coneflower)
Sedum spp. (sedums)
Salvia x *superba* (violet sage)
Veronica spicata (spike speedwell)
Yucca filamentosa (Adam's needle)

Handling Hillsides

With a little imagination, you can transform a sloping site from a maintenance headache to an eye-catching landscape asset. Hillsides are awkward to mow and weed, so the best strategy is to cover them with plants that take care of themselves. Or, if you're willing to invest some time and money, you can build retaining walls or terraced beds that will safely and attractively support a wide range of beautiful perennials.

Terraces or low walls can turn a troublesome slope into an eye-catching landscape feature.

Super Perennials for Slopes

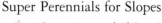

Grass is probably the most common groundcover used to hold the soil on slopes, but it isn't especially interesting, and it can be a real pain to mow every week. For an attractive and easy-care solution, replace the turf grass with tough, low-maintenance plants that look great and protect the soil, too. To get you started, "Great Groundcovers for Slopes" lists some of the most reliable options for sunny and shady sites.

Sunny Slopes One good option for sunny slopes is planting a mixture of sun-loving groundcovers, taller spreading perennials (such as daylilies), and spreading shrubs, such as creeping juniper (*Juniperus horizontalis*). Or, if you like a casual look and you're willing to mow the slope once a year, consider turning it into a wildflower meadow. You'll find more information on planning and planting a meadow garden in "Making a Meadow" on page 72.

Building a rock garden is another great solution for a sunny, well-drained slope. Place large rocks at irregular intervals throughout the area. Bury each so that over half is underground to keep it from rolling or washing away. Large, secure stones will give you a steady foothold so you can get into the garden for occasional weeding. Between the stones, plant sprawling, sun-loving perennials, such as wall rock cress (*Arabis caucasica*), snow-in-summer (*Cerastium tomentosum*), and basket-of-gold (*Aurinia saxatilis*), with small hardy bulbs, such as crocus and reticulated iris (*Iris reticulata*).

Shady Slopes On shady slopes, spreading species and cultivars of hostas make great groundcovers, alone or combined with other perennials. Other good companions include lily-of-the-valley (*Convallaria*

majalis), pachysandra (*Pachysandra terminalis*), and common periwinkle (*Vinca minor*). For extra interest, add spring-flowering bulbs to get early color from groundcover plantings.

If the slope is shaded by deciduous trees, create a woodland garden by combining groundcovers such as ajuga and European wild ginger (*Asarum europaeum*) with early-blooming wildflowers. Creeping phlox (*Phlox stolonifera*), wild bleeding heart (*Dicentra eximia*), and Allegheny foamflower (*Tiarella cordifolia*) are a few species that will bloom in spring before the trees leaf out fully and shade the area.

Establishing Plantings on a Slope Good soil preparation is a key part of successful slope landscaping. Remove the existing grass and weeds, and dig the soil to loosen it. If the slope is steep, you'll need

Choose drought-tolerant perennials for steep slopes and terraces; these sites tend to be very dry.

Plant low-growing perennials along the tops of walls and terraces so they can cascade over the side.

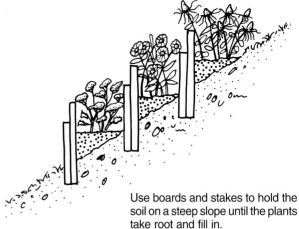

Use boards and stakes to hold the soil on a steep slope until the plants take root and fill in.

to build temporary terraces before you plant. Long, flat boards anchored behind 2-foot (60 cm) spikes driven partly into the ground hold the soil in place for a year or two. Once plants have gotten established and filled in, you can remove the boards and spikes.

Set the plants into the ground as you would for any other garden; see "Planting Is the Fun Part" on page 42 for details. Water thoroughly and add a generous layer of mulch. Weed and water regularly for the first year to get the plants off to a good start; after that, they should need little care.

Terraces for Trouble-free Slopes

Constructing permanent terraces requires more time, effort, and money up front, but the terraces last for years and dramatically increase the variety of perennials you can grow.

Planting perennials along walls (and even in the wall, if possible) will soften the look of the hard edges.

Low retaining walls (up to 2 feet [60 cm] high) are reasonably easy to construct from flat stones or lumber. Consult a professional landscaper or builder for any wall that must be taller than 2 feet (60 cm): Large retaining walls must be well anchored and properly designed to keep them from washing out, cracking, or tumbling down after a few years. It's easier to make walls correctly than to repair them.

Fill finished terraces with good topsoil. After the soil settles for a few weeks, add a bit more if needed to level the top of the beds; then you'll be ready to plant your perennials. Keep in mind that terraces may tend to dry out more quickly than regular in-ground beds, so you're better off looking for plants that can take dry conditions.

Great Groundcovers for Slopes

Here are some tough and trouble-free perennials that adapt well to life on a sloping site. To learn more about specific plants, look them up in "Perennials for Every Purpose," starting on page 86.

Groundcovers for Sun
Cerastium tomentosum (snow-in-summer)
Dianthus gratianopolitanus (cheddar pinks)
Phlox subulata (moss phlox)
Sedum spurium (two-row sedum)
Stachys byzantina (lamb's-ears)

Groundcovers for Shade
Ajuga reptans (ajuga)
Asarum europaeum (European wild ginger)
Epimedium x *rubrum* (red epimedium)
Galium odoratum (sweet woodruff)
Hosta hybrids (hostas, spreading types)
Lamium maculatum (spotted lamium)
Tiarella cordifolia (Allegheny foamflower)

Succeeding in Shade

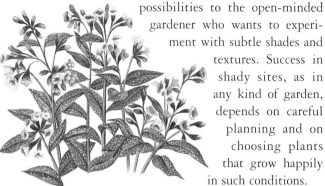

Shady nooks provide a cool, peaceful refuge for plants and people who can't take the hot summer sun. They may not glow with the vibrant colors of poppies and peonies, but they offer many wonderful possibilities to the open-minded gardener who wants to experiment with subtle shades and textures. Success in shady sites, as in any kind of garden, depends on careful planning and on choosing plants that grow happily in such conditions.

Picking Your Plants

The two main factors that determine which plants can grow well in your shade garden are how much light the garden gets and how much water is available.

Sites that get a few hours of direct sun or a full day of filtered light can support a wider range of plants than a spot that's in deep shade all day. Gardens under deciduous trees may get lots of sun until early summer, when the developing tree leaves begin to block the light. "Examine Your Exposure" on page 18 can help you figure out what type of shade you have. The individual plant entries in "Perennials for Every Purpose," starting on page 86, will tell you which kind of conditions each plant prefers.

Shady gardens can also vary widely in the amount of moisture that's available. Plants that grow well in moist woodland soils usually aren't happy in the dry shade under roof overhangs or shallow-rooted trees such as maples and beeches. In moist shade, you may need to seek out slug- and snail-resistant plants; some hostas that are less prone than others to slug damage include 'Blue Angel', 'Krossa Regal', 'Sum & Substance', *Hosta fortunei* 'Aureomarginata', and *H. sieboldiana* and its cultivar 'Frances Williams'.

As you would when planning any garden, look for perennials that are attractive as well as adaptable. Spring tends to be the primary bloom season in a shade garden, but you'll look at the plants all season long, so choose ones

Super Perennials for Shade

Here's a list of just some of the great-looking, easy-to-grow perennials that will thrive in a shady garden. You'll find more information in the individual entries in "Perennials for Every Purpose," starting on page 86.

Actea pachypoda (white baneberry)
Ajuga reptans (ajuga)
Aquilegia canadensis (wild columbine)
Arisaema triphyllum (Jack-in-the-pulpit)
Asarum europaeum (European wild ginger)
Astilbe x *arendsii* (astilbe)
Bergenia spp. (bergenias)
Brunnera macrophylla (Siberian bugloss)
Cimicifuga racemosa (black snakeroot)
Dicentra eximia (fringed bleeding heart)
Epimedium x *rubrum* (red epimedium)
Helleborus orientalis (Lenten rose)
Hosta hybrids (hostas)
Iris cristata (crested iris)
Lamium maculatum (spotted lamium)
Polygonatum odoratum (fragrant Solomon's seal)
Pulmonaria saccharata (Bethlehem sage)
Smilacina racemosa (Solomon's plume)
Tiarella cordifolia (Allegheny foamflower)
Uvularia grandiflora (great merrybells)

If your yard is partly sunny and partly shady, try a variety of plants to see which grow best in your conditions.

that also look good when they're not flowering. Include perennials that have showy, colored leaves, such as blue-leaved hostas, silver-dotted Bethlehem sage (*Pulmonaria saccharata*), maroon-leaved 'Palace Purple' heuchera (*Heuchera* 'Palace Purple'), and golden-leaved lamium (*Lamium maculatum aureum*). For extra summer color, remember annuals such as impatiens and begonias and the colorful foliage of coleus and caladiums.

Planning and Planting Tips

Take advantage of several strategies for succeeding in shade. First, direct traffic away from shallow-rooted trees and areas you wish to keep as deep shade so you can replace scraggly lawn with groundcovers. Use stepping stones or heavily mulched paths to guide visitors around planted areas. A bench on an informal stone patio makes an inviting destination and works well in the deepest shade or beneath the most shallow-rooted trees.

Second, enrich the soil with lots of organic matter. A good supply of organic matter may mean the difference between death and survival in shade, especially dry shade. If you are gardening under trees, you can't just till in the organic matter or dump a thick layer on the surface; either way, you'll harm the tree roots. Instead, try digging and enriching individual planting pockets close to the tree trunk, where there are few feeder roots. Dig a hole about 8 inches (20 cm) in diameter for each plant and mix in a handful or two of compost; then plant as usual.

Water hellebores (*Helleborus* spp.) regularly for the first few years; after that, they'll tolerate dry shade.

After planting, water thoroughly and apply a layer of mulch. In dry shade, water regularly until plants are established, and plan on watering even mature plants during dry spells. If slugs and snails become a problem, you may want to remove some or all of the mulch; despite all of its benefits, mulch also provides shelter for these troublesome pests.

Ajuga and hostas are two tough, dependable perennials that are excellent for easy-care shade gardens.

If you have a shallow-rooted tree that makes planting difficult, consider a patio with container plants instead.

A bog garden is a great site for many kinds of irises. The flowers are beautiful in early summer, and the spiky leaves look great all season.

Some tough perennials can even grow in standing water.

Turning Bogs into Beds

Don't let a wet yard or soggy spot deter you from gardening: Even a year-round spring or bog can be attractively landscaped with beautiful, easy-care perennials. You may decide to approach the area as you would any other garden, with a formal planting plan in mind. Or you may choose to go for an informal feel and create a casual-looking natural area.

Options for Organized Plantings

If your problem site is under water most of the year, go with the flow—leave it as a wetland or convert it into a small pond and plant perennials to cascade over its edges. Some of our most beautiful native plants, including cardinal flower (*Lobelia cardinalis*), queen-of-the-prairie (*Filipendula rubra*), white or pink turtle-heads (*Chelone* spp.), and some ferns, prefer to grow where their feet are wet. They look equally good in perennial beds and wild settings.

If you want a more traditional flower bed or border where soil is constantly soggy, raise the level of the soil in the planting area at least 4 inches (10 cm). Adding a healthy dose of organic matter and bringing in additional soil to make raised beds can often transform a constantly wet site into an evenly moist site—the ideal condition for many classic garden flowers. If the bed is still soggy, even in summer—that is, the soil never gets dry enough to crumble when you squeeze some—and you don't want to raise the bed any higher, stick with the plants that are suggested in "Perennials That Like Wet Feet."

A Natural Solution for Soggy Sites

If you enjoy the informal feel of naturalistic landscaping, wet spots are a perfect place to "go wild." Healthy wetlands serve important ecological roles by purifying groundwater, replenishing the water table, and supporting a wide variety of plants and wildlife.

A mixed planting of moisture-loving perennials can provide season-long interest in a wet spot. You don't need to carefully plan out different heights, textures, and colors—just set plants out in random order. Great blue lobelia (*Lobelia siphilitica*), swamp milkweed (*Asclepias incarnata*), marsh marigold (*Caltha palustris*), yellow flag (*Iris pseudacorus*), and blue flag (*Iris versicolor*) are a few colorful perennials that grow happily in constantly soggy soil. Angelica (*Angelica atropurpurea*) is a native perennial herb that forms lush, leafy clumps and tall flower clusters in

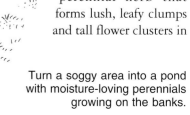

Turn a soggy area into a pond with moisture-loving perennials growing on the banks.

Spring-blooming marsh marigolds are a natural choice for planting in low spots or along ponds.

wet soil. Native cattails (*Typha latifolia*) thrive in standing water, but they may choke out everything else (which isn't a problem if you like them). Royal ferns (*Osmunda* spp.) and beech ferns (*Thelypteris* spp.) are also great additions for foliage interest.

If your soil is constantly moist but not saturated, your planting options expand dramatically. Most woodland plants and wildflowers prefer moist soil to dry soil. Many sun-loving wildflowers also grow happily in moist soil. If the area dries out enough to support grass, try a wet meadow, with rugged perennials like spotted Joe-Pye weed (*Eupatorium maculatum*) and New England asters (*Aster novae-angliae*). Cut the meadow with a string trimmer once a year (wear boots to keep your feet dry!) in late fall or early spring. You'll learn more about planning, planting, and maintaining such areas in "Making a Meadow" on page 72.

For more ideas, check out natural marsh, pond, or streamside habitats in your area to see what is thriving there and how it looks. You'll get lots of ideas about other plants that will grow well in your particular area and about how you can arrange them. (Just remember, gather ideas and inspiration from these natural areas, not from the plants themselves. Many garden centers are expanding their selection into water-garden plants as well, so you should have no trouble buying the plants you need.)

Perennials That Like Wet Feet

Here are some super perennials that will thrive in a spot with consistently moist soil. For more information on specific plants, look for their individual entries in "Perennials for Every Purpose," starting on page 86.

Arisaema triphyllum (Jack-in-the-pulpit)
Aruncus dioicus (goat's beard)
Asarum europaeum (European wild ginger)
Astrantia major (masterwort)
Brunnera macrophylla (Siberian bugloss)
Chelone glabra (white turtlehead)
Eupatorium maculatum (spotted Joe-Pye weed)
Filipendula rubra (queen-of-the-prairie)
Galium odoratum (sweet woodruff)
Iris sibirica (Siberian iris)
Ligularia dentata (big-leaved ligularia)
Lobelia cardinalis (cardinal flower)
Lysimachia punctata (yellow loosestrife)
Monarda didyma (bee balm)
Physostegia virginiana (obedient plant)
Polygonum affine (Himalayan fleeceflower)
Primula denticulata (drumstick primrose)
Smilacina racemosa (Solomon's plume)
Tradescantia x *andersoniana* (common spiderwort)

There's nothing like the colorful flower clusters of drumstick primroses to brighten up a bog garden.

Growing a Water-wise Landscape

If you live where rainfall is scant or undependable or if your soil is so sandy that water runs right through, it makes sense to plan your landscape accordingly. Choosing drought-adapted plants and using water-wise gardening techniques will save you more than just water—it can save you time and money, too! Plus, you'll be spared the disappointment of watching poorly chosen plants wither and die as the heat and drought take their toll. Instead, you'll have a great-looking landscape that can weather tough conditions with little extra help from you.

Water-saving Gardening Basics

Water-wise gardening involves a two-part approach. One is keeping the rainfall that you do get in the soil,

Plan an efficient, easy-care landscape by choosing drought-tolerant plants and using water-saving techniques such as drip irrigation and mulching.

or in storage, so it's available to plants when they need it. The other part is reducing the total amount of water that your garden needs to thrive.

Keeping Water Where You Need It

Good soil care is a key step in keeping moisture where plant roots can get it. Loose, crumbly soil can easily soak up rainfall that would just run off of compacted beds. Digging the soil thoroughly at planting time and keeping it loose by not walking on the beds will keep the soil in good shape.

Adding organic matter to your soil is another way to trap moisture. Organic matter is a natural sponge, soaking up water when it is available and releasing it later on to plant roots. Adding ample quantities of organic matter to your soil at planting time will help plants withstand dry spells. Also use liberal quantities of mulch to replenish the organic matter supply and to prevent moisture already in the soil from evaporating.

Channeling and storing rainfall are other ways to reduce the need for supplemental watering. Regrading areas of your yard may help to keep rainfall from running off into the street, or at least to slow down the water so it has more chance to soak in. Building terraces (as explained in "Handling Hillsides" on page 58) is a great way to slow or stop runoff on sloping sites. Place a large plastic trash can (cut a hole in the lid to let water in) or commercially available rain barrel under a downspout to collect rainwater for later use.

At planting, set plants out in shallow depressions, so the crowns and the soil immediately around them

'Autumn Joy' sedum is a tough, dependable perennial that offers nearly year-round interest with little care.

Yarrows and torch lilies (*Kniphofia* spp.) will thrive in loose, well-drained soil without regular watering.

If dry spells are common in your area, consider replacing some of your lawn with drought-tolerant perennials.

are slightly below the normal soil level. Or use extra soil to form a shallow basin around each plant (new or already established) to collect and hold available water.

Reducing Overall Water Needs Cutting down on the amount of water your yard actually needs is another important part of planning a water-wise landscape. Here are some ideas to try:

• Mulch, then mulch more! A thick layer of organic mulch will help hold moisture in the soil, where plant roots need it.

• Reduce the size of your lawn. Lush lawns just aren't compatible with arid climates. Prairie and meadow gardens are naturally adapted to drier conditions; once established, they don't need watering and need mowing only once a year (see "Making a Meadow" on page 72 for details).

• Group plants according to their water requirements. Locate thirsty plants closest to the house, rain barrel, or water faucet, where you can reach them easily. Landscape outlying areas with species that need little if any supplemental water, such as those listed in "Tough Perennials for Hot, Dry Sites."

• Leave a little extra space between all plants so their roots can reach farther for water without competing. (Mulch the bare soil between plants.)

• Block or moderate drying winds with a hedge or a windbreak. Or locate your garden on the sheltered side of an existing structure.

• If you must water, do it early or late in the day, preferably using drip systems or soaker hoses. "Watering" on page 44 will tell you how to judge when your plants really need to be watered.

Tough Perennials for Hot, Dry Sites

These plants don't mind heat and are happiest in soils that are very well drained and even sandy. Once established, they withstand extended dry spells. For more information on specific plants, check out the individual entries in "Perennials for Every Purpose," starting on page 86.

Achillea filipendulina (fern-leaved yarrow)
Allium giganteum (giant onion)
Artemisia absinthium (common wormwood)
Asclepias tuberosa (butterfly weed)
Aubrieta deltoides (purple rock cress)
Aurinia saxatilis (basket-of-gold)
Baptisia australis (blue false indigo)
Catananche caerulea (Cupid's dart)
Centranthus ruber (red valerian)
Cerastium tomentosum (snow-in-summer)
Coreopsis verticillata (thread-leaved coreopsis)
Dianthus gratianopolitanus (cheddar pinks)
Echinacea purpurea (purple coneflower)
Echinops ritro (globe thistle)
Eryngium amethystinum (amethyst sea holly)
Euphorbia epithymoides (cushion spurge)
Gaillardia x *grandiflora* (blanket flower)
Helianthus x *multiflorus* (perennial sunflower)
Oenothera tetragona (common sundrops)
Perovskia atriplicifolia (Russian sage)
Rudbeckia fulgida (orange coneflower)
Salvia officinalis (garden sage)
Salvia x *superba* (violet sage)
Sedum spectabile (showy stonecrop)
Sedum spurium (two-row sedum)
Stachys byzantina (lamb's-ears)
Verbascum chaixii (nettle-leaved mullein)
Yucca filamentosa (Adam's needle)

Foundation Planting with Perennials

When it comes time to landscape a newly built home, people traditionally head to the local nursery, fill up the car with yews, junipers, and rhododendrons, and plunk them in on a weekend to create a foundation planting. It's easy and fast, but after the first few years, you're stuck spending hours clipping and trimming the shrubs as they overgrow the space or buying new plants as the old ones die off.

Happily, more and more gardeners are discovering the advantages of using perennials, grasses, bulbs, and other colorful, adaptable plants to create a welcoming entrance that is both beautiful and low maintenance.

Hostas come in a wide range of sizes and colors. Their tidy growth habit makes them ideal for foundation plantings.

Perennials versus Shrubs

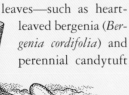

Evergreen shrubs are typically chosen for foundation planting because they grow quickly and are "interesting" all year. But the plants that look just right in 5 years often take over the house in 15 or 20. Shrubs may need frequent pruning not just for looks but to keep them from growing over windows, closing over doors, or (in humid areas) holding damaging moisture against the house itself. In cold areas, shrubs may be damaged by heavy, wet snow sliding off of the roof above. If you try to protect the shrubs from snow damage, then you're stuck looking at ugly wooden shrub shelters or burlap-covered lumps for several months each year.

Perennials, alone or in combination with hardy bulbs, trees, vines, and shrubs, offer attractive and more colorful alternatives to a boring row of clipped evergreens. Well-chosen perennials won't drastically outgrow their location, and they're dormant when snow falls off the roof. Mixing perennials that have evergreen leaves—such as heart-leaved bergenia (*Bergenia cordifolia*) and perennial candytuft (*Iberis sempervirens*)—with hardy bulbs and ornamental grasses can create a planting with year-round appeal. Plus, perennials change continually through the season, which is more than can be said for the most commonly planted foundation evergreens!

Planning a Perennial Foundation Planting

Planning a perennial garden next to your house is pretty much the same as planning one in any other part of the yard. In some cases, though, foundation sites have extreme growing conditions that you'll need to consider as you choose your plant.

Light levels and microclimates can vary dramatically on different sides of your house; a wall facing due north is cool and shady while one facing south or southwest bakes in the sun unless shaded by trees.

When you choose perennials and shrubs for foundation plantings, look for flower colors that will complement the colors of your house.

Ornamental grasses look great with all kinds of perennials and are attractive through much of the year.

Eaves may create a constant drought by blocking rainfall. At the drip line, the soil may be totally compacted by the impact of falling or dripping water.

Spend a little time learning about the site where you want to plant so you can select the best-adapted perennials for your conditions. (See "Learning about Your Landscape," starting on page 12, for complete details.) "Perennials for Every Purpose," starting on page 86, has individual entries on 130 great, easy-care perennials you might like to try. These entries will tell you what conditions the plants like, how tall they grow, when they bloom and how to care for them.

To cope with the problems of dry overhangs and compacted drip lines, plan to cover the strip from the house to just past the roof edge with mulch. For especially easy maintenance, use a layer of landscape fabric topped with 4 inches (10 cm) of gravel or bark chips. If this strip is too wide to be hidden behind a row of plants, top the mulch with driftwood or a few smooth river stones or other interesting rocks. If you'd really rather plant there, stick with drought-tolerant species that can take those tough conditions.

Foundation Planting Options

There are no special rules for designing foundation plantings—just choose the plants that can take the conditions and that look good to you. Including some fragrant flowers—such as peonies and cheddar pinks (*Dianthus gratianopolitanus*)—adds an extra welcoming touch. Many herbs offer fragrant flowers or leaves, and they're nearby when you need some for cooking.

Mix in culinary herbs, such as sage and thyme, to create a foundation planting that's practical as well as pleasing.

To shield high foundations, include some tall perennials that will continue to be interesting even after they've gone dormant. For instance, the gray seedpods of blue false indigo (*Baptisia australis*) look attractive all winter. A number of tall ornamental grasses are also pleasing to look at after they've dried. Enjoy the old stems and leaves all winter, then cut them back to the ground in early spring before the new growth sprouts.

For a formal look, keep the lines straight with a path of bricks or square or rectangular flagstones and straight edges to plantings. For a less formal design, curve the edge of the bed to create a gentle, casual feel and to allow a few of the plants in front to sprawl a bit onto the path.

Include a mix of rounded and spiky blooms to add interest to your planting. Fragrant leaves and flowers are nice, too!

PERENNIAL GARDENS
FOR EVERY SITE

From matched pairs of planted urns and formal herb gardens to casual meadow and cottage gardens, the possibilities for enjoying perennials in your landscape are endless. In this chapter, you'll find some fun and practical garden styles and themes that you can use when you are planning your perennial plantings. You'll learn the characteristics of several different kinds of gardens and find out which perennials work best for each.

A classic variation on the perennial border is the color-theme border. It's a natural choice for gardeners with a strong favorite color. You'll find lots of hints on planning your own color-based plantings in "Creating a Color-theme Garden" on page 70.

Meadows are the most informal type of perennial garden. Creating a beautiful meadow out of a lawn area does take some work, but the time you'll save in mowing only once or twice a year will more than repay the initial effort. "Making a Meadow" on page 72 gives you all the details you need for turning a boring lawn area into a beautiful mixture of grasses and flowers.

Whether your style is formal or informal, you can have the pleasure of growing perennials that will attract butterflies to your garden. "Gardening for Butterflies" on page 74 tells you how to create a great butterfly habitat right in your own yard.

Herbs are a natural choice for any kind of landscape. If you have a formal landscape, you could include a knot garden, with an intricate design of herbs clipped into tiny hedges and laid out in patterns. But herbs are equally at home in more casual settings, either alone or mixed with traditional perennials in a bed or border. In "Landscaping with Perennial Herbs" on page 76, you'll find out how to incorporate these colorful, fragrant, and flavorful plants into all parts of your perennial landscape.

Cottage gardens are another fun way to group your perennials. No two cottage gardens are alike, but they're all informal, exuberant, and colorful. Usually they're mixtures of reseeding annuals, easy-care perennials, shrubs, roses, and herbs, often planted so closely that you can barely distinguish one plant from another. "Creating a Cottage Garden" on page 78 covers the basics of planning your own informal plantings. Fragrance is an essential element of the romance and charm of the cottage style; "Gardening with Fragrance" on page 80 offers special tips for choosing delightfully scented perennials for any planting.

Growing perennials in pots is a great way to create movable, easily changed displays to perk up an otherwise plain patio or front porch. "Growing Perennials in Containers" on page 82 will help you to choose perennials that adapt well to container culture and to care for them so they look their best.

If you enjoy having lots of flowers to bring inside, a cutting garden could be for you. In "Creating a Cutting Garden" on page 84, you'll find out which perennials work best for fresh arrangements and how to pick them for best results.

You may like one of these garden themes so much that you decide to use it throughout your yard. Or you may enjoy tucking several different smaller theme gardens into various areas, so each part of your yard has a different feel. Either way, you'll have a great time planning, planting, and appreciating your special perennial gardens.

The options for landscaping with perennials are limitless. Plant perennials alone in a formal border, grow them with grasses in a meadow garden, or combine them with a bounty of bulbs, herbs, and shrubs in a cottage garden.

Creating a Color-theme Garden

You can design beautiful gardens around a theme as simple as a single color. This may sound plain, but it's anything but that—color-theme gardens are attractive and dramatic additions to any landscape. Even gardens that are based on green leaves contain varying tints and shades, as well as textures and patterns, from the frosty blue-greens of some hostas to the deep glossy green of European wild ginger (*Asarum europaeum*). When you start including flower colors against the greens, you add an extra level of interest. Even if the flowers you choose are all in the same color group, the many different shades and tints create a mosaic of changing colors throughout the season.

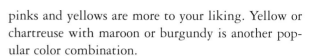

Planning a color-theme garden starts by picking the color you want to work with. Try a monochrome (based on one flower color) border if you have a favorite color or love collecting flowers of a particular color. Or make a small monochromatic section part of a long mixed-color border, perhaps using silver foliage to separate it from flowers of other colors.

If you have a couple of unconnected small beds, you might want to try a different color in each. Or choose a single color for the whole garden in each season: perhaps pink for spring, white for summer, and yellow for fall, or whatever colors appeal to you.

Another option to consider is a two-color border. Blue and white make a classic combination. Or perhaps pinks and yellows are more to your liking. Yellow or chartreuse with maroon or burgundy is another popular color combination.

The key to creating a beautiful and effective color-theme garden is to pick the colors that *you* like and those that blend well with your house. White flowers, for instance, can look dirty against cream-colored siding, while bright pinks can clash unmercifully with rusty orange brick.

If you're not sure how certain colors will look in a given setting, try growing the plants there in a container for a year. If the colors look good to you, go ahead and plan a full-scale garden; if they don't fit the bill, move the pot elsewhere, and try a different combination in that spot next year. You'll save yourself a lot of time and money this way, and you'll be more confident about the results. In the sections below, you'll find more tips for planning gardens around some of the most popular colors.

Beautiful Blue Gardens

Blue is a popular color theme for perennial plantings. Many beloved summer-blooming perennials have blue flowers, including delphiniums, Siberian iris (*Iris*

Gardens based on blue flowers and foliage are peaceful and soothing—a perfect place to relax after a rough day.

Red flowers look marvelous against green leaves. The contrast of these colors is dynamic and exciting.

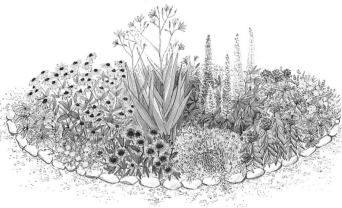

sibirica), bellflowers (*Campanula* spp.), and pincushion flower (*Scabiosa caucasica*).

To extend the season, add blue-flowered shrubs, such as caryopteris (*Caryopteris* x *clandonensis*), and annuals, such as ageratum and lobelia (*Lobelia erinus*). For spring color, plant bulbs such as Spanish bluebells (*Hyacinthoides hispanicus*) and Siberian squills (*Scilla sibirica*). For even more choices, expand your list to include the many flowers in the blue-violet range.

Several plants offer bluish foliage; amethyst sea holly (*Eryngium amethystinum*) and blue false indigo (*Baptisia australis*) offer blue flowers as well. Many of the finest hosta cultivars—including 'Krossa Regal', 'Blue Giant', and 'Hadspen Blue'—have cool blue leaves that look super in shady gardens. Rue (*Ruta graveolens*) and blue fescue (*Festuca cinerea*) produce their best blues in full sun. Also include silver foliage, which is stunning in blue borders.

Pretty Pink Gardens

Pink is an easy choice for a color theme, since so many perennials, hardy bulbs, and flowering shrubs come in this color. Use pink flowers alone, or try a two-color combination of pink and red, pink and white, or pink

and pale yellows. Pink foliage is hard to find, but purples—like purple garden sage (*Salvia officinalis* 'Purpurascens')—and silvers—such as lamb's-ears (*Stachys byzantina*)—are perfect additions to pink borders.

Wonderful White Gardens

Elegant white theme gardens offer perhaps the widest range of flower choice, as so many perennials, hardy bulbs, annuals, and flowering shrubs and trees come in bright white, off-white, or cream.

All-white designs are sometimes called "moon gardens" because the flowers almost glow under the light of a full moon. This effect can also be achieved under street lights in urban gardens or at the edge of a well-lit patio. Moon gardens include many plants with silver or gray foliage; they may also include flowers in the palest pastels, as these reflect moonlight almost as well as white. For gardens near the house, include fragrant types of white roses, lilies, and peonies, along with fragrant annuals such as sweet alyssum (*Lobularia maritima*) and flowering tobacco (*Nicotiana alata*).

Rousing Reds, Oranges, and Yellows

Hot-color borders are exciting and vibrant. Yellow gardens have a sunny, cheerful look and are fairly easy to arrange without fear of clashing colors. Reds and oranges make the loudest statements of the various color themes, but red flowers also have the greatest potential to clash with each other. Before planting a whole border of these bright colors, consider trying a small bed or part of a border first to see if you like the effect.

White gardens are especially charming at night, when the pale blooms and leaves reflect any available light.

Gardens with lots of yellow flowers and foliage look cheerful and sunny, even on dreary days.

Start your meadow off in spring with masses of naturalized bulbs, such as bluebells (*Hyacinthoides* spp.).

Making a Meadow

Meadows are informal blends of flowers and grasses growing in a sunny, open spot. They provide food and shelter for birds, beneficial insects, and butterflies. They also add a casual, country touch to any yard. Best of all, established meadows require little upkeep.

Steps to a Great-looking Meadow

Creating a vigorous, beautiful meadow involves more than simply shaking seeds out of a can onto a grassy or dusty spot. For best results, you'll need to give your meadow the same care you'd use to start any garden: prepare the soil well, choose the best-adapted perennials, and plant them properly. Just follow these simple steps:

1. Pick a site with well-drained soil and at least 6 hours of sun a day.

2. In spring, summer, or fall, remove existing grasses and aggressive weeds; lawn grasses can spread vigorously and smother small, new plants. Skim off slices of turf with a spade. Compost the pieces of sod you remove or use them to fill holes in the remaining lawn.

3. Spread 1 to 2 inches (2.5 to 5 cm) of compost over the area, and dig or till it into the top 4 to 6 inches (10 to 15 cm) of soil. Use a rake to remove any rocks and smooth the soil.

4. To reduce the bank of weed seeds in the soil, water the area thoroughly to encourage surface weed seeds to sprout; then rake or hoe shallowly to kill the seedlings. Repeat the process several times before planting. Or use mulch instead of watering and hoeing; cover the area with black plastic or at least 12 layers of newspaper for an entire season.

5. In fall, set out your meadow perennials, grasses, and bulbs, and mulch them well. By spring, the roots will be well established, and your plants will be ready to put on great growth.

6. In spring, if you wish, rake away some mulch to sow annual wildflower seeds between the perennial meadow plants. Annuals will provide quick color the first year while the perennials are growing new roots and getting established.

Birds enjoy the seeds and insects they find in a meadow garden.

7. Through the first growing season, water your meadow when the top 1 to 2 inches (2.5 to 5 cm) of soil is dry to help the growing young plants get established.

Routine Meadow Maintenance

Mow your meadow once a year to keep it looking good and to keep weeds, shrubs, and trees from invading. Late fall to early winter, after plants have formed seeds, is the best time. If you want to feed the birds, leave seed heads standing until late winter or early spring; just be aware that they'll be harder to mow after winter rain and snow have beaten them down.

A mixture of bulbs, perennials, annuals, and grasses creates a cheerful garden scene with little maintenance.

In a meadow garden, you can combine many perennials in one area without worrying much about colors and sizes.

Cut the whole meadow to a height of about 6 inches (15 cm). Use a sickle-bar mower for large areas; a string trimmer or hand clippers can handle small patches. A regular lawn mower won't work; it cuts too low. Leave trimmings in place so plants can self-sow, or collect them for your compost pile.

Aside from the yearly trim, your only maintenance is to dig out tree seedlings and aggressive weeds such as quack grass, poison ivy, bindweed, and burdock as soon as they appear. Established meadows don't require water, fertilizer, or mulch. As the plants get established, your meadow garden will look different each year, but it will always be beautiful.

Obedient plant and other spreading perennials can be invasive in borders, but they're perfect for meadow gardens.

Marvelous Meadow Perennials

The recipe for a magnificent meadow includes a blend of tough perennial flowers and noninvasive perennial grasses, with a dash of daffodils and other naturalized spring bulbs for early color. Below you'll find some suggested flowers you can consider for your moist or dry site, along with some great meadow grasses. For more information on the perennials, look in their individual entries in "Perennials for Every Purpose," starting on page 86.

Perennials for Dry Meadows

Achillea filipendulina (fern-leaved yarrow)
Asclepias tuberosa (butterfly weed)
Baptisia australis (blue false indigo)
Echinacea purpurea (purple coneflower)
Gaillardia x *grandiflora* (blanket flower)
Helianthus x *multiflorus* (perennial sunflower)
Liatris spicata (spike gayfeather)
Oenothera tetragona (common sundrops)
Rudbeckia fulgida (orange coneflower)
Solidago rigida (stiff goldenrod)

Perennials for Moist Meadows

Aster novae-angliae (New England aster)
Chelone glabra (white turtlehead)
Eupatorium maculatum (spotted Joe-Pye weed)
Eupatorium rugosum (white snakeroot)
Filipendula rubra (queen-of-the-prairie)
Helenium autumnale (common sneezeweed)
Lobelia cardinalis (cardinal flower)
Physostegia virginiana (obedient plant)
Thermopsis caroliniana (Carolina lupine)

Great Grasses for Meadows

Andropogon virginicus (broomsedge)
Bouteloua curtipendula (sideoats grama grass)
Festuca spp. (fescues)
Schizachyrium scoparium (little bluestem)
Sporobolus heterolepis (prairie dropseed)

Gardening for Butterflies

Planting a landscape for butterflies is a great way to add an exciting element of moving color to your yard. Choosing and growing the right perennials will supply the food butterflies need throughout their lives. You'll also want to provide water and shelter to encourage the butterflies that come to stay in your yard.

Growing Food for Butterflies

To find out what will attract the butterflies in your area, look for them in nearby gardens, old fields, and at the edges of woods. Observe which flowers they prefer and where they stop to sun themselves. If you see a pretty butterfly sipping nectar from a particular flower, consider growing that plant. Imitating nature is the secret to successful butterfly gardening.

To have a great butterfly garden, you must get used to a few holes in the leaves of your perennials. You need to let the caterpillars feed in order to keep the adult butterflies around. Many "flowers" listed for butterfly gardens—including violets, parsley, hollyhocks (*Alcea rosea*), and milkweeds (*Asclepias* spp.)—are really food sources (leaves) for the caterpillars.

Adult butterflies that are ready to lay eggs are attracted by the plants that will feed their developing larvae. Some adults also feed on flower nectar. Plants that have clusters of short, tubular, brightly colored flowers are especially popular. You'll find a list of beautiful butterfly-attracting perennials in "Best Bets for Butterflies." Many annuals and shrubs—including butterfly bush (*Buddleia davidii*) and abelia (*Abelia* x *grandiflora*)—are also natural choices.

Arranging Your Butterfly Plantings

If you have an informal landscape, consider planting a meadow garden (as explained in "Making a Meadow" on page 72). If you don't have room for a meadow, grow some of the many wildflowers that double as garden perennials, such as asters and coneflowers (*Echinacea* and *Rudbeckia* spp.). Scatter these plants throughout your landscape, or put several of them together in a special butterfly garden. Large splashes of color are easier for butterflies to find than a single plant, so group several plants of the same color together.

Hollyhock leaves are a favorite food source for the common checkered skipper and the painted lady butterfly.

Providing a Safe Haven for Butterflies

Along with growing their favorite food and nectar plants, you can take a number of steps to encourage butterflies to stay in your yard.

Make a Spot for Sunbathing Butterflies like sun and dislike wind, so plant flowers in sunny spots where fences, walls, or shrubs act as windbreaks. Set flat stones in a sheltered, sunny spot for butterflies to bask on.

Just Add Water Butterflies are attracted to shallow

Besides adding colorful blooms to your garden, orange coneflowers offer nectar for fritillaries, crescentspots, and other butterflies.

Butterflies like to bask in sheltered, sunny areas. Set out some flat stones there for them to rest on.

puddles and muddy soil. Dig a small, shallow basin, line it with plastic, and cover it with sandy soil and gravel to form a butterfly-luring water source.

Diversify Your Yard Adding diversity to your landscape means creating different mini-environments as well as increasing the number of different plants. Edge habitats—where woods meet lawn or meadow and lawn meets garden or shrub plantings—provide great environments for butterflies. If you can, allow a corner of your yard to go wild; a tangle of brush provides protection from predators.

Most butterflies have very specific tastes, so increase the variety of plants to provide a smorgasbord of food and nectar sources and attract many different species from early spring through fall.

Avoid Using Pesticides One of the most important steps in having a butterfly haven is creating a safe, pesticide-free habitat. Even organically acceptable pesticides such as rotenone and pyrethrin kill butterflies and their larvae. BT, a biological control used against many garden pests, is also fatal to the larvae of desirable butterflies. Use safer techniques such as handpicking and water sprays to remove pests from plants. If you don't want butterfly larvae to munch on your vegetable garden (carrots, celery, cabbage, broccoli, and parsley are a few favorite targets), protect those crops with floating row covers.

The flowers of showy stonecrop are a magnet for a variety of different butterflies, including tortoiseshells.

Attract butterflies with a water source and a variety of different plants.

Herbs look wonderful any way you use them—grouped into a special herb garden or mixed with perennials and bulbs.

Landscaping with Perennial Herbs

Versatile, colorful, and flavorful, herbs have a place in any landscape. Mix them with other perennials in beds and borders, or group them together in a formal herb garden. Either way, you can enjoy their delightful scents and colors in crafts and in the kitchen as well as in the garden.

Using Herbs around Your Yard

Deciding which herbs you'll grow and where you'll grow them is basically no different than choosing other perennials for your garden. You either need to make a list of the herbs that you want to grow and then find a place for them or to pick a site and look for herbs that will thrive there.

Creating an Herb Garden Some gardeners like to group a collection of herbs into a special herb garden. This makes it easier to find the ones you want so you can enjoy their various scents or harvest them for cooking or crafts.

Plan your herb garden as a regular perennial bed or border, or give it a more formal look with paths, edgings, and separate growing beds. A basic herb garden could consist of several square raised beds edged with wooden sides and separated by paths. For even more formality, you could lay out the garden beds in geometric shapes, wheel

spokes, or intricate knots.

Define the edges of formal beds with low, clipped hedges of bluish rue, green hyssop, or silvery santolina—or even a combination of all three. Or be more casual and allow the herbs that are growing along the edge to sprawl a little onto the paved or gravel paths. For a traditional touch, plan a small round bed in the center of the garden, and accent it with a sundial, statue, domed straw bee skep, or large potted bay (*Laurus nobilis*) or rosemary as a special focal point.

Locate culinary herb gardens as close to the kitchen as possible for easy access. Grow what you'll use fresh in cooking plus extra to dry or freeze for winter. Remember to include attractive, edible herbs such as silver thyme and variegated sages for color contrast. Add annual herbs and edible flowers such as purple basil, nasturtium, and borage for even more color.

Adding Herbs to Other Plantings If you don't have room for a separate herb garden, tuck your favorite herbs into other perennial beds and borders. Most herbs look good in formal designs; many make a natural addition to casual cottage gardens as well. A number of herbs are also well suited to container gardening, so you can move them around to add fragrance and color wherever you need it.

Herb Gardening Basics

If you meet herbs' simple needs, you'll find them to be among the least demanding plants to grow.

Sunny sites will suit the widest range of herbs. It is possible to grow some herbs in partial to full shade,

Preventing Mint from Spreading

Sink a bottomless bucket into the soil at the planting spot.

Fill the bucket with soil and plant the mint in the center.

Lavender is a traditional part of an herb garden. It is beloved for its beautiful flowers and delightful fragrance.

A statue or urn makes a charming accent in a small herb garden.

but your choices will be limited. (Mints, lemon balm, and sweet woodruff are your most likely subjects for success in shade.)

Make sure the soil is well drained, ideally with a pH near neutral to slightly alkaline. Build raised beds to improve drainage if your soil tends to be wet all season. Work in some compost as you prepare the soil. The compost will supply the nutrients your herb plants need, so don't add extra fertilizer before planting.

Allow ample room for ornamental herbs to grow without crowding. Space culinary herbs closer together, since the frequent trimming for harvest will also keep the plants smaller.

Some herbs will spread so quickly that they need special control measures. Sweet woodruff is a charming, low-growing perennial with whorled leaves and white spring flowers, but it spreads too much to work well in herb beds; grow it as a groundcover under shrubs instead. Mints are also notorious for spreading rampantly. To keep them from taking over the rest of the yard, bury open-bottomed buckets in the garden and plant the mints inside. Many invasive herbs also adapt well to growing in pots.

Double-duty Perennial Herbs

If you want to get the most possible enjoyment out of your yard, why not grow perennials that are useful as well as attractive? Listed below are some popular perennial herbs, with notes on their ornamental features and other uses, including crafts such as dried arrangements and wreaths.

Achillea filipendulina (fern-leafed yarrow): showy yellow flowers; crafts

Artemisia absinthium (common wormwood): silvery leaves; crafts

Chrysanthemum parthenium (feverfew): small white, daisy-like flowers; crafts

Hyssopus officinalis (hyssop): evergreen leaves and blue flowers; culinary, tea

Lavandula angustifolia (lavender): scented gray leaves and purple flowers; crafts, culinary

Melissa officinalis (lemon balm): lemon-scented leaves and white flowers; tea

Monarda didyma (bee balm): scented leaves and showy red flowers; crafts, tea

Nepeta x *faassenii* (catmint): gray leaves and blue flowers; crafts

Ruta graveolens (rue): aromatic blue-green leaves; crafts

Salvia officinalis (garden sage): scented gray leaves and blue flowers; culinary, tea

Sage is useful in the garden for its attractive foliage and in the kitchen for its flavor.

It's hard to beat tall, spiky flowers for adding a dramatic touch to a cottage garden.

Plant oriental poppies with bushy plants that will fill in when the poppies go dormant in midsummer.

Creating a Cottage Garden

The ultimate in informality, cottage gardens display a glorious riot of colors, textures, heights, and fragrances. Cottage gardens defy many gardening "rules": Plants are packed closely together, ignoring standard spacing; colors aren't organized into large drifts; tall plants pop up in front of shorter ones; flowers are allowed to flop over and grow through each other to create a delightful, casual mixture.

While cottage gardens may appear effortless and unorganized, they need to be planned, planted, and maintained just like any other perennial garden. In this section, you'll learn the tricks to capturing the informal cottage garden effect without creating a messy-looking mixture.

Choosing a Site

Locate cottage gardens next to the house, especially by a door. If your front or side yard is small, you may want to devote the whole space to the garden. In this case, a gravel, brick, stone, or even cement path is essential; make it wide (at least 3 feet [90 cm]) to allow room for plants to spill out onto it.

Picking the Plants

To create a pleasing jumble rather than a chaotic mess, combine a variety of different flower shapes and sizes. Thinking of flowers in terms of their visual impact will help you get the right balance.

"Feature" flowers are the ones that first catch your eye; they have strong shapes— like spiky lupines (*Lupinus polyphyllus*) and massive peonies—or bright colors.

Enjoy the orchid-like flowers of bearded irises in early summer and the spiky foliage the rest of the season.

The delicate blooms of peach-leaved bellflower have long been a favorite in cottage gardens.

Pretty Perennials for Cottage Gardens

These colorful and dependable, great cottage garden flowers have been favorites for years. Use feature flowers for bold colors and textures, edging plants to line the front, and filler flowers to tie the whole design together. You can learn more about specific plants listed below by looking them up in "Perennials for Every Purpose," starting on page 86.

Feature Flowers

Alcea rosea (hollyhock)
Campanula persicifolia (peach-leaved bellflower)
Delphinium x *belladonna* (Belladonna delphinium)
Dictamnus albus (gas plant)
Iris, bearded hybrids (bearded iris)
Iris sibirica (Siberian iris)
Lilium hybrids (lilies)
Lupinus polyphyllus (garden lupine)
Paeonia lactiflora (common garden peony)
Papaver orientale (oriental poppy)
Phlox paniculata (garden phlox)
Verbascum chaixii (nettle-leaved mullein)

Edging Plants

Aubrieta deltoidea (purple rock cress)
Aurinia saxatilis (basket-of-gold)
Campanula portenschlagiana (Dalmatian bellflower)
Cerastium tomentosum (snow-in-summer)
Dianthus gratianpolitanus (cheddar pinks)
Euphorbia epithymoides (cushion spurge)
Heuchera sanguinea (coral bells)
Nepeta x *faassenii* (catmint)
Primula vulgaris (English primrose)
Pulmonaria saccharata (Bethlehem sage)

Filler Flowers

Alchemilla mollis (lady's mantle)
Aquilegia x *hybrida* (hybrid columbine)
Aster novae-angliae (New England aster)
Astrantia major (masterwort)
Centaurea hypoleuca (knapweed)
Centranthus ruber (red valerian)
Chrysanthemum x *superbum* (shasta daisy)
Coreopsis verticillata (thread-leaved coreopsis)
Geranium sanguineum (blood-red cranesbill)
Gypsophila paniculata (baby's-breath)
Lychnis coronaria (rose campion)

"Filler" flowers tend to be smaller and less obvious than the feature plants. Baby's-breath is a classic filler flower.

"Edgers" are low plants used in the fronts of beds or spilling over onto paths; think of thymes and catmint (*Nepeta* x *faassenii*).

These categories aren't rigid: Lavender and the flowers of lady's mantle (*Alchemilla mollis*) make nice fillers, but both are often used to edge paths as well. Rose campion (*Lychnis coronaria*) works as a filler, but if set among flowers with contrasting colors, its bright magenta flowers may stand out as a feature. The key is to use some flowers that serve each purpose, so you don't have all bright (and probably clashing) feature flowers, all small filler flowers, or all low edging plants.

As you choose plants for the garden, include some that have scented foliage or flowers; fragrance is a traditional part of the cottage garden feeling. It's also important to choose flowers that bloom at different times for a continuous display.

Perennials aren't the only plants you can grow in your cottage garden: Annuals, herbs, shrubs, vines, and bulbs all can have a place in your cottage garden, too. Old-fashioned roses, either shrub types or climbers, are a classic ingredient and an important source of fragrant flowers. Climbing roses or honeysuckles look great trained over a door or archway; let clematis climb up lampposts or railings.

Including unusual and unlikely plants is a long-standing cottage tradition. Accent your cottage garden with dwarf fruit trees, and tuck in some other edibles for surprise: try colorful lettuces, curly parsley, red-stemmed 'Ruby' chard, and maroon-podded 'Burgundy' okra.

Gardening with Fragrance

Perennials with fragrant leaves and flowers have a place in any landscape. There's nothing like the fresh scent of mint to perk you up after a long day at the office. And who could resist resting on a cozy garden bench near a patch of peonies in full, fragrant bloom? In beds, borders, cottage gardens, and foundation plantings, mixing in some scented perennials will add an extraspecial touch to your yard.

Fragrance in Flowers

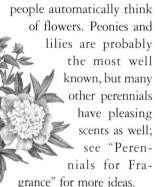

When you mention fragrance in the garden, most people automatically think of flowers. Peonies and lilies are probably the most well known, but many other perennials have pleasing scents as well; see "Perennials for Fragrance" for more ideas.

Traditionally, scented flowers were grown close to the house so their fragrance could be appreciated Through open doors and windows. They're equally nice near outdoor eating areas, patios, and porches—any place where people linger. Raised planters are great for short, fragrant flowers so you don't have to get down on your hands and knees to enjoy the scents.

Many fragrant flowers are also beautiful, so you can enjoy looking at them and sniffing them as you walk

Many bearded irises have a lovely scent. If fragrance is important to you, sniff the blooms before you buy.

around or work in the yard. Cutting these flowers for arrangements brings this pleasure indoors.

Fragrance in Foliage

A number of plants have fragrant foliage, but you need to touch these to smell them. Plant lavender and bee balm (*Monarda didyma*) where you'll brush against them as you walk by. Grow lemon balm (*Melissa officinalis*) near a garden seat or in a raised container so you can easily rub the leaves to release their delicious lemony odor. Wormwood (*Artemisia absinthium*) and rue (*Ruta graveolens*) leaves have pungent scents that some people find pleasing and others find disagreeable; try sniffing these plants before you buy.

Buying and Growing Fragrant Perennials

The real key to having a scented garden that you enjoy is smelling plants before you buy them. The fragrance that a friend raves about may be undetectable or even unpleasant to you. Visit nurseries or public gardens when the plants you want are blooming, and sniff the flowers or foliage to see what you think. Different cultivars of the same plant may vary widely in their scents, so smell them all before you choose. "Perennials for Fragrance"

Catmint has gray-green leaves that have a pungent, minty scent. It looks wonderful with other perennials and shrubs.

Heady-scented roses are a classic part of a fragrance garden. Combine them with perennials for extra color.

gives you some ideas of specific perennials and cultivars that most gardeners agree are great additions to any scented garden.

Just as a bed of many different flowers colors can look jumbled, a mixture of many strong fragrances can be distracting or even downright repulsive. As you plan your garden, try to arrange it with just one or two scented plants in bloom at any given time. That way, you can enjoy different fragrances all through the season without being overwhelmed by too many at once.

Grow lemon balm in a pot, near a bench, or along a path, where you can rub the leaves and enjoy the lemon scent.

Perennials for Fragrance

Here's a list of some popular perennials you can include for fragrance in your landscape. If a plant's cultivars aren't always fragrant, the list includes the names of a few cultivars that are scented.

Centranthus ruber (red valerian): flowers, especially those of the white form

Convallaria majalis (lily-of-the-valley): flowers

Dianthus gratianopolitanus (cheddar pinks): flowers

Hemerocallis hybrids (daylilies): flowers of a few (mainly yellow) types, including 'Hyperion' and lemon daylily (*H. lilioasphodelus*)

Hyacinthus orientalis (hyacinth): flowers

Iris, bearded hybrids (bearded iris): flowers of most types

Lavandula angustifolia (lavender): leaves and flowers

Lilium hybrids (lilies): flowers of some types, including regal lilies, trumpet hybrids, oriental hybrids (such as 'Casa Blanca'), and *L. speciosum* 'Rubrum'

Narcissus hybrids (daffodils): flowers of some cultivars, including 'Geranium', 'Cragford', 'Actaea', 'Minnow', 'Baby Moon', 'Pipit', and 'Cheerfulness'

Nepeta x *faassenii* (catmint): leaves

Paeonia lactiflora (common garden peony): flowers of some cultivars, including 'Festiva Maxima', 'Pink Parfait', 'Sara Bernhardt', 'Edulis Superba', and 'Big Ben'

Phlox paniculata (garden phlox): flowers

Polygonatum odoratum (fragrant Solomon's seal): flowers

Growing Perennials in Containers

No matter what size or style of garden you have, growing perennials in pots can greatly expand your planting options. Try a few container perennials and discover how fun, practical, and versatile these movable gardens can be.

Low-growing perennials look wonderful cascading out of window boxes. Water regularly to keep plants healthy.

Solving Challenges with Containers

With a little creativity, you'll find many different ways to use containers to solve problem spots. If you can't kneel or if you garden from a wheelchair, you can grow plants at a convenient height in raised planters. If your soil is too hard or rocky to dig, grow flowers in half-barrel planters instead of in the ground.

If you've got a shady spot that's crying out for color, use potted perennials to create a rotating display: As flowers fade, move the shady pot to a sunnier spot and replace with one that's robust from sunshine. Or tuck a few pots into a dull planting to add quick color. If space is really limited, create your own garden paradise on a rooftop, porch, or window box.

Don't limit your container gardens to just practical uses, though. Growing perennials in pots is a great way to experiment with different plant combinations before you commit to putting them in the ground. If

you don't like a combination, just separate the pots and group them with other possibilities.

Containers can also make great garden accents. Choose bold, sculptural perennials such as Adam's needle (*Yucca filamentosa*) for formal designs; mix lots of different colors and cascading plants for a cottage look.

Choosing a Container

Pot possibilities are endless. You may buy commercially made plastic or clay containers or make your own out of old barrels, washtubs, or even buckets. Be creative; almost anything you can put drainage holes in—from clay drainage tiles to old leather work boots—can be pressed into service.

Solid-sided containers, such as plastic pots, hold water longer than porous clay. Plastics are great if your summers tend to be hot and dry, since you'll have to water less often. But if you live in a wet climate, or if you tend to overwater, porous containers are probably best. Plastic pots are lighter, making them easier to move, but they are more prone to blowing over. Clay pots are heavy and less likely to blow over, but they often crack when they do tip.

Potted perennials add mobile spots of color to beds and borders. Replace containers as needed through the season.

Evergreen perennials such as bergenia provide year-round interest in pots and planters.

Large containers offer a variety of possibilities. Start with spring bulbs and plant perennials for later bloom.

Slip nursery pots of perennials or bulbs into decorative baskets to cover the unattractive plastic containers.

In windy areas or for tall plants, place rocks in the bottom of any pot to increase stability. Empty clay pots or bring them indoors before freezing weather; wet soil expands as it freezes and will crack the pot. Dark pots heat up in bright sun and dry out quickly; avoid black plastic pots for container gardens that are growing in full sun.

Picking Perennials for Containers

Just about any perennial will grow well in a pot, as long as you give it the growing conditions and routine care that it needs. Plant several perennials in one pot or group several in individual containers. Include plants with attractive foliage—such as spotted lamium (*Lamium maculatum*), heart-leaved bergenia (*Bergenia cordifolia*), and ornamental grasses—to extend the period of interest. Hardy bulbs add spring color to all containers; choose crocuses and other small types, as their fading foliage is easier to camouflage.

Caring for Container Gardens

Keeping the right water balance is a key part of successful container gardening. First, you need to choose a growing medium that will hold some water but not too much. Straight garden soil isn't a good choice; improve it by mixing 2 parts soil with 1 part finished compost (or peat moss) and 1 part perlite. Or use sterilized, premixed "soil-less" potting mixes;

these are free of soilborne diseases and they weigh much less, an important consideration for rooftop gardeners and for plants in large pots.

Regular watering is another way you'll balance each container's water supply. Some containers may need watering every day, others only once a week. A good general rule is to wait until the top 1 inch (2.5 cm) of soil is dry; then water thoroughly, until some comes out of the bottom. If the water seems to run right through the container, put a tray or saucer underneath; empty any water that remains the next day.

Since their rooting space is limited, plants in pots need fertilizer much more often than plants growing in the ground. After they've been growing for a month or so, give plants dilute liquid fertilizer every couple of weeks. Use fish emulsion, liquid seaweed, or a balanced organic fertilizer; follow the instructions on the package to find out how often and how much fertilizer you should apply.

Fertilize containers several times during the season.

Creating a Cutting Garden

If you enjoy having armloads of flowers to bring indoors for fresh arrangements, consider adding a cutting garden to your perennial landscape. A cutting garden is simply one or more beds where you grow flowers just for arrangements. You can collect beautiful blooms from your cutting garden without raiding your carefully planned displays in the rest of the yard.

For easy picking and arranging, look for perennials and bulbs that have long, sturdy stems.

Cutting Garden Basics

Few people have enough space to put a cutting garden truly out of sight, but the more removed it is, the less you'll worry about making it look nice. Some gardeners turn over a corner of their vegetable garden to cut flowers; others create separate cutting beds along a garage, in a sunny side yard, or in a sheltered corner of the backyard.

Wherever you put your cutting beds, you want them to be easy to reach and maintain. Prepare the soil well, and mulch and water as needed to keep plants vigorous and blooming. Stake floppy or long-stemmed flowers—including peonies, baby's-breath, and delphiniums—to keep the stems upright and the flowers clean.

Choosing Plants for Cutting

Selecting plants for your cutting garden is much like choosing perennials for any planting. Most important,

you need to choose plants that will thrive in your growing conditions; if they aren't growing well, they won't produce many flowers. Here are some other things you'll want to consider when you're deciding what to include:

- If space is limited, concentrate on growing perennials in your favorite flower colors; if you have lots of room, plant a variety of colors to have lots of options.
- Grow perennials that have different shapes to keep your arrangements from looking monotonous. Include spiky flowers and foliage for height, flat or round flowers and leaves for mass, and small, airy flowers and leaves for fillers.
- Look for perennials with long stems. Cultivars described as dwarf or compact are great for ornamental

Handling Cut Flowers

Pick flowers in the morning, just as they begin to open.

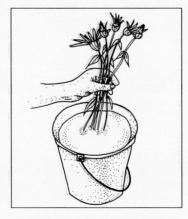

Put the just-picked flowers into a bucket of warm water.

Make the final cuts under water before arranging the blooms.

The daisy-like blooms of asters and orange coneflowers add bright color and dramatic form to any arrangement.

plantings, but their stems are usually too short for easy arranging.

- For extraspecial arrangements, include some fragrant flowers; see "Perennials for Fragrance" on page 81 for ideas.
- Don't forget to include foliage—it adds body and filler to arrangements. Use subtle greens and silvers to emphasize individual flowers or colors; variegated leaves make striking accents.

To add extra excitement to your arrangements, include other plants—annuals, grasses, and hardy bulbs—in your cutting garden. Cosmos, snapdragon, larkspur (*Consolida ambigua*), and calendula (*Calendula officinalis*) are a few of the easy-to-grow annuals that are wonderful for fresh arrangements. Ornamental grasses are great for both flowers and foliage. Spray their delicate flowers with lacquer or cheap hairspray to make them last longer.

Collecting Cut Flowers

Taking a little extra care when you collect your flowers and foliage will help them look great over a longer period. In the cool of the morning, harvest flowers that haven't fully opened using sharp clippers or a knife; immediately plunge the stems into a bucket of warm water. As you arrange the flowers, cut the stems to their final lengths under water so no air bubbles enter. Remove leaves that will be below the waterline in the finished arrangement.

After arranging your flowers, fill the vase to the top with water; refill as soon as the level drops. Add a shot of lemon-lime soda or a commercial floral preservative to keep the water fresh. Flowers will last longest in a cool room out of direct light.

Favorite Perennials for Flower Arranging

Here's a list of some of the best perennials you can grow for cut flowers. For more information, look up their individual entries in "Perennials for Every Purpose," starting on page 86.

Achillea filipendulina (fern-leaved yarrow)
Alchemilla mollis (lady's-mantle)
Aster novae-angliae (New England aster)
Astrantia major (masterwort)
Baptisia australis (blue false indigo)
Boltonia asteroides (boltonia)
Chrysanthemum x *superbum* (shasta daisy)
Delphinium x *belladonna* (belladonna delphinium)
Dictamnus albus (gas plant)
Echinacea purpurea (purple coneflower)
Echinops ritro (globe thistle)
Eryngium amethystinum (amethyst sea holly)
Gaillardia x *grandiflora* (blanket flower)
Gypsophila paniculata (baby's-breath)
Helenium autumnale (common sneezeweed)
Heuchera sanguinea (coral bells)
Iris spp. (irises)
Liatris spicata (spike gayfeather)
Lilium hybrids (lilies)
Monarda didyma (bee balm)
Narcissus hybrids (daffodils)
Nepeta x *faassenii* (catmint)
Paeonia lactiflora (common garden peony)
Phlox paniculata (garden phlox)
Physostegia virginiana (obedient plant)
Platycodon grandiflorus (balloon flower)
Rudbeckia fulgida (orange coneflower)
Salvia x *superba* (violet sage)
Scabiosa caucasica (pincushion flower)
Stachys byzantina (lamb's-ears)
Thermopsis caroliniana (Carolina lupine)
Veronica spicata (spike speedwell)

PERENNIALS FOR EVERY PURPOSE

With so many wonderful perennials to choose from, it can be very difficult to decide which ones you want to grow. Lured by the glossy plant catalogs filled with gorgeous photographs, you may find it very hard to resist the urge to buy one of everything—but be strong! If you really want to succeed with perennials, you need to ask yourself these two questions before buying any plant:

Will it thrive in the growing conditions I have to offer? If you have a hot, sunny yard, shade-loving woodland plants like wild gingers (*Asarum* spp.) and foamflowers (*Tiarella* spp.) are likely to just curl up and die. And sun-worshippers like yarrow and pinks (*Dianthus* spp.) are doomed to fail in a damp, shady spot. Fortunately, there are perennials adapted to just about every garden condition, so you can have a lush, beautiful, easy-care landscape if you grow the ones that are adapted to your site.

Will the plant serve the purpose I want it for? Do you need a perennial that blooms in a certain color, or is the foliage more important for all-season interest? Do you want a low-growing plant to fill in along the front of a border or a tall one with long flower stems that are good for cutting? By keeping your plans in mind as you pick your plants, you can choose perennials that will be useful as well as attractive.

At this point, you may be asking yourself a third question: Where can I find this information about each plant? Catalog descriptions are often long on the plant's virtues and short on actual growing information. Plant labels usually offer some cryptic growing advice like "sun/dry" and no suggestions on what the plant is good for. But now you have all the information you need in one place—here in "Perennials for Every Purpose."

This guide is arranged in an easy-to-use, quick-reference format. Since many perennials have several common names, all of the perennials are listed alphabetically by their botanical name. Knowing the botanical name when you buy from a garden center or catalog will help to ensure that you get the exact plant you're looking for. If you only know a plant's common name, look it up in the index; the index entry will tell you the botanical name.

For each perennial, you'll find a color photograph and a detailed description, along with guidelines for growing the plant successfully. The "Landscape Uses" section offers tips on where the plant fits best: in a formal border, a cottage garden, a meadow, a woodland, or perhaps a cutting garden. In "Compatible Companions," you'll find suggestions of other wonderful plants that look great and grow well with that particular perennial.

Before you buy any perennial, read through its entry to make sure it fits your needs and conditions. If you're looking for ideas of new plants to try, browse through the pictures and read about the plants you're interested in. Or, if you want to spruce up an existing planting, check the entries of the perennials you already have to find suggestions of companion plants you can grow with them. By selecting the appropriate plants for your site and needs, you'll be well on your way to successful landscaping with perennials.

Perennials are available in a dazzling array of colors, shapes, and sizes. Your local garden centers and nurseries should have a wide variety; check out mail-order sources to find even more uncommon kinds and colors.

FERN-LEAVED YARROW

BICOLOR MONKSHOOD

Fern-leaved yarrow is a tough, adaptable perennial that looks great in herb gardens, perennial borders, wildflower meadows, cutting gardens—even containers!

Bicolor monkshood is a showy, fall-flowering perennial for borders or informal gardens. It thrives in climates with cool summer nights and warm days with low humidity.

DESCRIPTION: Fern-leaved yarrow is an aromatic herb with ferny, olive green leaves. The wide-spreading plants produce dozens of tall, leafy stems bearing flattened flower clusters. The 4–5-inch (10–12.5 cm) heads contain dozens of tightly packed, golden yellow flowers. Plants grow from fibrous roots.

SEASON OF INTEREST: Flowers open in summer and last for several weeks; plants rebloom if deadheaded.

HEIGHT AND SPREAD: Height 3–4 feet (90–120 cm); width 3 feet (90 cm); forms broad, tight clumps.

BEST SITE AND CLIMATE: Plant in average, dry to moist, well-drained soil in full sun or light shade. Thrives where summer humidity is low to moderate. Zones 3–9.

GROWING GUIDELINES: Plants spread rapidly and need frequent division. Lift clumps every 3 years in early spring or fall; replant vigorous portions into amended soil. For propagation, divide clumps or take tip cuttings in spring or early summer.

LANDSCAPE USES: Plant at the front or middle of formal perennial borders or with grasses in wildflower meadows and other informal gardens. Use on dry, sunny banks to control erosion.

COMPATIBLE COMPANIONS: Combine with drought-tolerant perennials such as catmints (*Nepeta* spp.), pinks (*Dianthus* spp.), and globe thistle (*Echinops ritro*). Strap-leaved plants such as ornamental grasses contrast with the yarrow's rounded form.

DESCRIPTION: Lush, five- to seven-lobed, dissected leaves clothe sturdy stems topped with dense flower spikes. The dark blue or two-toned flowers have protruding helmet-like hoods above three lower petals. Plants grow from thickened, spidery roots. All parts of the plant are poisonous if eaten.

SEASON OF INTEREST: Late summer and fall bloom. The foliage is attractive before flowering.

HEIGHT AND SPREAD: Height 3–4 feet (90–120 cm); width 2 feet (60 cm). Habit is variable, but generally open and vase-shaped, especially in shade.

BEST SITE AND CLIMATE: Plant in fertile, humus-rich, moist but well-drained soil in full sun or light shade. Afternoon shade is advised in warmer zones. Zones 3–7.

GROWING GUIDELINES: Space plants 2–3 feet (60–90 cm) apart, with the crowns just below the surface. Divide in fall or early spring only if plants become overcrowded and bloom diminishes.

LANDSCAPE USES: Plant near the middle or rear of perennial borders, in informal settings such as open woodlands and meadows, or as a mass planting in front of trees and shrubs.

COMPATIBLE COMPANIONS: Combine with other fall-blooming perennials and ornamental grasses or use in groups with fruiting shrubs such as beautyberries (*Callicarpa* spp.) and viburnums.

WHITE BANEBERRY

Mature clumps of white baneberry in full fruit are stunning in the fall garden. The red-stalked berries are poisonous to people but savored by birds.

DESCRIPTION: White baneberries are shrubby woodland plants noted for their showy fall fruits. The spring flowers lack petals and are composed of a fuzzy cluster of broad stamens. The blooms are carried on sturdy stems above deeply dissected, compound leaves. The oval white fruits are 1/4 inch (6 mm) long and borne on showy stalks. Plants grow from a woody crown with wiry yellow roots.

SEASON OF INTEREST: Spring bloom; late summer to fall berries.

HEIGHT AND SPREAD: Height 2–4 feet (60–120 cm). Mature clumps may reach 3 feet (90 cm) across.

BEST SITE AND CLIMATE: Plant in moist, humus-rich soil in partial to full shade. Zones 3–9.

GROWING GUIDELINES: Top-dress clumps with compost or shredded leaves in spring or fall. Plants seldom need division. Sow fresh seed outdoors in early fall to midfall after removing the pulp.

LANDSCAPE USES: Plant baneberries for dramatic accent at the edge of the path in a woodland garden or at the end of a shady walk. Mass plantings are breathtaking among ferns and foliage plants.

COMPATIBLE COMPANIONS: Combine with wild bleeding heart (*Dicentra eximia*) and violets. In fall, the berried plants look terrific with ferns, cardinal flower (*Lobelia cardinalis*), blue lobelia (*Lobelia siphilitica*), white wood aster (*Aster divaricatus*), and monkshoods (*Aconitum* spp.).

AJUGA

Ajuga spreads rapidly to form a dense, weedproof ground-cover; it may even be somewhat invasive, especially in lawns. Try it as an underplanting for flowering shrubs.

DESCRIPTION: Ajuga, also commonly known as bugleweed, spreads by creeping, aboveground stems. The wrinkled, spoon-shaped leaves are evergreen in mild climates. Plants grow from thin, fibrous roots. The small, intense blue flowers are carried in tiered whorls on short stalks.

SEASON OF INTEREST: Late spring and early summer bloom. The foliage is attractive all season.

HEIGHT AND SPREAD: Height in bloom 4–10 inches (10–25 cm); width 8–10 inches (20–25 cm). Low, leafy clumps may spread to several feet (60 cm or more) across from a single plant.

BEST SITE AND CLIMATE: Plant in sun or shade in average to rich, moist but well-drained soil. Plants do not tolerate extended drought or excessive moisture. Zones 3–9.

GROWING GUIDELINES: Plants are easy to establish in spring or fall. Propagate by division any time during the growing season. Take stem cuttings from sideshoots in spring or summer.

LANDSCAPE USES: Choose ajuga as a groundcover under trees and hedges or for edging beds.

COMPATIBLE COMPANIONS: Give groundcover plantings of ajuga a lift with flowering plants such as sedums, Siberian iris (*Iris sibirica*), daylilies, cranesbills (*Geranium* spp.), and ferns.

CULTIVARS: 'Atropurpurea' has bronze-purple leaves. 'Burgundy Glow' has white, pink, and green foliage.

| *Alcea rosea* | Malvaceae | *Alchemilla mollis* | Rosaceae |

HOLLYHOCK

LADY'S-MANTLE

Hollyhocks are old-fashioned garden favorites. The foliage may look unattractive after bloom; combine with ornamental grasses and bushy perennials to hide the leaves.

Lady's-mantle is a mounded, clump-forming perennial with round, pleated foliage. If the leaves look tattered after flowering, cut plants to the ground; new foliage will appear.

DESCRIPTION: Hollyhocks are tall, coarse biennials or short-lived perennials with rounded or lobed foliage that clothes the stout stalks. The 2–4-inch (5–10 cm), five-petaled, saucer-shaped flowers mingle with the foliage on the upper half of the stem. Flower color ranges from white and pale yellow to pink, rose, and deep red. Plants grow from coarse, fibrous roots and a woody crown.

SEASON OF INTEREST: Summer and early fall bloom. Each plant may bloom for 2 months.

HEIGHT AND SPREAD: Height 2–8 feet (60–240 cm); width 2–3 feet (60–90 cm).

BEST SITE AND CLIMATE: Plant in average to rich, well-drained soil in full sun or partial shade. Prefers cool nights and low humidity. Zones 2–8.

GROWING GUIDELINES: These short-lived plants benefit from annual division after blooming. Sow seed indoors in winter for bloom in the summer or outdoors in summer for bloom the following summer. Dust rust-infected (orange-spotted) foliage with sulfur. Spray mite-infested plants (those with yellow-stippled leaves) with insecticidal soap.

LANDSCAPE USES: Hollyhocks are perfect as an accent by a garden shed or planted along a fence or wall.

COMPATIBLE COMPANIONS: Combine with full, leafy perennials such as yarrows, sages (*Salvia* spp.), and sundrops (*Oenothera* spp.).

DESCRIPTION: The 4–6-inch (10–15 cm), pale green leaves are densely clothed in soft hairs that catch beads of water like jewels on velvet. Plants grow from stout, creeping crowns with fibrous roots. Small chartreuse flowers in foamy clusters cover the plant.

SEASON OF INTEREST: Spring and early summer bloom. The foliage forms a distinctive, soft green carpet throughout the season.

HEIGHT AND SPREAD: Height 6–12 inches (15–30 cm); width 12–24 inches (30–60 cm).

BEST SITE AND CLIMATE: Grow in humus-rich, evenly moist soil in sun or shade. Where summer heat and humidity are high, provide afternoon shade. Excessive heat and humidity can damage the foliage. Zones 4–8.

GROWING GUIDELINES: Set the stout crowns at the soil surface. Divide the crowns in spring or fall. Sow fresh seed outdoors in summer or early fall.

LANDSCAPE USES: Choose lady's-mantle for the front of formal and informal beds and borders or for edging walks. Seedlings may appear in cracks in walls and stairs to happy effect.

COMPATIBLE COMPANIONS: Combine with other plants that enjoy moist soil such as Siberian iris (*Iris sibirica*), astilbes, primroses, and sedges (*Carex* spp.). Plant them with large-leaved perennials such as ligularias (*Ligularia* spp.) and hostas.

Allium giganteum   Liliaceae   *Amsonia tabernaemontana*   Apocynaceae

GIANT ONION

WILLOW BLUE STAR

Giant onions create a showstopping display in summer. Combine them with bushy perennials that will fill the gap when the foliage goes dormant after flowering.

Grow willow blue star as an herbaceous hedge or combine it with other plants. The foliage is an excellent background for other perennials; its golden fall color is a bonus.

DESCRIPTION: Giant onion produces strap-like, gray-green leaves that arch outward from the bulbs. The starry, purple flowers radiate in 4-inch (10 cm) spheres from stout stalks. Plants grow from a large bulb.

SEASON OF INTEREST: Early- to mid-summer bloom. Foliage dies to the ground soon after flowering.

HEIGHT AND SPREAD: Height 3–5 feet (90–150 cm); width 1–2 feet (30–60 cm).

BEST SITE AND CLIMATE: Plant in rich, well-drained soil in full sun. Dormant bulbs tolerate considerable drought. Zones 4–8.

GROWING GUIDELINES: Plant new bulbs in fall. Plants go dormant in midsummer to late summer; divide as the foliage turns yellow. Sow ripe seed outdoors or indoors in summer or fall.

LANDSCAPE USES: Plant a generous supply of bulbs at the middle or rear of the border or in front of flowering shrubs.

COMPATIBLE COMPANIONS: Combine with full-bodied perennials such as lavender (*Lavandula* spp.), yarrows, wallflowers (*Erysimum* spp.), and sages (*Salvia* spp.). The purple flowers are perfect in combination with the chartreuse flowers of lady's-mantle (*Alchemilla mollis*). For a jazzy combination, contrast them with the spiky forms of foxgloves (*Digitalis* spp.) and mulleins (*Verbascum* spp.), along with ornamental grasses.

DESCRIPTION: Willow blue star is a tough, shrubby plant with lance-shaped leaves that clothe the stout stems. The $1/2$-inch (12 mm), five-petaled, starry, steel-blue flowers are carried in rounded terminal clusters. Plants grow from a woody, fibrous-rooted crown.

SEASON OF INTEREST: Primarily spring bloom, with some secondary shoots blooming in early summer.

HEIGHT AND SPREAD: Height 1–3 feet (30–90 cm); width 3 feet (90 cm).

BEST SITE AND CLIMATE: Plant in average or rich, moist but well-drained soil in full sun or partial shade. Tolerates heat and cold. Zones 3–9.

GROWING GUIDELINES: If plants flop, prune stems back to 6–8 inches (15–20 cm) after flowering; new shoots will form an attractive compact mound. To expand your stock, divide plants in early spring or fall, take 4–6-inch (10–15 cm) stem cuttings in early summer, or sow fresh seed outdoors in fall.

LANDSCAPE USES: Use the shrubby clumps to add structure to the garden, either alone as a mass planting or combined with other perennials in both formal and informal settings.

COMPATIBLE COMPANIONS: Combine willow blue star with spiky perennials such as irises and ornamental grasses. Use bold-textured plants like oriental poppy (*Papaver orientale*), peonies, globe thistle (*Echinops ritro*), and hostas for contrast.

Anaphalis triplinervis   Compositae

THREE-VEINED EVERLASTING

Unlike most silver-leaved plants, three-veined everlasting grows well in moist soil. The papery white flowers and soft leaves add bright spots to the late-summer garden.

DESCRIPTION: Three-veined everlasting is a lovely plant with soft, silver-gray leaves and papery, white, double flowers that dry right on the plant and persist for weeks. The flowers have dark centers and are borne in open, flattened clusters. Plants form broad clumps from creeping stems.

SEASON OF INTEREST: Plants produce a profusion of flowers in July, August, and September. The neat, attractive foliage is an asset throughout the season. The flowers are excellent for cutting and drying.

HEIGHT AND SPREAD: Height 1–1¹/₂ feet (30–45 cm); width 1 foot (30 cm).

BEST SITE AND CLIMATE: Plant three-veined everlasting in moist, average to humus-rich soil in full sun to partial shade. Zones 3–8.

GROWING GUIDELINES: This easy-care perennial spreads to form large clumps in moist soil. Divide the vigorous clumps every 2–4 years to control their spread. Cuttings root freely in early summer. No serious pests or diseases.

LANDSCAPE USES: Grow them in the front or middle of beds and borders or in informal gardens and meadow plantings.

COMPATIBLE COMPANIONS: Combine with the vertical leaves of Siberian iris (*Iris sibirica*) or sweet flag (*Acorus calamus*). Ornamental grasses are excellent companion plants, as are astilbes, daylilies, and garden phlox (*Phlox paniculata*).

Anemone tomentosa 'Robustissima'   Ranunculaceae

GRAPE-LEAVED ANEMONE

Grape-leaved anemone lights up the fall garden with pink flowers atop tall stems. Once established, plants spread by creeping underground stems to form broad clumps.

DESCRIPTION: Grape-leaved anemone produces clouds of fragile, soft rosy pink flowers atop slender stems. The foliage is mostly basal, with three-lobed, thrice-divided, hairy leaves. Plants grow from thick tuberous roots.

SEASON OF INTEREST: Late summer and fall bloom.

HEIGHT AND SPREAD: Height 3–5 feet (90–150 cm); width 2–3 feet (60–90 cm).

BEST SITE AND CLIMATE: Plant in rich, evenly moist soil in sun or light shade. In warmer zones, protect plants from hot afternoon sun. Zones 3–8.

GROWING GUIDELINES: Divide overgrown clumps in spring if bloom was sparse the previous fall. Propagate by division or sow fresh seed outdoors in summer or fall. Provide a winter mulch for plants in Northern gardens. No serious pests or diseases.

LANDSCAPE USES: Plant them in formal or informal gardens or as a mass planting with shrubs.

COMPATIBLE COMPANIONS: In fall borders, combine with garden phlox (*Phlox paniculata*), asters, goldenrods (*Solidago* spp.), maiden grass (*Miscanthus sinensis*), and monkshoods (*Aconitum* spp.). In moist, open shade, plant them with ferns.

OTHER SPECIES:

A. x *hybrida,* Japanese anemone, is similar but grows taller and comes in a variety of colors with single or double flowers. Zones 5–8.

Aquilegia canadensis   Ranunculaceae

WILD COLUMBINE

Wild columbines may be short-lived in the garden, but self-sown seedlings are plentiful and will replenish your plantings. The flowers are popular with hummingbirds.

DESCRIPTION: The red-and-yellow blooms of these beloved wildflowers nod atop delicate stalks laced with divided, gray-green leaflets. The basal leaves arise directly from a stout taproot.

SEASON OF INTEREST: Wild columbines produce a profusion of flowers in early spring to midspring. The winter rosettes turn purple-blue at the onset of cool weather.

HEIGHT AND SPREAD: Height 1–3 feet (30–90 cm); width 1 foot (30 cm). Foliage rosettes are 6–12 inches (15–30 cm) high when not in flower.

BEST SITE AND CLIMATE: Plant in poor to average, well-drained soil in full sun or partial shade. Established plants are drought-tolerant. Zones 3–8.

GROWING GUIDELINES: Set out young plants in spring or fall. Columbines are plagued by leafminers, which form pale tunnels and blotches in the leaves. Remove and destroy affected foliage; in severe cases, spray weekly with insecticidal soap.

LANDSCAPE USES: Plant as an airy group in beds, borders, woodlands, and open meadows. Use them as a mass planting with flowering shrubs and small trees.

COMPATIBLE COMPANIONS: Combine with ferns and woodland wildflowers such as wild ginger (*Asarum canadense*) and foamflower (*Tiarella cordifolia*). In sunny meadows, plant them with wild geranium (*Geranium maculatum*) and ornamental grasses.

Aquilegia x *hybrida*   Ranunculaceae

HYBRID COLUMBINE

Hybrid columbines are graceful plants with curious nodding flowers. The blooms may be bicolored or of a single color— yellow, red, purple, white, and pink are common.

DESCRIPTION: Each flower has five spurred petals surrounded by five petal-like sepals. The spurs may be $1/2$–4 inches (12–100 mm) long. The ferny foliage has many fan-shaped leaflets. Plants grow from a thick taproot.

SEASON OF INTEREST: Spring and early summer bloom.

HEIGHT AND SPREAD: Height 2–3 feet (60–90 cm); width 1–2 feet (30–60 cm).

BEST SITE AND CLIMATE: Tolerates heat and cold. Plant in light, average to rich, well-drained soil in full sun or partial shade. Excess nitrogen promotes weak growth. Zones 3–9.

GROWING GUIDELINES: Hybrid columbines generally live only 2–4 years, but plants self-sow prolifically, so new plants are always developing. They hybridize readily and some seedlings may be misshapen; remove unattractive plants. Sow seed outdoors in spring or summer; indoors, place pot-sown seeds in a refrigerator for 4–6 weeks before moving them to room temperature. See the Wild Columbine entry for details on pests.

LANDSCAPE USES: Columbines look best in groups or drifts. Plant in formal beds and borders or in informal settings such as open woodlands and meadows.

COMPATIBLE COMPANIONS: Combine with spring and early-summer perennials, tulips, and daffodils. In light shade, combine them with wildflowers, ferns, and hostas.

WALL ROCK CRESS

JACK-IN-THE-PULPIT

Wall rock cress looks wonderful tumbling over a stone wall or creeping through a rock garden. It spreads quickly in cool climates to form an attractive, evergreen groundcover.

Jack-in-the-pulpits are beloved spring wildflowers that have enchanted children of all ages with their silent sermons. They are long-lived and easy to grow.

DESCRIPTION: The 1-inch (2.5 cm) leaves are clothed in soft hairs. Plants produce so many white or pink flowers that the leaves are obscured. The creeping stems produce a sparse network of fibrous roots.

SEASON OF INTEREST: Late winter and early spring bloom.

HEIGHT AND SPREAD: Height 6–10 inches (15–25 cm); width 12–18 inches (30–45 cm).

BEST SITE AND CLIMATE: Plant in average, well-drained soil in full sun or light shade. Plants are widely tolerant of soil moisture and fertility. Wall rock cress languishes in warmer zones, especially in the humid Southeast. Zones 3–7.

GROWING GUIDELINES: After flowering, cut plants back to encourage new shoots. Divide every 2–4 years to keep plants healthy. For propagation, take cuttings in spring or layer stems; division is also effective. No serious pests or diseases.

LANDSCAPE USES: In beds and borders, grow it as an informal edger or as a front-of-the-border plant.

COMPATIBLE COMPANIONS: Combine with taller border perennials such as cranesbills (*Geranium* spp.), bellflowers (*Campanula* spp.), and sea thrift (*Armeria maritima*). Interplant clumps with spring bulbs and early perennials such as moss phlox (*Phlox subulata*) and columbines (*Aquilegia* spp.). Use sedums and creeping baby's-breath (*Gypsophila repens*) to fill in as plants cease flowering.

DESCRIPTION: The unusual flowers hide beneath single or paired leaves, each with three broad leaflets. Each consists of a leaf-like hood (called a spathe) and a fleshy central column (called the spadix) that bears the sexual parts. The green flowers are striped with yellow or purple. Plants grow from a button-like tuber.

SEASON OF INTEREST: Flowers appear in spring. Glossy red berries ripen in late summer.

HEIGHT AND SPREAD: Height 1–3 feet (30–90 cm); width 1–1½ feet (30–45 cm).

BEST SITE AND CLIMATE: Zones 3–9. Plant in evenly moist, humus-rich soil in partial to full shade. Plants tolerate wet soil.

GROWING GUIDELINES: Clumps develop slowly from offsets or seeds. Remove the pulp from ripe berries and sow the seed outdoors. Seedlings develop slowly and may take several years to bloom.

LANDSCAPE USES: Plant among low wildflowers in the shade garden, where they create an eye-catching vertical accent. Grow them along woodland paths and in other informal settings.

COMPATIBLE COMPANIONS: Combine with wild bleeding heart (*Dicentra eximia*), bloodroot (*Sanguinaria canadensis*), columbines (*Aquilegia* spp.), hostas, and ferns. Plant them under shrubs or flowering trees such as viburnums and serviceberries (*Amelanchier* spp.).

| *Armeria maritima* | Plumbaginacea | *Artemisia absinthium* | Compositae |

COMMON THRIFT

Common thrift forms dense, evergreen tufts of grass-like, gray-green leaves that are attractive all year. The ball-shaped flower clusters add color in late spring and summer.

DESCRIPTION: Leafless bloom stalks arise from the centers of many tightly packed rosettes that grow from thickened fibrous roots. The small pink flowers are crowded into rounded 1-inch (2.5 cm) heads.

SEASON OF INTEREST: Flowers in late spring and summer. The foliage is decorative all season.

HEIGHT AND SPREAD: Height 10–14 inches (25–35 cm) in flower, 2–4 inches (5–10 cm) in leaf; width 8–10 inches (20–25 cm).

BEST SITE AND CLIMATE: Plant in average to rich, moist but well-drained soil in full sun. Plants prefer cool nights and low humidity. Zones 4–8.

GROWING GUIDELINES: Plants can tolerate drought once they are established and will grow in rock crevices where water is scarce. Common thrift also tolerates air- and soil-borne salt. Divide clumps in early spring or fall. Sow seed indoors in winter on a warm seedbed. No serious pests or diseases.

LANDSCAPE USES: Choose them for rock and wall gardens or along paths. They are perfect for seaside gardens.

COMPATIBLE COMPANIONS: Combine with low plants such as snow-in-summer (*Cerastium tomentosum*) and rock cress (*Arabis caucasica*), or use them in rock gardens with dwarf conifers and ornamental grasses.

CULTIVARS: 'Alba' has white flowers on 5-inch (12.5 cm) stems.

COMMON WORMWOOD

Common wormwood is a stout perennial that grows to shrub-like proportions. The silvery foliage adds a cool touch to perennial borders, herb gardens, and shrub plantings.

DESCRIPTION: The deeply lobed, aromatic foliage is covered with soft hairs, creating a soft, gray-green tone. The inconspicuous yellow flowers are borne in compound terminal clusters.

SEASON OF INTEREST: Blooms in late summer and fall. Foliage is the plant's main asset all season.

HEIGHT AND SPREAD: Height 2–3 feet (60–90 cm); width 2 feet (60 cm).

BEST SITE AND CLIMATE: Plant in average, sandy or loamy, well-drained soil in full sun. Zones 3–9.

GROWING GUIDELINES: Thrives in all but the most inhospitable garden spots. Avoid overly rich soil, which encourages weak growth. If plants become floppy or open in habit, prune them back by at least half to encourage compact growth. Grow from cuttings (a new shoot with a piece of older stem at the base) taken in late summer. Dust the cut surfaces with a rooting hormone to speed production of new roots. No serious pests or diseases.

LANDSCAPE USES: Use in formal or informal dry-soil gardens. Wormwoods are perfect for cottage and herb gardens as well as rock gardens. Plants also respond well to container culture.

COMPATIBLE COMPANIONS: Combine with yarrows, sages (*Salvia* spp.), ornamental onions (*Allium* spp.), and other drought-tolerant perennials. The soft foliage is lovely with ornamental grasses or in the foreground of conifers.

| *Aruncus dioicus* | Rosaceae | *Asarum europaeum* | Aristolochiaceae |

GOAT'S BEARD

EUROPEAN WILD GINGER

Goat's beards mix well with shrubs and other perennials in beds and borders. Try them as a replacement for shrubs to add excitement to foundation plantings.

The glossy, evergreen leaves of European wild ginger reflect the light of the sky, brightening shaded gardens. With age, plants will spread to form dense clumps.

DESCRIPTION: Goat's beard is a showy, shrub-like perennial with large, thrice-divided leaves and airy flower plumes. The plants are dioecious, meaning that male and female flowers are borne on separate plants. The male flowers have many fuzzy, creamy white stamens, making them more showy. Plants grow from a stout, fibrous-rooted crown.

SEASON OF INTEREST: Late spring and early summer bloom. The shrub-like proportions of this plant add season-long structure to the garden.

HEIGHT AND SPREAD: Height 3–6 feet (90–180 cm); width 3–5 feet (90–150 cm).

BEST SITE AND CLIMATE: Plant in moist, humus-rich soil in partial shade. In cooler zones, plants grow well in full sun. Goat's beards do not grow well in areas with hot nights. Zones 3–7.

GROWING GUIDELINES: Set plants 4–5 feet (1.2–1.5 m) apart to allow for their ultimate size; mature plants are quite impressive. Divide plants in early spring. Sow seed outdoors or inside on a warm seedbed. No serious pests or diseases.

LANDSCAPE USES: Use in a lightly shaded woodland garden or as an accent with flowering shrubs.

COMPATIBLE COMPANIONS: Combine with spiky-leaved irises, shrub roses, and bushy perennials such as cranesbills (*Geranium* spp.), peonies, and bee balms (*Monarda* spp.). In shaded retreats, plant them with ferns, wildflowers, and hostas.

DESCRIPTION: European wild ginger is a slow-creeping groundcover with glossy, kidney-shaped leaves mottled along the veins. The aromatic rhizomes, with a scent reminiscent of commercial ginger, creep at or just below the soil surface. The unusual, jug-like flowers are dull brown and usually hidden under the foliage.

SEASON OF INTEREST: The stunning foliage looks great all year.

HEIGHT AND SPREAD: Height 6–12 inches (15–30 cm); width 12 inches (30 cm).

BEST SITE AND CLIMATE: Plant in moist, humus-rich soil in partial to full shade. Wild gingers are quite drought-tolerant once established, but the foliage looks best when moisture is adequate. Zones 4–8.

GROWING GUIDELINES: The clumps of this groundcover spread steadily to form tight mats of weedproof foliage. If plants become too crowded, divide them in early spring or fall. No serious pests or diseases.

LANDSCAPE USES: Plant these exceptionally beautiful groundcovers along a garden path, in woodland wildflower gardens, or in a shaded rock garden.

COMPATIBLE COMPANIONS: Bulbs, woodland wildflowers, and shade-loving perennials such as lungworts (*Pulmonaria* spp.), barrenworts (*Epimedium* spp.), primroses, and hostas are excellent companions.

| *Asclepias tuberosa* | Asclepidaceae | *Aster novae-angliae* | Compositae |

BUTTERFLY WEED

The bright flowers of butterfly weed are perfect for enlivening borders, cottage gardens, meadows, and container plantings. The plants can even tolerate seaside conditions.

DESCRIPTION: Butterflies adore the masses of brilliant orange flowers that crown the mounded, shrub-like clumps in summer. The fuzzy, lance-shaped leaves densely clothe sturdy stems that arise from a thick, deep-seated taproot.

SEASON OF INTEREST: The flowers open in profusion in May and June but may be followed by sporadic bloom throughout summer. Rocket-shaped seedpods explode in the fall, releasing clouds of silken parachutes carrying the flattened seeds aloft.

HEIGHT AND SPREAD: Height 2–3 feet (60–90 cm); width 2 feet (60 cm).

BEST SITE AND CLIMATE: Plant in poor to average, well-drained soil in full sun or light shade. Plants thrive in sandy soil and tolerate seaside conditions. Zones 3–9.

GROWING GUIDELINES: Established plants are extremely drought-tolerant and thrive for years with little care. Take tip cuttings in late spring or early summer; they root quickly. Sow fresh seed outdoors in fall.

LANDSCAPE USES: Grow butterfly weed in formal borders, rock gardens, and meadow plantings.

COMPATIBLE COMPANIONS: Combine with blue and purple flowers such as sages (*Salvia* spp.) and lavenders (*Lavandula* spp.) for a lively display. Ornamental grasses, asters, and goldenrods (*Solidago* spp.) are natural companions in meadows.

NEW ENGLAND ASTER

As they mature, New England asters form broad, bushy clumps topped with daisy-like fall flowers. Cultivars vary in bloom color, from white to purple, pink, and rose.

DESCRIPTION: New England aster is a tall, stately plant with hairy stems clothed in clasping, lance-shaped leaves. The $1^1/_2$–2-inch (35–50 mm) lavender to purple flowers have bright yellow centers.

SEASON OF INTEREST: Late summer through fall bloom.

HEIGHT AND SPREAD: Height 3–6 feet (90–180 cm); width 3 feet (90 cm). Forms broad, bushy clumps when mature.

BEST SITE AND CLIMATE: Plant in moist, humus-rich soil in full sun or light shade. Plants will tolerate consistently moist or wet soil. Zones 3–8.

GROWING GUIDELINES: Divide clumps every 3–4 years in spring. Plants may need staking. For propagation, take 4–6-inch (10–15 cm) tip cuttings in late spring or early summer. Àsters are susceptible to powdery mildew, which turns the leaves dull gray. Thin the stems to promote good air circulation; keep water off the leaves. Dust affected plants with sulfur to control the spread of the disease.

LANDSCAPE USES: Plant in formal and informal garden settings or in meadows and prairies. Most selections are suited to the back of the border.

COMPATIBLE COMPANIONS: Combine these showy asters with fall perennials such as sunflowers (*Helianthus* spp.), Japanese anemone (*Anemone* x *hybrida*), chrysanthemums, and sedums, as well as the foliage of artemisias and ornamental grasses.

| *Astilbe* x *arendsii* | Saxifragaceae | *Astrantia major* | Umbelliferae |

ASTILBE

Astilbes are lovely plants for moist shade gardens or beside pools. The airy plumes of red, pink, rose, lilac, cream, or white flowers add grace and motion to the garden.

DESCRIPTION: The ferny, dissected leaves have shiny broad leaflets and remain attractive all summer. The emerging spring shoots are often tinged with red. The upright, often plumed bloom clusters bear tightly packed, fuzzy flowers. Plants grow from woody crowns with fibrous roots.

SEASON OF INTEREST: Spring and early summer bloom. The foliage is a season-long asset, and the dried seed heads are attractive in the snowy landscape.

HEIGHT AND SPREAD: Height 2–4 feet (60–120 cm); width 2–3 feet (60 –90 cm).

BEST SITE AND CLIMATE: Plant in consistently moist, slightly acid, humus-rich soil in full to partial shade. Plants tolerate more sun where summer temperatures are cool. Zones 3–9.

GROWING GUIDELINES: These heavy feeders benefit from an annual application of balanced organic fertilizer. If crowns rise above the soil, top-dress with compost or lift and replant the clumps. Divide clumps every 3–4 years.

LANDSCAPE USES: Plant masses beside a stream or pond where their plumes are reflected in the water. In beds and borders, plant them at the front or toward the center, depending on their size.

COMPATIBLE COMPANIONS: Combine with ferns, daylilies, lady's-mantle (*Alchemilla mollis*), and other plants that appreciate moist soil.

MASTERWORT

Masterwort is a trouble-free perennial that thrives in areas with cool summers. Its unusual, button-like flower heads are surrounded by starry, pointed bracts.

DESCRIPTION: Masterwort is a showy perennial with bold, deeply lobed leaves rising directly from a stout, fibrous-rooted crown. Leafy, branched flower stalks rise from the center of the clumps. The flower heads are surrounded by stiff bracts that remain after the flowers fade, prolonging the display.

SEASON OF INTEREST: Early to late summer flowers; reblooms frequently if deadheaded. The foliage is attractive all season.

HEIGHT AND SPREAD: Height 2–3 feet (60–90 cm); width 1–2 feet (30–60 cm).

BEST SITE AND CLIMATE: Plant masterwort in evenly moist, humus-rich soil in full sun or partial shade. Zones 4–7.

GROWING GUIDELINES: Clumps increase by creeping underground stems and may outgrow their position. Divide plants in fall or early spring, or remove runners from the main clump. Sow fresh seed outdoors in late summer.

LANDSCAPE USES: Choose masterwort for the mixed border where its bold foliage and unusual flowers complement perennials and shrubs.

COMPATIBLE COMPANIONS: Combine with airy meadow rues (*Thalictrum* spp.), spiky mulleins (*Verbascum* spp.), foxgloves (*Digitalis* spp.), ornamental onions (*Allium* spp.), lilies, and grasses. Plant them beside a pond with irises, ligularias (*Ligularia* spp.), and ferns.

PURPLE ROCK CRESS

Purple rock cress is an excellent choice for sunny rock gardens and rock walls. The mats of evergreen leaves are covered with white, rose, or purple flowers in spring.

DESCRIPTION: Purple rock cress is a low, mounding plant with weak stems clothed in sparsely toothed, evergreen leaves. Plants spread by thin rhizomes to form broad clumps. The ³/₄-inch (19 mm), four-petaled flowers may be white, rose, or purple.

SEASON OF INTEREST: Early spring bloom.

HEIGHT AND SPREAD: Height 6–8 inches (15–20 cm); width 8–12 inches (20–30 cm).

BEST SITE AND CLIMATE: Plant in average, well-drained, sandy or loamy, neutral soil in full sun or light shade. Thrives where summer humidity and temperatures are not excessive and nights are cool. Zones 4–8.

GROWING GUIDELINES: Plants tend to flop after flowering; shear clumps to promote compact growth and encourage repeat bloom. Divide clumps in fall to promote fresh growth. Take stem cuttings after flowering. Plants are susceptible to rot when grown in heavy, sodden soil or where nighttime temperatures are high.

LANDSCAPE USES: Grow in cracks and crevices of walls or among rocks in a rock garden. Plant them at the edge of walks or at the front of beds and borders.

COMPATIBLE COMPANIONS: Combine with spring bulbs, coral bells (*Heuchera* spp.), sedums, red valerian (*Centranthus ruber*), and basket-of-gold (*Aurinia saxatilis*).

BASKET-OF-GOLD

Give basket-of-gold sun and good drainage, and it will produce masses of yellow blooms. It tolerates hot, dry conditions but suffers in very hot and humid climates.

DESCRIPTION: Basket-of-gold produces mounds of 6-inch (15 cm), oblong, gray-green leaves from a thick crown. Its hairy leaves and deep, thickened roots help the plants to endure dry soil and warm temperatures. The brilliant yellow flowers have four rounded petals and are carried in upright, branched clusters.

SEASON OF INTEREST: Early spring bloom. Foliage stays attractive if summers are cool.

HEIGHT AND SPREAD: Height 10–12 inches (25–30 cm); width 12 inches (30 cm).

BEST SITE AND CLIMATE: Plant basket-of-gold in average, well-drained, loamy or sandy soil in full sun. Zones 3–7.

GROWING GUIDELINES: Clumps spread by creeping stems and may flop after flowering. Cut stems back by two-thirds after flowering to encourage compact growth. For propagation, divide in fall or take stem cuttings in spring or fall. Plants are susceptible to root rot in heavy, moist soil and where humidity is high. Grow only in well-drained soil.

LANDSCAPE USES: Use generous plantings to add a spot of bright color to rock walls, rock gardens, and along walks.

COMPATIBLE COMPANIONS: Combine with rock cress (*Aubrieta* spp.), pinks (*Dianthus* spp.), columbines (*Aquilegia* spp.), dwarf conifers, and grasses.

| *Baptisia australis* | Leguminosae | *Belamcanda chinensis* | Iridaceae |

BLUE FALSE INDIGO

BLACKBERRY LILY

Blue false indigo looks equally attractive in formal borders or informal prairie and meadow plantings. It forms dense, rounded mounds that reach shrub-like proportions.

Blackberry lily has showy curved "fans" of foliage that resemble those of irises. The orange summer flowers are followed by clusters of black seeds in fall.

DESCRIPTION: The stout, branching stems bear 1–3-inch (2.5–7.5 cm), three-lobed, blue-green leaves. The 1-inch (2.5 cm) deep blue flowers are carried in narrow, open clusters. Plants grow from thick, deep taproots.

SEASON OF INTEREST: Late spring and early summer bloom. The foliage looks lovely all season, and the dried pods persist well into the winter.

HEIGHT AND SPREAD: Height 2–4 feet (60–120 cm); width 3–4 feet (90–120 cm).

BEST SITE AND CLIMATE: Plant in average to rich, moist but well-drained soil in full sun or partial shade. Zones 3–9.

GROWING GUIDELINES : Space young plants 3–4 feet (90–120 cm) apart. Division is seldom necessary except for propagation; then divide clumps in fall using a sharp knife or shears. Keep at least one eye (bud) per division. Take tip cuttings after flowering or sow fresh seed outdoors in summer. No serious pests or diseases.

LANDSCAPE USES: Plant toward the middle or rear of the border, where its shrubby stems form a backdrop for other plants.

COMPATIBLE COMPANIONS: Combine with Siberian iris (*Iris sibirica*), peonies, and other bold-textured plants. In wild settings, plant them with wildflowers such as butterfly weed (*Asclepias tuberosa*) and asters as well as ornamental grasses.

DESCRIPTION: The branched clumps grow from creeping rhizomes and may consist of dozens of decorative fans. The six-petaled, 2-inch (5 cm), orange flowers are speckled with red. In fall, the inflated seed capsules split to expose the berry-like clusters of black seeds that give the plant its common name.

SEASON OF INTEREST: Mid- to late-summer bloom. The summer foliage and fall fruits are decorative.

HEIGHT AND SPREAD: Height 2–4 feet (60–120 cm); width 1–2 feet (30–60 cm).

BEST SITE AND CLIMATE: Plant in average to rich, well-drained soil in full sun or light shade. Afternoon shade may prolong the life of the individual flowers. Zones 4–10; may need winter protection in colder areas of Zone 4.

GROWING GUIDELINES: Plants spread by creeping rhizomes to form dense clumps. Divide in late summer as necessary to control their spread. Self-sown seedlings will appear. Propagate by division or by sowing fresh seed outdoors.

LANDSCAPE USES: Choose blackberry lily for the front or middle of formal borders as well as for informal gardens and meadows.

COMPATIBLE COMPANIONS: Combine with garden phlox (*Phlox paniculata*), daylilies, and other plants with large flowers that will contrast with the small, starry flowers. Contrast the bold foliage with fine textures.

Bergenia cordifolia   Saxifragaceae

HEART-LEAVED BERGENIA

Grow bergenias under shrubs for a glossy green groundcover, or use them in borders or containers. Use foliage plants such as ferns and small-leaved hostas for contrast.

DESCRIPTION: Bergenias are handsome foliage plants with broad, oval, leathery, evergreen leaves. The 10–12-inch (25–30 cm) leaves emerge from a stout, creeping rhizome with fibrous roots. Fleshy pink or rose flowers are carried on thick stems.

SEASON OF INTEREST: Early spring bloom, with occasional flowers in summer or fall. The foliage turns red in fall and stays attractive into winter.

HEIGHT AND SPREAD: Height 12–14 inches (30–35 cm); width 12 inches (30 cm).

BEST SITE AND CLIMATE: Plant in moist, humus-rich soil in sun or partial shade. In warmer zones, provide afternoon shade to protect leaves from burning. Plants are drought-tolerant once established. Zones 3–9.

GROWING GUIDELINES: As clumps age, they become bare in the center. Lift plants in spring and remove old portions of the rhizome with a sharp knife; replant into amended soil. Protect foliage and growing tips with a winter mulch of evergreen boughs or marsh hay. Trap slugs in shallow cups of beer sunken so the rims are flush with the soil surface.

LANDSCAPE USES: Use as accents in beds and borders, at the base of rock walls, or along the garden path.

COMPATIBLE COMPANIONS: Combine with small-flowered plants such as bellflowers (*Campanula* spp.), pinks (*Dianthus* spp.), cranesbills (*Geranium* spp.), and asters.

Boltonia asteroides   Compositae

BOLTONIA

Boltonia is an adaptable perennial that looks attractive all season. It prefers moist soil, but the stems tend to be sturdier and more compact in dry conditions.

DESCRIPTION: Boltonias are tall, late-season perennials. They produce masses of 1-inch (2.5 cm) white daisies with bright yellow centers in open clusters that smother the 3–5-inch (7.5–12.5 cm), gray-green, willow-like foliage.

SEASON OF INTEREST: Late summer through fall bloom. The mounded plants are lovely in foliage; the flowers are a bonus.

HEIGHT AND SPREAD: Height 4–6 feet (1.2–1.8 m); width 4 feet (1.2 m).

BEST SITE AND CLIMATE: Grow boltonia in moist, humus-rich soil in full sun or light shade. Plants will tolerate dry soil. Zones 3–9.

GROWING GUIDELINES: Plants form sturdy, dense stems that seldom need staking. Divide oversized clumps in spring. Division is also an easy way to propagate the species; take early-summer tip cuttings to increase a cultivar. No serious pests or diseases.

LANDSCAPE USES: Choose boltonia for the rear of formal beds and borders or for informal plantings and cottage gardens. Enjoy their open form in meadows or beside ponds or streams.

COMPATIBLE COMPANIONS: Combine with fall-blooming perennials such as asters, Japanese anemones (*Anemone* x *hybrida*), goldenrods (*Solidago* spp.), Joe-Pye weeds (*Eupatorium* spp.), and ornamental grasses.

Brunnera macrophylla Boraginaceae	*Campanula persicifolia* Campanulaceae
# SIBERIAN BUGLOSS	# PEACH-LEAVED BELLFLOWER

The bold summer foliage of Siberian bugloss is a perfect foil for fine-textured plants like astilbes, ferns, and grasses. Its blue blooms blend well with spring wildflowers.

DESCRIPTION: The 8-inch (20 cm), heart-shaped leaves rise in a tight mound from a short, fibrous-rooted rhizome. Sprays of $^1/_4$ inch (6 mm), forget-me-not blue flowers cover the plants in spring.

SEASON OF INTEREST: Early spring bloom; flowering often continues for 3–4 weeks. The foliage is stunning all season long.

HEIGHT AND SPREAD: Height 1–1$^1/_2$ feet (30–45 cm); width 2 feet (60 cm).

BEST SITE AND CLIMATE: Plant in evenly moist, humus-rich soil in partial to full shade. Plants are tolerant of short dry spells once established; if drought persists, plants will go dormant. In Northern gardens, bugloss can take considerable sun. Zones 3–8.

GROWING GUIDELINES: This tough perennial seldom needs division. Self-sown seedlings will appear regularly around the parent clumps. Divide clumps in early spring or fall, or take 3–4-inch (7.5–10 cm) root cuttings in fall or early winter. Transplant self-sown seedlings to their desired position.

LANDSCAPE USES: Plant as a groundcover under trees or shrubs, in shade and woodland gardens, or in partially shaded borders.

COMPATIBLE COMPANIONS: Combine with tulips, daffodils, and other spring bulbs, along with wildflowers such as Jacob's ladder (*Polemonium reptans*), phlox, and foamflower (*Tiarella cordifolia*).

Peach-leaved bellflower is a dependable favorite for cottage gardens and borders. The blooms are also long-lasting as cut flowers in indoor arrangements.

DESCRIPTION: Peach-leaved bellflower produces mounds of narrow, 8-inch (20 cm), evergreen leaves from a fibrous-rooted crown. Tall, narrow stalks carry a profusion of open, bell-shaped, lavender-blue flowers.

SEASON OF INTEREST: Summer bloom.

HEIGHT AND SPREAD: Height 1–3 feet (30–90 cm); width 2 feet (60 cm).

BEST SITE AND CLIMATE: Plant in moist but well-drained, humus-rich soil in full sun to partial shade. Provide protection from hot afternoon sun in warmer zones. Peach-leaved bellflower prefers cool summer temperatures. Zones 3–8.

GROWING GUIDELINES: Plants may be short-lived in warmer zones. For propagation, take tip cuttings in early summer or divide clumps in early spring; gently tease the tightly packed crowns apart. Slugs may damage the leaves; trap the pests in shallow pans of beer set flush with the soil surface.

LANDSCAPE USES: Place toward the middle or rear of the border. Use them in drifts as an accent along a stone wall or garden fence.

COMPATIBLE COMPANIONS: The showy flower spikes combine well with yarrows, Russian sage (*Perovskia atriplicifolia*), cranesbills (*Geranium* spp.), bee balm (*Monarda* spp.), phlox, and other fine- to medium-textured plants. Use them with shrub and climbing roses as well as flowering vines such as clematis.

Campanula portenschlagiana   Campanulaceae

DALMATIAN BELLFLOWER

Dalmatian bellflower is a free-flowering, easy-care groundcover that spreads over rocks and open soil to form extensive clumps. It also looks great cascading over walls.

DESCRIPTION: Dalmatian bellflower forms low, creeping mats of small triangular leaves. At bloom time, the leaves are practically obscured by scads of starry, blue-purple, bell-shaped flowers. Plants grow from fibrous-rooted crowns and root along the stems as they rest on the ground.

SEASON OF INTEREST: Spring and early summer bloom.

HEIGHT AND SPREAD: Height 3–6 inches (7.5–15 cm); width 10–12 inches (25–30 cm).

BEST SITE AND CLIMATE: Plant in average to rich, well-drained soil in full sun or partial shade. Dalmatian bellflower tolerates drought and heat. Zones 4–8.

GROWING GUIDELINES: For propagation, divide plants in spring or fall or take tip cuttings in late spring. Plants are also easy to grow from seed sown indoors or out.

LANDSCAPE USES: Dalmatian bellflowers were made for rock and wall gardens: Plant them in crevices and watch them spread to form breathtaking clumps. Also use them at the front of borders or as edging for beds.

COMPATIBLE COMPANIONS: Combine with spring bulbs, purple rock cress (*Aubrietia deltoidea*), columbines (*Aquilegia* spp.), basket-of-gold (*Aurinia saxatilis*), sedums, and grasses.

Catananche caerulea   Compositae

CUPID'S DART

Grow Cupid's darts in rock gardens, cutting gardens, and dry, sunny borders. The long-lasting straw-like blooms dry easily and are prized by flower arrangers.

DESCRIPTION: Cupid's dart produces tufts of narrow, woolly leaves from a fibrous rootstock. The 2-inch (5 cm), daisy-like, blue flowers resemble asters but lack the bold yellow center. They are carried singly on wiry stems.

SEASON OF INTEREST: Summer bloom.

HEIGHT AND SPREAD: Height 1½–2 feet (45–60 cm); width 10–12 inches (25–30 cm).

BEST SITE AND CLIMATE: Plant in light, well-drained, humus-rich soil in full sun. Good drainage is imperative. Plants are heat-tolerant. Zones 4–9.

GROWING GUIDELINES: Plants may be short-lived, especially in heavy soil. Divide clumps each fall to promote longevity. For propagation, sow seed indoors in early spring or take 2–3-inch (5–7.5 cm) root cuttings in fall or winter; plants will bloom the first year. No serious pests or diseases.

LANDSCAPE USES: Use in mass plantings in rock gardens or at the front of a dry, sunny perennial garden. Plant them in the cutting garden, too.

COMPATIBLE COMPANIONS: Combine with yarrows, sundrops (*Oenothera* spp.), catmints (*Nepeta* spp.), cranesbills (*Geranium* spp.), thyme, and sedums. Set them out among creeping plants where they show to good advantage.

CULTIVARS: 'Blue Giant' is a stout cultivar with dark blue flowers. 'Major' has lavender-blue flowers on 3-foot (90 cm) stems.

Centaurea hypoleuca   Compositae

KNAPWEED

Knapweed is a bushy, fast-spreading perennial that bears loads of fringed pink flowers in late spring and early summer. It may even rebloom if you remove the spent flowers.

DESCRIPTION: Knapweed grows from a fibrous-rooted crown to produce a clump of pinnately lobed leaves with eight to ten woolly divisions. The leaves clothe thick, weakly upright, flowering stems. The fringed pink flowers have broad, white centers; they resemble annual bachelor's buttons (*Centaurea cyanus*) and are borne one to a stem. The flowers are long-lasting in dried or fresh arrangements.

SEASON OF INTEREST: Late spring and early summer bloom.

HEIGHT AND SPREAD: Height 1½–2½ feet (45–75 cm); width 1½ feet (45 cm).

BEST SITE AND CLIMATE: Plant in moist but well-drained, humus-rich soil in full sun. Plants become lanky in too much shade. Zones 3–7.

GROWING GUIDELINES: Remove flower heads as they fade to promote rebloom. When flower production wanes, cut plants back to remove floppy stems. Divide clumps every 2–3 years to keep plants vigorous. Sow seed outdoors in fall or indoors in late winter. No serious pests or diseases.

LANDSCAPE USES: Use in cottage gardens and in other informal settings as well as in meadow plantings.

COMPATIBLE COMPANIONS: Combine with ornamental grasses, orange coneflowers (*Rudbeckia* spp.), and yarrows.

CULTIVARS: 'John Coutts' has rosy purple flowers on 2-foot (60 cm) stems.

Centranthus ruber   Valerianaceae

RED VALERIAN

The bright coral red flowers of red valerian add vibrant color to the spring and summer border. Pink-, rose-, and white-flowered selections are also available.

DESCRIPTION: Red valerian is an upright perennial with opposite, gray-green, oval leaves on branching stems. Plants grow from a fibrous-rooted crown. The flowers are carried in branched clusters.

SEASON OF INTEREST: Spring and summer bloom.

HEIGHT AND SPREAD: Height 1–3 feet (30-90 cm); width 2 feet (60 cm).

BEST SITE AND CLIMATE: Plant in average, sandy or loamy, neutral or alkaline soil in full sun. Red valerian grows readily in rock crevices where soil is at a premium. Plants perform best where summers are cool. Zones 4–8.

GROWING GUIDELINES: Plants may become floppy after blooming; shear them back to promote compact growth and reblooming. Sow seed outdoors in summer. Plants often self-sow prolifically, but seedlings may not be the same color as their parents. To reproduce plants of a specific color, remove basal shoots and treat them like tip cuttings.

LANDSCAPE USES: Perfect for wall and rock gardens and borders.

COMPATIBLE COMPANIONS: Red valerian shows off to great advantage in mass plantings in walls. The often harsh coral red flower color combines well with the neutral colors of stone or with creamy yellow flowers. In the border, plant it with yarrows, marguerites (*Anthemis tinctoria*), shasta daisies (*Chrysanthemum* x *superbum*), sedums, and grasses.

| *Cerastium tomentosum* | Caryophyllaceae | *Chelone glabra* | Scrophulariaceae |

SNOW-IN-SUMMER

WHITE TURTLEHEAD

Snow-in-summer is a distinctive groundcover for sunny, well-drained sites. It is very cold-tolerant but doesn't adapt well to hot and humid conditions.

White turtlehead thrives in wet soil, but it can adapt to drier conditions, too. For extra color, you could also grow a pink-flowered species, such as C. lyonii.

DESCRIPTION: Snow-in-summer is a low, mounding plant with small, woolly leaves on wiry stems. Plants grow from a dense tangle of fibrous roots. The 1-inch (2.5 cm), snow white flowers have five deeply notched petals. They are borne in open clusters held well above the foliage.

SEASON OF INTEREST: Late spring and early summer bloom.

HEIGHT AND SPREAD: Height 6–10 inches (15–25 cm); width 12 inches (30 cm).

BEST SITE AND CLIMATE: Plant in average, sandy or loamy, well-drained soil in full sun. Zones 2–7.

GROWING GUIDELINES: After flowering, shear plants to the ground to promote fresh, compact growth. Clumps may overgrow their position; divide in spring or fall to control their spread. For propagation, take tip cuttings in early summer or remove divisions from the outside of the clump. Plants may suffer from fungal rot that blackens the leaves and stems. Well-drained soil and cool summer temperatures are the best preventives.

LANDSCAPE USES: Choose for cascading over a wall, planting in a rock garden, or edging a path.

COMPATIBLE COMPANIONS: The profusion of flowers is a bright addition to the spring garden with late bulbs, Johnny-jump-ups (*Viola tricolor*), pinks (*Dianthus* spp.), bellflowers (*Campanula* spp.), and catmint (*Nepeta* spp.).

DESCRIPTION: White turtlehead is a bushy perennial with tall, leafy stems that grow from a stout, fibrous-rooted crown. The 4–7-inch (10–17.5 cm), opposite leaves are lance-shaped with toothed margins. The unusual creamy white, tubular flowers are inflated, with a puckered lip that resembles the head of a turtle with jaws agape.

SEASON OF INTEREST: Late summer into fall bloom.

HEIGHT AND SPREAD: Height 1–3 feet (30–90 cm); width 1–2 feet (30–60 cm).

BEST SITE AND CLIMATE: Plant in evenly moist, humus-rich soil in full sun or partial shade. Zones 3–8; intolerant of excessive heat.

GROWING GUIDELINES: Divide the fleshy-rooted crowns in spring or after flowering to reduce their size or to increase your stock. Another propagation option is to take stem cuttings in early summer; remove the flower buds if present. No serious pests or diseases.

LANDSCAPE USES: Turtleheads look great in both formal and informal gardens. Grow them in borders or meadows or near ponds or water gardens.

COMPATIBLE COMPANIONS: Combine with asters, phlox, grasses, and goldenrods (*Solidago* spp.) for late-summer color. Turtleheads are lovely with pale pink Japanese anemones (*Anemone* x *hybrida*) and spiky Canadian burnet (*Sanguisorba canadensis*).

Chrysanthemum x *morifolium*   Compositae

GARDEN MUM

The bright flowers of mums signal the end of summer and the return of cold weather. They bloom in a variety of colors, from white, pink, and red to gold and yellow.

DESCRIPTION: Mums have stout stems clothed in lobed leaves and grow from creeping stems with tangled, fibrous roots. Flower size ranges from 1–6 inches (2.5–15 cm). Also known as *Dendranthema* x *grandiflorum*.

SEASON OF INTEREST: Late summer through fall bloom.

HEIGHT AND SPREAD: Height 1¹/₂–5 feet (45–150 cm); width 1–3 feet (30–90 cm). Quite variable, depending on the cultivar.

BEST SITE AND CLIMATE: Plant in light, humus-rich, well-drained soil in full sun or light shade. Mums vary in their hardiness; usually Zones 3–9.

GROWING GUIDELINES: Pinch the stems once or twice in May or June to promote compact growth. Divide the fast-growing clumps in spring every 1–2 years to keep them vigorous. Take tip cuttings in late spring or early summer.

LANDSCAPE USES: Use mums to breathe new life into tired annual displays. Place them in formal beds and borders or cottage gardens. They also grow well in pots.

COMPATIBLE COMPANIONS: Combine with asters, goldenrods (*Solidago* spp.), sedums, grasses, and anemones (*Anemone* spp.) for a showy fall display. Use them with foliage plants such as yuccas (*Yucca* spp.) and ornamental grasses.

Chrysanthemum x *superbum*   Compositae

SHASTA DAISY

Shasta daisies look delightful in borders, cottage gardens, and meadows. The plants are extremely heat- and cold-tolerant; they can even take seaside conditions.

DESCRIPTION: Shasta daisies are showy, summer-blooming plants with dense clusters of shiny 10-inch (25 cm), deep green, toothed leaves from short, creeping, fibrous-rooted stems. The 3-inch (7.5 cm) bright white daisies have large, bright yellow centers; they are carried on stout, leafy stems. Also known as *Leucanthemum* x *superbum*.

SEASON OF INTEREST: Produces flowers freely throughout the summer months.

HEIGHT AND SPREAD: Height 1–3 feet (30–90 cm); width 2 feet (60 cm).

BEST SITE AND CLIMATE: Plant in average to rich, well-drained soil in full sun. Zones 3–10; exact zones vary by cultivar.

GROWING GUIDELINES: Deadhead plants to promote continued bloom. These easy-care plants grow quickly but may be short-lived, especially in warmer zones. Divide and replant clumps every 3–4 years to keep them vigorous. For propagation, remove offsets from the main clump or divide in spring. No serious pests or diseases.

LANDSCAPE USES: Plant in beds and borders, cottage gardens, and meadow gardens.

COMPATIBLE COMPANIONS: Combine with summer-blooming perennials such as yarrows, daylilies, irises, and poppies. In a seaside garden, plant them with blanket flowers (*Gaillardia* spp.), butterfly weed (*Asclepias tuberosa*), grasses, and coreopsis.

Cimicifuga racemosa   Ranunculaceae

BLACK SNAKEROOT

Walls, vines, and shrubs make an excellent background for the showy flowers of black snakeroot. The plants also combine well with ferns, hostas, and shade wildflowers.

DESCRIPTION: The wand-like spires of black snakeroot wave above an open cluster of large, compound leaves with toothed leaflets. The small, $^1/_2$-inch (12 mm), white flowers have a dense whorl of fuzzy stamens (male reproductive structures) and no petals. Plants grow from a stout, fibrous-rooted crown.

SEASON OF INTEREST: Early summer to midsummer bloom. The foliage is attractive all season.

HEIGHT AND SPREAD: Height 4–7 feet (1.2–2.1 m); width 3–4 feet (90–120 cm).

BEST SITE AND CLIMATE: Plant in moist, humus-rich soil in sun or shade. Protect plants from afternoon sun in warmer zones. Plants are somewhat drought-tolerant once established. Zones 3–8.

GROWING GUIDELINES: Young plants take several years to reach flowering size. Clumps increase gradually each year and may have 10–15 bloom stalks at maturity. For propagation, divide clumps with a sharp knife in fall, leaving at least one eye (bud) per division. Or sow fresh seed outdoors in fall; it may take two seasons to germinate.

LANDSCAPE USES: Place at the rear of the border or in a cottage garden. The plants make distinctive accents along or at the end of a garden path. They are equally suitable for a woodland garden.

COMPATIBLE COMPANIONS: Combine the striking spikes of black snakeroot with bold flowers such as phlox, peonies, and daylilies.

Colchicum autumnale   Liliaceae

AUTUMN CROCUS

The splendor of autumn crocus in full bloom is a high point of the season. Combine these bulbs with groundcovers to hide the spring foliage as it ripens.

DESCRIPTION: Dozens of 2–4-inch (5–7.5 cm) rose, pink, or white flowers crowd together to create a breathtaking display. Rosettes of coarse, glossy, oval leaves emerge early in spring but disappear by midsummer. The flowers emerge from the bare soil naked and unashamed.

SEASON OF INTEREST: September bloom; the new foliage is attractive in the spring garden.

HEIGHT AND SPREAD: Height 1–1$^1/_2$ feet (30–45 cm) in foliage; 4–6 inches (10–15 cm) in bloom. Plants 4–6 inches (10–15 cm) wide.

BEST SITE AND CLIMATE: Give them average to rich, moist but well-drained soil in full sun to light shade. Zones 4–9.

GROWING GUIDELINES: Set out the corms in August or early September; they will bloom soon after. Remove the leaves only after they turn brown. Divide clumps every 3–4 years after the foliage has ripened.

LANDSCAPE USES: Use a generous planting in formal borders, in cottage and rock gardens, along garden paths, or in drifts with shrubs.

COMPATIBLE COMPANIONS: Combine with Japanese anemones (*Anemone* x *hybrida*), asters, and chrysanthemums. In partial shade, plant them with lungworts (*Pulmonaria* spp.), bleeding hearts (*Dicentra* spp.), and ferns.

THREAD-LEAVED COREOPSIS

Thread-leaved coreopsis bears masses of starry yellow flowers over several months. This easy-care perennial demands little attention once established.

DESCRIPTION: Thread-leaved coreopsis is an airy, rounded plant with thread-like, three-lobed leaves. Plants grow from a fibrous-rooted crown. The 1–2-inch (2.5–5 cm) starry flowers are butter to golden yellow.

SEASON OF INTEREST: Plants bloom throughout the summer.

HEIGHT AND SPREAD: Height 1–3 feet (30–90 cm); width 2–3 feet (60–90 cm).

BEST SITE AND CLIMATE: Plant in average to rich, moist but well-drained soil in full sun or light shade. Coreopsis are drought-tolerant once established. Overly rich soil promotes floppy growth. Zones 3–9.

GROWING GUIDELINES: Plants eventually die out at the center; divide old clumps and replant into amended soil. For propagation, take tip cuttings in early summer or remove small divisions from the edge of the clump. No serious pests or diseases.

LANDSCAPE USES: Perfect for the front of the border in exuberant masses or along walks and paths. They are also well suited to cottage and rock gardens.

COMPATIBLE COMPANIONS: Combine with cranesbills (*Geranium* spp.), yarrows, daylilies, orange coneflowers (*Rudbeckia* spp.), and purple coneflowers (*Echinacea* spp.). Try them with ornamental grasses or use a mass planting with shrubs.

DUTCH CROCUS

Crocuses thrive in spring sun but can take shade once they're done blooming. They grow well under deciduous trees because they go dormant as the trees leaf out.

DESCRIPTION: Bright flowers in a rainbow of colors herald the return of spring. The six-petaled flowers are 2–4 inches (5–10 cm) tall and emerge with grass-like foliage. Plants grow from a button-like corm and go dormant by early summer.

SEASON OF INTEREST: Early spring bloom.

HEIGHT AND SPREAD: Height 4–6 inches (10–15 cm); width 6 inches (15 cm).

BEST SITE AND CLIMATE: Plant bulbs in fall in moist but well-drained, humus-rich soil in full sun or partial shade. Zones 3–9.

GROWING GUIDELINES: Buy top-quality, fresh, fleshy corms and set them out as soon as you receive them. Plants form dense clumps and can be divided every 4 years or so; lift clumps as the foliage turns yellow and separate the corms.

LANDSCAPE USES: Crocuses are a welcome addition to any garden. Plant generous groups of them in beds and borders, cottage and rock gardens, or woodlands and shaded spots. Mass plantings in lawns create a welcome relief from the monotony of turf.

COMPATIBLE COMPANIONS: Combine with a wealth of other spring bulbs including daffodils, species tulips, and squills (*Scilla* spp.). Plant them under groundcovers that will fill the spot left when they go dormant. Spring-blooming perennials such as bleeding hearts (*Dicentra* spp.) and barrenworts (*Epimedium* spp.) make excellent companions.

Delphinium x *belladonna*   Ranunculaceae

BELLADONNA DELPHINIUM

Delphiniums are traditional favorites for borders and cottage gardens. The showy flowers range in color from white through all shades of blue, lavender, and purple.

DESCRIPTION: Plants form multistemmed clumps from stout crowns with thick, fleshy roots. The deeply cut, lobed leaves are 6–8 inches (15–20 cm) long. In each flower, five petal-like sepals surround two to four small, true petals that are often called the "bee." The top sepal has a long spur.

SEASON OF INTEREST: Late spring through summer flowers; plants may rebloom in fall.

HEIGHT AND SPREAD: Height $4^1/_2$–6 feet (1.3–1.8 m); width 2–3 feet (60–90 cm).

BEST SITE AND CLIMATE: Plant in evenly moist but well-drained, fertile, humus-rich soil in full sun. A neutral to slightly acid soil is preferable. Usually Zones 4–7; many hybrids are hardy to Zone 3.

GROWING GUIDELINES: Delphiniums are heavy feeders and benefit from an annual spring topdressing of a balanced organic fertilizer or well-rotted manure. Thin the clumps to three to five stems as they emerge. To encourage rebloom, remove the old flowering stems above the first leaf below the lowest flowers. Divide overgrown plants in spring and replant into amended soil.

LANDSCAPE USES: Choose delphiniums for the rear of the border where their showy spires will tower over other summer-blooming perennials.

COMPATIBLE COMPANIONS: Combine with shrubby perennials such as phlox, lilies, lupines (*Lupinus* spp.), and ornamental grasses.

Dianthus gratianopolitanus   Caryophyllaceae

CHEDDAR PINKS

Cheddar pinks bear sweet-scented flowers you'll enjoy outdoors in the garden or indoors as cut flowers. They grow well in sunny rock gardens or cascading over walls.

DESCRIPTION: The broad, mounded plants produce dense clusters of 3-inch (7.5 cm), blue-green, grass-like leaves. Plants grow from trailing stems with fibrous roots. The fragrant white, rose, or pink flowers are borne on wiry stems.

SEASON OF INTEREST: Early- to mid-summer bloom.

HEIGHT AND SPREAD: Height 9–12 inches (22.5–30 cm); width 12 inches (30 cm).

BEST SITE AND CLIMATE: Plant in average, well-drained, sandy or loamy soil in full sun. The soil should be neutral or only slightly acid for best growth. Zones 3–9.

GROWING GUIDELINES: Divide clumps every 2–3 years to keep them vigorous. Remove flowers as they fade to promote continued bloom. Take stem cuttings from the foliage rosettes in summer. Pinks are susceptible to rust, a fungus that causes yellow blotches on the upper surface of the leaves and raised, orange spots on the lower surface. Thin clumps to promote air circulation, and dust affected plants with sulfur.

LANDSCAPE USES: Place cheddar pinks at the front of the border or use them as an edging along paths.

COMPATIBLE COMPANIONS: Combine with other front-of-the-border plants such as sedums, thyme, and lamb's-ears (*Stachys byzantina*). Interplant them with spiky foliage such as yuccas (*Yucca* spp.) and grasses.

| *Dicentra eximia* | Fumariaceae | *Dictamnus albus* | Rutaceae |

FRINGED BLEEDING HEART

GAS PLANT

Fringed bleeding hearts bloom mostly in spring, but flowers can appear any time during the growing season. The ferny foliage looks great from spring through fall.

Gas plants take a few years to get established, but once they're settled in, they need little care. White, violet purple, and red-violet selections are available.

DESCRIPTION: Bleeding hearts bear a profusion of small clusters of pink, heart-shaped flowers held above finely divided, blue-green foliage. Plants form dense rosettes of deeply cut foliage from thick, fleshy roots.

SEASON OF INTEREST: Early spring to early summer flowering, with sporadic bloom throughout the season.

HEIGHT AND SPREAD: Height 1–2¹/₂ feet (30–75 cm); width 2–3 feet (30–90 cm).

BEST SITE AND CLIMATE: Plant in evenly moist, humus-rich soil in partial shade. Plants tolerate full sun in Northern gardens. Protect plants with a winter mulch in colder zones. Zones 3–9.

GROWING GUIDELINES: Top-dress with compost in early spring. If plants lose vigor, lift and divide clumps and replant into amended soil. For propagation, sow fresh seed outdoors in summer or divide plants in fall. Self-sown seedlings are common. No serious pests or diseases.

LANDSCAPE USES: Plant in formal and informal gardens, in rockeries, or in masses along garden paths. The plants are exquisite and delicate in foliage and flower, so place them where they are easy to admire.

COMPATIBLE COMPANIONS: Combine with bulbs, primroses, and wildflowers for a striking spring display. For summer interest, plant them with hostas, ferns, and groundcovers.

DESCRIPTION: Gas plant forms shrub-like clumps, with stout stems clothed in deep green, pinnately lobed leaves, and erect flower spikes. The 1-inch (2.5 cm), showy white flowers have five starry petals and ten long, curled stamens (male reproductive structures) that protrude from the flower. The starry seed capsules are attractive throughout the summer. Plants grow from thick, woody crowns with fibrous roots.

SEASON OF INTEREST: Late spring or early summer bloom. The clean foliage and starry seed capsules remain attractive all season.

HEIGHT AND SPREAD: Height 1–4 feet (30–120 cm); width 1–3 feet (30–90 cm).

BEST SITE AND CLIMATE: Plant in well-drained, average to rich soil in sun or light shade. Zones 3–8.

GROWING GUIDELINES: Sow fresh seed outdoors in late summer; seedlings appear the next season but grow slowly. Transplant young plants to their permanent position after 3 years of growth. Plants are subject to root rot in soggy soil; provide good drainage and do not overwater.

LANDSCAPE USES: Choose gas plants for formal and cottage gardens with dry soil or for meadow plantings.

COMPATIBLE COMPANIONS: Combine with dry-soil perennials such as oriental poppy (*Papaver orientale*), yarrows, and sundrops (*Oenothera* spp.).

Digitalis grandiflora   Scrophulariaceae

YELLOW FOXGLOVE

Yellow foxgloves bloom dependably with little care. The tall flower spikes of these popular, old-fashioned perennials are familiar to generations of gardeners.

DESCRIPTION: The stems are clothed in fuzzy, broad, lance-shaped leaves. Foliage rosettes form at the base of the flowering stem and persist over winter. The 2-inch (5 cm), soft yellow flowers are carried on erect 1–3-foot (30–90 cm) stalks. Plants grow from fibrous-rooted crowns. Also known as *D. ambigua*.

SEASON OF INTEREST: Plants flower in early summer; they often rebloom if cut back after flowering.

HEIGHT AND SPREAD: Height 2–3 feet (30–90 cm); width 1 foot (30 cm).

BEST SITE AND CLIMATE: Plant in moist but well-drained, humus-rich soil in full sun to partial shade. Zones 3–8.

GROWING GUIDELINES: Divide overgrown clumps in spring or fall. Remove spent bloom stalks to promote rebloom; leave one stalk to self-sow. Sow fresh seed outdoors in fall.

LANDSCAPE USES: Plant at the middle or rear of perennial gardens. Use mass plantings along a wall or fence or in combination with flowering shrubs.

COMPATIBLE COMPANIONS: Combine with garden phlox (*Phlox paniculata*), tall bellflowers (*Campanula* spp.), cranesbills (*Geranium* spp.), peonies, violas, and irises. In informal woodland gardens, plant them with clustered bellflowers (*Campanula glomerata*), Solomon's seals (*Polygonatum* spp.), ferns, and ornamental grasses.

Dodecatheon meadia   Primulaceae

SHOOTING-STAR

Shooting-stars spread slowly to form thick clumps with many bloom stalks. Plants go dormant after flowering, so grow them with bushy perennials that will fill the gap.

DESCRIPTION: Shooting-star is a delicate wildflower with elongated oval leaves. The bloom stalk is crowned with a cluster of pink or white flowers. Each flower resembles a dart, with a forward-pointing cluster of stamens and five reflexed petals. Plants grow from shallow, spidery, white roots.

SEASON OF INTEREST: Spring bloom.

HEIGHT AND SPREAD: Height 1–2 feet (30–60 cm) in flower; leaves to 1 foot (30 cm) tall. Width to 1 foot (30 cm).

BEST SITE AND CLIMATE: Grow shooting-star in average to humus-rich, moist soil with a near-neutral or slightly alkaline pH. Plant in sun or shade; direct sun in spring is necessary for best bloom. As plants go dormant after flowering, the soil can become somewhat dry. Zones 4–8.

GROWING GUIDELINES: For propagation, divide clumps in summer or fall. Lift plants and tease the crowns apart; replant. No serious pests or diseases.

LANDSCAPE USES: Plant shooting-stars in shade and woodland gardens or at the edge of a moist meadow or prairie garden. Use them in rock gardens or in drifts with shrubs and spring-flowering trees.

COMPATIBLE COMPANIONS: Combine with spring wildflowers such as wild columbine (*Aquilegia canadensis*) and wild gingers (*Asarum* spp.). In a summer-shaded corner, plant them with lungworts (*Pulmonaria* spp.), anemones, and ferns.

| *Echinacea purpurea* | Compositae | *Echinops ritro* | Compositae |

PURPLE CONEFLOWER

The bright blooms of purple coneflower add a splash of color to ornamental grasses and combine well with most perennials. Established plants tolerate heat and drought.

DESCRIPTION: Purple coneflowers are showy summer daisies with sparse, 6-inch (15 cm), oval or broadly lanced-shaped leaves on stout, hairy stems. Plants grow from thick, deep taproots. The red-violet to rose pink flowers have broad, drooping rays (petal-like structures) surrounding raised, bristly cones.

SEASON OF INTEREST: Mid- to late-summer bloom; the dried seed heads are attractive through winter.

HEIGHT AND SPREAD: Height 2–4 feet (60–120 cm); width 1–2 feet (30–60 cm).

BEST SITE AND CLIMATE: Plant in average to rich, moist but well-drained soil in full sun. Zones 3–8.

GROWING GUIDELINES: Purple coneflowers increase from basal buds to form broad, long-lived clumps. Division is seldom necessary and is not recommended. Self-sown seedlings may appear. For propagation, sow seed outdoors in fall.

LANDSCAPE USES: Plant in formal perennial gardens or meadow and prairie gardens.

COMPATIBLE COMPANIONS: Combine the bold heads of purple coneflower with fine-textured flowers such as yarrows, baby's-breath (*Gypsophila paniculata*), and Russian sage (*Perovskia atriplicifolia*) as well as border phlox (*Phlox paniculata*) and coreopsis. In meadows and prairies, plant them with goldenrods (*Solidago* spp.), asters, sunflowers, blazing stars (*Liatris* spp.), and a generous supply of ornamental grasses.

GLOBE THISTLE

Globe thistles are tough, long-lived perennials. They are drought-tolerant once established and thrive for many years without staking or division.

DESCRIPTION: Globe thistles are stout, coarse perennials with erect stems clothed in spiny, lobed leaves. They grow from thick, deep-branched taproots. Small, five-petaled, steel-blue flowers are packed into 1–2-inch (2.5–5 cm) spherical heads.

SEASON OF INTEREST: Midsummer bloom. The spiny, lobed foliage is attractive all summer.

HEIGHT AND SPREAD: Height 2–4 feet (60–120 cm); width 2–3 feet (60–90 cm).

BEST SITE AND CLIMATE: Plant in average to rich, well-drained soil in full sun. Good drainage is essential, especially in winter; soggy soil is sure death. Heat-tolerant. Zones 3–8.

GROWING GUIDELINES: For propagation, remove sideshoots from the main clump without disturbing the crown or take root cuttings in spring or fall. No serious pests or diseases.

LANDSCAPE USES: Position near the middle or rear of the border, or use in cottage gardens or meadows. Butterflies and bees relish the flowers. The round heads are perfect for cutting fresh or for drying.

COMPATIBLE COMPANIONS: Combine showy globe thistles with other drought-tolerant perennials such as sedums, Russian sage (*Perovskia atriplicifolia*), catmints (*Nepeta* spp.), and oriental poppy (*Papaver orientale*). Surround them with fine-textured ornamental grasses, baby's-breath (*Gypsophila paniculata*), and asters.

Epimedium x *rubrum*   Berberidaceae

RED EPIMEDIUM

Epimediums are great woodland groundcovers that will grow happily for years with little attention. They perform well under adverse conditions, even in dry shade under trees.

DESCRIPTION: The leaves are divided into glossy, heart-shaped leaflets. The wiry, trailing stems have matted, fibrous roots. The unusual flowers have four red, petal-like sepals and four spurred, ivory petals. They are held in clusters above the emerging new leaves.

SEASON OF INTEREST: Early- to mid-spring flowers. The foliage emerges tinged with red and darkens to a deep green that is attractive all season.

HEIGHT AND SPREAD: Height 10–12 inches (25–30 cm); width 12 inches (30 cm).

BEST SITE AND CLIMATE: Plant in moist, humus-rich soil in partial to full shade. Avoid waterlogged soil, especially during the winter. Zones 4–8.

GROWING GUIDELINES: Mulch plants in winter to protect the crowns when growing them at the edge of their range. Cut foliage to the ground in early spring to allow the flowers to emerge unobscured. Divide overgrown clumps in late summer.

LANDSCAPE USES: Plant in drifts in woodland gardens, along paths, or under shrubs and trees.

COMPATIBLE COMPANIONS: Combine with spring bulbs, Lenten roses (*Helleborus* spp.), primroses, hostas, wildflowers, and ferns. Plant them under spring-flowering shrubs such as fothergillas (*Fothergilla gardenii*), winterhazels (*Corylopsis* spp.), daphnes (*Daphne* spp.), and rhododendrons.

Erigeron speciosus   Compositae

DAISY FLEABANE

Daisy fleabane is lovely with low grasses in dry meadows and prairie gardens. The blooms make long-lasting cut flowers for indoor arrangements.

DESCRIPTION: The floriferous fleabanes form leafy clumps of hairy, 6-inch (15 cm), lance-shaped leaves that spring from fibrous-rooted crowns. The $1^1/_2$-inch (3.5 cm) aster-like flowers of daisy fleabane have white, pink, rose, or purple rays surrounding bright yellow centers.

SEASON OF INTEREST: Early- to mid-summer flowers, with occasional rebloom.

HEIGHT AND SPREAD: Height $1^1/_2$–$2^1/_2$ feet (45–75 cm); width 1–2 feet (30–60 cm).

BEST SITE AND CLIMATE: Plant in moist but well-drained, average to rich soil in full sun or light shade. Tolerant of heat and cold. Zones 2–9.

GROWING GUIDELINES: Fleabanes are long-lived perennials that benefit from fall division every 2–3 years. If division isn't enough to increase your stock, take tip cuttings in spring before the flower buds form. Another option is to sow seed outdoors in fall or indoors in spring.

LANDSCAPE USES: Plant daisy fleabanes at the front of beds and borders or in rock gardens.

COMPATIBLE COMPANIONS: Combine with summer-blooming perennials such as pinks (*Dianthus* spp.), cranesbills (*Geranium* spp.), cinquefoils (*Potentilla* spp.), sundrops (*Oenothera* spp.), and phlox. Plant them in informal settings with yarrows, butterfly weed (*Asclepias tuberosa*), ornamental onions (*Allium* spp.), and ornamental grasses.

| *Eryngium amethystinum* | Umbelliferae | *Eupatorium maculatum* | Compositae |

AMETHYST SEA HOLLY

SPOTTED JOE-PYE WEED

The rounded flower clusters and spiny bracts of amethyst sea holly add excitement to any perennial planting. These trouble-free plants tolerate heat, cold, and drought.

Spotted Joe-Pye weed is a tall, stately perennial that's perfect for moist borders and meadow plantings. The flowers will attract bees and butterflies to your garden.

DESCRIPTION: Amethyst sea holly is an architectural plant with stiff, flowering stems and mostly basal, pinnately divided leaves. Plants grow from thick taproots. The small, steel-blue, globose flower heads are surrounded by thin, spiny bracts. The flowering stems are also blue.

SEASON OF INTEREST: Summer bloom. The glossy foliage is attractive all season.

HEIGHT AND SPREAD: Height 1–1¹/₂ feet (30–45 cm); width 1–2 feet (30–60 cm).

BEST SITE AND CLIMATE: Plant in average, well-drained soil in full sun. Sea holly is extremely drought-tolerant once established. Zones 2–8.

GROWING GUIDELINES: Set plants out in their permanent location while they are young; older plants resent disturbance. Division is seldom necessary. For propagation, sow fresh seed outdoors in fall. Self-sown seedlings may be plentiful.

LANDSCAPE USES: Plant amethyst sea holly in the middle of the border as an accent, or use it as a mass planting against a hedge or wall. The showy blue bracts combine well with yellow-leaved shrubs.

COMPATIBLE COMPANIONS: Combine with goldenrods (*Solidago* spp.), asters, phlox, and ornamental grasses. Surround the colorful heads with fine-textured plants such as sea lavenders (*Limonium* spp.), baby's-breath (*Gypsophila paniculata*), and coral bells (*Heuchera* spp.).

DESCRIPTION: Spotted Joe-Pye weed produces whorled tiers of broad lance-shaped leaves on stout stems spotted with purple. The showy terminal flower clusters are domed to rounded and consist of hundreds of small, fuzzy, mauve flowers. Plants grow from thick, fibrous roots.

SEASON OF INTEREST: Mid- to late-summer bloom. The dark green foliage is attractive all season, and the dried seed heads are a valuable addition to the winter landscape.

HEIGHT AND SPREAD: Height 4–6 feet (1.2–1.8 m); width 3–4 feet (90–120 cm).

BEST SITE AND CLIMATE: Plant in moist, humus-rich soil in full sun or light shade. Zones 2–8.

GROWING GUIDELINES: Plants take 2–3 years to mature, so leave ample room when planting small transplants. For propagation, divide plants in early spring or in fall, or take stem cuttings in early summer. Leafminers may cause large pale patches on the leaves; remove and destroy the affected foliage.

LANDSCAPE USES: Choose Joe-Pye weeds for the middle or back of the border for a bold accent. Plant them as a screen with ornamental grasses.

COMPATIBLE COMPANIONS: Combine spotted Joe-Pye weed with tall perennials such as culver's root (*Veronicastrum virginicum*), rose mallow (*Hibiscus* spp.), ironweed (*Vernonia* spp.), goldenrods (*Solidago* spp.), asters, and grasses.

| *Eupatorium rugosum* | Compositae | *Euphorbia epithymoides* | Euphorbiaceae |

WHITE SNAKEROOT

CUSHION SPURGE

Brighten up late-season shade gardens with the fall flowers of white snakeroot. These easy-care perennials grow quickly to form multistemmed clumps.

Cushion spurge blooms at the same time as tulips, so you can create many striking color combinations. The plants are long-lived garden residents that need little care.

DESCRIPTION: White snakeroot is a late-blooming perennial with foamy terminal clusters of white flowers. The thin stems are clothed in paired, oval leaves. Plants grow from fibrous-rooted crowns.

SEASON OF INTEREST: Early fall bloom. The silvery seed heads are showy into winter.

HEIGHT AND SPREAD: Height 3–4 feet (90–120 cm); width 1–2 feet (30–60 cm).

BEST SITE AND CLIMATE: Plant white snakeroot in average to rich, moist soil in partial sun or shade. Zones 3–7.

GROWING GUIDELINES: To propagate, divide in early spring or after flowering. Self-sown seedlings may be numerous. No serious pests or diseases.

LANDSCAPE USES: Plant white snakeroot in informal situations, such as along woodland paths or in meadow gardens. Grow them in groups in shaded recesses where few other plants will grow.

COMPATIBLE COMPANIONS: Combine white snakeroot with other late-season plants such as asters, grasses, and goldenrods (*Solidago* spp.). In shaded areas, plant them with Solomon's seals (*Polygonatum* spp.), astilbes, and ferns.

OTHER SPECIES:

E. perfoliatum, boneset, is well suited for wet-soil sites. It offers hairy, lance-shaped leaves and flat clusters of white flowers in summer. Zones 3–8.

DESCRIPTION: Cushion spurge is a creeping plant with thick stems clothed in succulent, blue-gray, wedge-shaped leaves. The stems grow from fleshy, fibrous roots. The unusual flower heads consist of tiny yellow flowers surrounded by showy, funnel-shaped, yellow bracts (modified leaves).

SEASON OF INTEREST: Spring bloom. The lush foliage is handsome all summer and turns apricot and orange in the fall.

HEIGHT AND SPREAD: Height 6–10 inches (15–25 cm); width 12–24 inches (15–30 cm).

BEST SITE AND CLIMATE: Plant in average to rich, well-drained soil in full sun or light shade. Plants will grow in poor, gravelly soil. Zones 3–8.

GROWING GUIDELINES: Divide the congested clumps if they overgrow their position. Propagate by taking stem cuttings in summer; place them in a well-drained medium before the cut end dries out. No serious pests or diseases.

LANDSCAPE USES: Plant at the front of the border, in a sunny rock garden, or in a rock wall.

COMPATIBLE COMPANIONS: Combine with early-blooming perennials such as columbines (*Aquilegia* spp.), rock cress (*Arabis* and *Aubrieta* spp.), creeping phlox (*Phlox stolonifera*), and daisy fleabane (*Erigeron speciosus*). Use them with bulbs such as ornamental onions (*Allium* spp.), fritillaries (*Fritillaria* spp.), and daffodils.

| *Filipendula rubra* | Rosaceae | *Fritillaria imperialis* | Liliaceae |

QUEEN-OF-THE-PRAIRIE

CROWN IMPERIAL

Mature clumps of queen-of-the-prairie make an arresting display in bloom. If the leaves look tattered after flowering, cut plants to the ground; new leaves will emerge.

The leafy stalks of crown imperials tower over lower spring perennials. Grow them with ferns and bushy perennials to fill the gaps left as they go dormant in summer.

DESCRIPTION: Queen-of-the-prairie is a towering perennial with huge flower heads on stout, leafy stalks. The showy, 1-foot (30 cm) leaves are deeply lobed and starry. Plants grow from stout creeping stems. The small, five-petaled, pink flowers are crowded into large heads that resemble cotton candy.

SEASON OF INTEREST: Late spring and early summer bloom. The foliage remains attractive with sufficient watering, and the seed heads are decorative.

HEIGHT AND SPREAD: Height 4–6 feet (1.2–1.8 m); width 2–4 feet (60–120 cm).

BEST SITE AND CLIMATE: Plant in evenly moist, humus-rich soil in full sun to light shade. Plants will not tolerate prolonged dryness. Zones 3–9.

GROWING GUIDELINES: Plants spread quickly and will need division every 3–4 years to keep them from overtaking their neighbors. Plants spread more slowly in drier soil. For propagation, divide clumps in spring or fall, or remove crowns from the edge of the clump. No serious pests or diseases.

LANDSCAPE USES: Plant at the rear of the border, along streams, beside ponds, and in moist meadow and prairie gardens.

COMPATIBLE COMPANIONS: Combine with shrub roses, irises, daylilies, and phlox. Use them beside ponds with ferns, ornamental grasses, and bold foliage plants such as hostas and rodgersias.

DESCRIPTION: Crown imperial is a stout perennial with thick stems crowded with thin, lance-shaped leaves. The terminal flower cluster boasts nodding waxy bells with a tufted crown resembling a pineapple top. Plants grow from a large, fleshy bulb.

SEASON OF INTEREST: Spring bloom.

HEIGHT AND SPREAD: Height $2^1/_2$–3 feet (75–90 cm); width 1 foot (30 cm).

BEST SITE AND CLIMATE: Plant crown imperials 6–8 inches (15–20 cm) deep in the fall. They need humus-rich, moist but well drained soil in full sun or light shade. Zones 5–8.

GROWING GUIDELINES: Crown imperial is often short-lived under most garden conditions. Some gardeners treat them as annuals and replant them each year. In the right spot, however, crown imperials can return to grace your spring garden for many years. No serious pests.

LANDSCAPE USES: Plant in beds and borders, in cottage gardens, and along open woodland walks.

COMPATIBLE COMPANIONS: Combine crown imperials with tulips, bleeding hearts (*Dicentra* spp.), columbines (*Aquilegia* spp.), and other spring flowers. Grow them with foliage plants such as ferns to fill the gaps left as they go dormant.

CULTIVARS: 'Aurora' has orange-red flowers. 'Lutea Maxima' has large yellow flowers. 'Rubra Maxima' is similar with fiery orange flowers.

| *Gaillardia* x *grandiflora* | Compositae | *Galium odoratum* | Rubiaceaé |

BLANKET FLOWER

SWEET WOODRUFF

Give blanket flowers a sunny, well-drained spot, and they'll bear dazzling orange-and-yellow blooms all summer. They make super companions for ornamental grasses.

DESCRIPTION: Showy hybrid blanket flower blooms on loose stems with hairy, lobed leaves. The larger basal leaves are 8–10 inches (20–25 cm) long. Plants grow from fibrous-rooted crowns. The ragged yellow and orange daisy-like flowers have single or double rows of toothed, petal-like rays surrounding a raised center.

SEASON OF INTEREST: Blooms throughout summer.

HEIGHT AND SPREAD: Height 2–3 feet (60–90 cm); width 2 feet (60 cm).

BEST SITE AND CLIMATE: Plant in average to poor, well-drained soil in full sun. Rich, moist soil causes plants to overgrow and flop. Zones 4–9

GROWING GUIDELINES: Blanket flowers are drought-tolerant and thrive under seaside conditions. They may be short-lived and should be divided every 2–3 years to keep them vigorous. Divide for propagation, or sow seed outdoors in fall.

LANDSCAPE USES: Choose blanket flowers for rock gardens, borders, or seaside gardens. They are beautiful in drifts in meadows and prairies.

COMPATIBLE COMPANIONS: Combine with other drought-tolerant perennials such as coreopsis (*Coreopsis* spp.), butterfly weed (*Asclepias tuberosa*), yarrows, and yuccas (*Yucca* spp.). Plant them with ornamental grasses such as blue oat grass (*Helictotrichon sempervirens*) and variegated purple moor grass (*Molinia caerulea* 'Variegata').

Sweet woodruff produces whorls of light to dark green leaves that form an enchanting groundcover in shady gardens. The dainty white spring flowers are a bonus.

DESCRIPTION: Sweet woodruff is a showy groundcover with whorls of glossy, dark green leaves that emerge bright green in early spring. The small white flowers are carried at the tip of each stem in spring. Plants grow from fibrous roots.

SEASON OF INTEREST: Spring bloom; plants form an attractive groundcover throughout the growing season.

HEIGHT AND SPREAD: Height 4–10 inches (10–25 cm); width 1–2 feet (30–60 cm).

BEST SITE AND CLIMATE: Plant sweet woodruff in average to rich, moist soil in partial sun to shade. Zones 3–9.

GROWING GUIDELINES: Plants spread by creeping stems to form broad clumps. Propagate by dividing overgrown plants in early spring or after flowering, or take stem cuttings in early summer. No serious pests.

LANDSCAPE USES: Plant sweet woodruff in shade and woodland gardens, as an edging for paths, or as a groundcover under trees and shrubs.

COMPATIBLE COMPANIONS: Combine sweet woodruff with large-leaved plants such as hostas, wild gingers (*Asarum* spp.), lungworts (*Pulmonaria* spp.), and bergenia. Plant them with spring bulbs, primroses, bleeding hearts (*Dicentra* spp.), and ferns.

BLOOD-RED CRANESBILL

Even when blood-red cranesbills aren't in flower, you can still enjoy the finely cut foliage all season. The leaves even turn a burgundy-red color in fall.

DESCRIPTION: Cranesbills of the genus *Geranium* are hardy, long-lived perennials often confused with annual bedding geraniums of the genus *Pelargonium*. Blood-red cranesbill is a spreading to low-mounding plant with deeply cut, five-lobed leaves arising from a slow-creeping, fibrous-rooted crown. The bright magenta, saucer-shaped, five-petaled flowers are carried singly above the foliage.

SEASON OF INTEREST: Early- to mid-summer bloom, with some flowers thereafter. The foliage is attractive all season.

HEIGHT AND SPREAD: Height 9–12 inches (22.5–30 cm); width 12–18 inches (30–45 cm).

BEST SITE AND CLIMATE: Plant in evenly moist, well-drained, humus-rich soil in full sun or partial shade. Zones 3–8.

GROWING GUIDELINES: Divide plants when they overgrow their position; lift clumps in spring or fall, tease the stems apart, and replant into amended soil. Only the species comes true from seed; sow seed outdoors in fall or indoors in early spring on a warm 70°F (21°C) seedbed. Propagate cultivars by division or stem cuttings in summer. No serious pests or diseases.

LANDSCAPE USES: Place cranesbills at the front of the border to tie plantings together, or use them as an edging along walks.

COMPATIBLE COMPANIONS: Combine with sundrops

The hybrid cranesbill 'Johnson's Blue' is popular for its neat foliage and lovely flowers. Like many other cranesbills, it is excellent at the front of a border.

(*Oenothera* spp.), catmints (*Nepeta* spp.), bellflowers (*Campanula* spp.), phlox, and irises.

CULTIVARS: 'Album' is an excellent cultivar with clear, white, cup-shaped flowers. *G. sanguineum* var. *striatum* (also listed as 'Lancastriense') is a prostrate cultivar with light pink flowers lined with rose.

OTHER SPECIES: The genus *Geranium* includes many garden-worthy species. A few of the best ones are listed here.

G. dalmaticum, Dalmatian cranesbill, is a low, rounded plant with small, curly, lobed leaves and 1-inch (2.5 cm) mauve flowers. Plants spread rapidly by creeping stems. *G. dalmaticum* var. *album* has white flowers. 'Biokovo' is a hybrid with pale pink flowers. Zones 4–8.

G. macrorrhizum, bigroot cranesbill, is a fast-spreading plant with fragrant, seven-lobed leaves and bright pink flowers. 'Album' has white flowers with pink sepals. 'Ingwersen's Variety' has light pink flowers and glossy leaves. 'Spessart' has white flowers with pale pink sepals. Zones 3–8.

G. maculatum, wild cranesbill, is a woodland plant with five-lobed leaves and tall, sparsely flowered stalks of clear pink or white flowers. Zones 4–8.

G. pratense, meadow cranesbill, has deeply incised leaves and 1¹⁄₂-inch (3.5 cm) purple flowers with red veins. 'Mrs. Kendall Clarke' has lilac-blue flowers. Zones 3–8.

| *Gillenia trifoliata* | Rosaceae | *Gypsophila paniculata* | Caryophyllaceae |

BOWMAN'S-ROOT

BABY'S-BREATH

Grow bowman's root in borders and meadows, along driveways and roadsides, and at the edges of woodlands. Be patient: It will take several years to form large clumps.

*Clouds of baby's-breath look great in combination with perennials that have spiky leaves or flowers, such as foxgloves (*Digitalis *spp.) or yuccas (*Yucca *spp.).*

DESCRIPTION: Bowman's-root is a shrubby perennial with wiry stems clothed in alternate, compound leaves. Each leaf has three lance-shaped, toothed leaflets. The white flowers have five slender, twisted petals and are carried in loose terminal clusters. Plants grow from deep, thickened roots. Also known as *Porteranthus trifoliatus.*

SEASON OF INTEREST: Late spring and early summer bloom. The foliage and shrubby habit make the plant a season-long asset.

HEIGHT AND SPREAD: Height 2–4 feet (60–120 cm); width 2–3 feet (60–90 cm).

BEST SITE AND CLIMATE: Plant bowman's-root in average to rich, moist soil in full sun or partial shade. Plants tolerate sandy, dry soils. Zones 4–8.

GROWING GUIDELINES: Set out young transplants, as mature plants resent disturbance. Clumps seldom need division. Propagate by taking stem cuttings in spring or by sowing seed when it ripens.

LANDSCAPE USES: Choose bowman's-root for an airy accent in beds and borders. Use it as a "weaver" in cottage gardens to link bolder flowers such as delphiniums and poppies.

COMPATIBLE COMPANIONS: Combine bowman's-root with coarser-textured plants such as peonies, yarrow, and sedums. Use the airy sprays to fill the voids left by summer-dormant plants such as oriental poppies (*Papaver orientale*).

DESCRIPTION: Baby's-breath is an old-fashioned perennial with airy flower clusters and sparse, smooth, blue-green foliage. The stems and basal leaves grow from a thick, deep taproot. The small, single or double, white flowers are carried in large, domed clusters.

SEASON OF INTEREST: Summer bloom.

HEIGHT AND SPREAD: Height 3–4 feet (90–120 cm); width 2–3 feet (60–90 cm).

BEST SITE AND CLIMATE: Plant in near-neutral to alkaline, moist, humus-rich soil in full sun or light shade. Tolerates heat and cold. Zones 3–9.

GROWING GUIDELINES: Set plants out in spring and do not disturb the crowns once plants are established. Good drainage is essential for longevity. Tall cultivars may need staking. Take stem cuttings in summer and place them in a high humidity environment. Sow seed outdoors in spring or fall. No serious pests or diseases.

LANDSCAPE USES: Baby's-breath is an excellent "filler" plant in the perennial garden. Use the airy sprays to hide the yellowing foliage of bulbs and past-bloom perennials.

COMPATIBLE COMPANIONS: For a dramatic effect, combine baby's-breath with spiky perennials such as gayfeathers (*Liatris* spp.). It also combines well with plants that go dormant in summer, such as tulips and oriental poppy (*Papaver orientale*).

Helenium autumnale   Compositae

COMMON SNEEZEWEED

Sneezeweeds prefer cool temperatures and tend to "stretch" in warm weather; either stake them or pinch the stem tips in early summer to promote compact growth.

DESCRIPTION: Common sneezeweed is a late-season perennial with tall, leafy stems that spring from a fibrous-rooted crown. The hairy, lance-shaped leaves have a few large teeth along the margins. The 2-inch (5 cm), yellow, daisy-like flowers have broad, petal-like rays and spherical centers.

SEASON OF INTEREST: Late summer and fall bloom. Some cultivars bloom in midsummer and again in fall if cut back.

HEIGHT AND SPREAD: Height 3–5 feet (90–150 cm); width 2–3 feet (60–90 cm).

BEST SITE AND CLIMATE: Plant in evenly moist, humus-rich soil in full sun or light shade. Tolerates wet soil. Zones 3–8.

GROWING GUIDELINES: Cut plants back by half after flowering to promote a second bloom. Divide the clumps every 3–4 years to keep them vigorous. For propagation, take stem cuttings in early summer, or sow seed of the species outdoors in fall. Propagate cultivars by division or cuttings only. No serious pests or diseases.

LANDSCAPE USES: Plant them with other late-summer perennials at the middle or rear of the border or in mass plantings in meadows and prairie gardens.

COMPATIBLE COMPANIONS: Combine with asters, goldenrods (*Solidago* spp.), boltonias, garden phlox (*Phlox paniculata*), and ornamental grasses.

Helianthus x *multiflorus*   Compositae

PERENNIAL SUNFLOWER

Sunflowers are easy to grow but need room to spread. Their cheerful flowers add bold splashes of color to the summer border, meadow, or cutting garden.

DESCRIPTION: The showy summer blooms of perennial sunflowers have stout stems clothed in wide, 8-inch (20 cm), wedge-shaped leaves. The 5-inch (12.5 cm), daisy-like flowers have bright yellow rays and yellow centers. Plants grow from stout, fibrous-rooted crowns.

SEASON OF INTEREST: Mid- to late-summer bloom. Bold spring and summer foliage. Drooping fall seed heads are attractive to birds.

HEIGHT AND SPREAD: Height 4–5 feet (1.2–1.5 m); width 2–3 feet (60–90 cm).

BEST SITE AND CLIMATE: Plant in moist, average to rich soil in full sun. Plants will tolerate wet soil. Zones 4–8.

GROWING GUIDELINES: Divide in fall every 3–4 years. The stems are usually self-supporting, except when plants are grown in partial shade. Take stem cuttings in early summer or sow seed outdoors in fall. No serious pests or diseases.

LANDSCAPE USES: Plant them at the middle or rear of beds and borders, in meadows and prairies, and in the cutting garden.

COMPATIBLE COMPANIONS: Combine with garden phlox (*Phlox paniculata*), asters, goldenrods (*Solidago* spp.), sedums, and ornamental grasses. Plant them in masses in front of evergreens and in mixed plantings of shrubby conifers and grasses.

Helleborus orientalis	Ranunculaceae

LENTEN ROSE

Lenten roses may take 2 or 3 years to get established; after that, they'll bloom dependably every spring. Try them as a groundcover under shrubs and flowering trees.

DESCRIPTION: Lenten roses are classic winter or early-spring perennials with deeply lobed, leathery leaves growing from a stout crown with fleshy roots. The reddish purple, pink, or white flowers have five petal-like sepals surrounded by green leafy bracts. The flowers fade to soft pink with age.

SEASON OF INTEREST: Flowering time varies from early winter through spring. The evergreen foliage is attractive year-round.

HEIGHT AND SPREAD: Height 1–1^1/$_2$ feet (30–45 cm); width 1–2 feet (30–60 cm).

BEST SITE AND CLIMATE: Plant in evenly moist, humus-rich soil in light to partial shade. Established plants tolerate dry soil and deep shade. Zones 4–8.

GROWING GUIDELINES: In spring, remove any damaged leaves. Divide only if needed for propagation. Lift clumps after flowering in spring and separate the crowns. Replant the divisions immediately. Plant fresh seed outdoors in late summer. Self-sown seedlings usually appear.

LANDSCAPE USES: Plant Lenten roses in shade gardens, along woodland walks, and in spring borders.

COMPATIBLE COMPANIONS: Combine Lenten roses with early-spring bulbs, wildflowers, lungworts (*Pulmonaria* spp.), and ferns. Plant them with the colored stems of shrubby dogwoods (such as *Cornus sericea*) for a lovely late-winter display.

Hemerocallis hybrids	Liliaceae

DAYLILIES

Each daylily flower lasts only one day, but a profusion of new buds topping multiple bloom stalks keeps the plants in bloom for a month or more.

DESCRIPTION: Daylilies are one of the most popular summer perennials. Their colorful flowers consist of three petals and three narrower, petal-like sepals. The strap-like leaves have a central vein that forms a keel when viewed in cross section. The crowns increase from short sideshoots. Daylily flowers vary in color and form. The majority of the wild species are orange or yellow with wide petals and narrow, petal-like sepals. Modern hybrids come in a rainbow of colors with the exceptions of blues and true white. Many have blazes, eyes, and blotches on the petals. Flower shape varies from traditional form to narrow-petaled, spider-like forms and fat, tubular or saucer-shaped flowers.

SEASON OF INTEREST: Late spring through summer bloom.

HEIGHT AND SPREAD: Height varies from 1–5 feet (30–150 cm). The common height range for most hybrids is 2–4 feet (60–120 cm); width 2–3 feet (60–90 cm).

BEST SITE AND CLIMATE: Plant in evenly moist, average to rich soil in full sun or light shade. Most modern hybrids need at least 8 hours of direct sun in order to flower well. Some of the older selections and the species will bloom in partial shade. Usually Zones 3–9.

GROWING GUIDELINES: Plant container-grown or bareroot plants in spring or fall, placing the crowns

DAYLILIES—CONTINUED

CORAL BELLS

Thousands of daylily cultivars are available in a dizzying range of colors. It's best to buy plants after you see them to make sure they are the color you want.

The airy blooms of coral bells dance in the wind over rounded, evergreen leaves. The flower colors range from white through shades of pink and red.

just below the soil surface. Plants take a year to become established, then spread quickly to form dense clumps. Remove spent flowers regularly to keep plants looking their best. If leaves yellow, grasp them firmly and give them a quick tug to remove them from the base. Lift overcrowded, sparse-flowering clumps and pull or cut the tangled crowns apart. Division is also the way to propagate named cultivars. Although daylilies are usually pest-free, aphids and thrips may attack the foliage and flower buds. Wash off aphids with a stream of water or spray them with insecticidal soap. Thrips make small white lines in the foliage and may deform flower buds if damage is severe. Spray with insecticidal soap or a botanical insecticide such as pyrethrin.

LANDSCAPE USES: Daylilies are perfect for mass plantings. Use them in beds and borders, in meadow plantings, and at the edge of a woodland with shrubs and trees.

COMPATIBLE COMPANIONS: Combine daylilies with summer-blooming perennials and ornamental grasses. Use them with fine-textured flowers such as coral bells (*Heuchera* spp.), baby's-breath (*Gypsophila paniculata*), and yarrows. Plant them with generous quantities of garden phlox (*Phlox paniculata*), cranesbills (*Geranium* spp.), and daisies (*Chrysanthemum* spp).

DESCRIPTION: The leaves may be deep green, gray-green, or mottled with silver. Plants grow from woody, fibrous-rooted crowns. The small, fringed flowers are carried in slender, branching clusters.

SEASON OF INTEREST: Late spring through summer bloom. The foliage is attractive all season.

HEIGHT AND SPREAD: Height 1–2½ feet (30–75 cm); width 1–2 feet (30–60 cm).

BEST SITE AND CLIMATE: Plant in moist but well-drained, humus-rich soil in full sun or partial shade. In warmer zones, provide shade from hot afternoon sun. Zones 3–8.

GROWING GUIDELINES: Remove old flower stalks to promote reblooming. As plants grow, they rise above the soil on woody crowns. Lift plants every 3–4 years and replant the crowns in amended soil. Do not crowd the plants by packing in too many in a small space; crowded plants lose vigor and bloom less. Hybrids do not come true from seed; divide plants instead in spring or early fall.

LANDSCAPE USES: Plant coral bells at the front of the border, as an edging for beds, along walkways, or in a lightly shaded rock garden. They respond well to container culture.

COMPATIBLE COMPANIONS: Combine with cranesbills (*Geranium* spp.), catmints (*Nepeta* spp.), ornamental onions (*Allium* spp.), sundrops (*Oenothera* spp.), and columbines (*Aquilegia* spp.).

HOSTAS

Hostas are indispensable foliage plants for shaded gardens. Hundreds of cultivars are available; many, such as 'Gold Standard', have striking leaf colors.

Plant a variety of hostas in borders or as groundcovers. They make excellent companions for spring bulbs, since their leaves fill the space left when bulbs go dormant.

DESCRIPTION: The thick, pleated or puckered leaves vary in size from 1 inch (2.5 cm) to 3 feet (90 cm) or more. Leaf color varies from deep green to chartreuse, yellow-gold, and many shades of blue. Both yellow and white variegations are common. Lavender, purple, or white flowers are carried in slender spikes. Individual flowers have three petals and three petal-like sepals. Plants grow from stout crowns with thick, fleshy roots.

SEASON OF INTEREST: Summer or fall bloom. The foliage is decorative all season, and many selections develop nice golden fall color.

HEIGHT AND SPREAD: Varies widely. Height 6 inches (15 cm) to 3 feet (90 cm) or more in leaf or flower; width from 6 inches (15 cm) to 5 feet (1.5 m).

BEST SITE AND CLIMATE: Plant hostas in evenly moist, humus-rich soil in light to full shade. They are tough and versatile plants, adaptable to both dry and wet soil. Filtered sun encourages the best leaf color in the gold- and blue-leaved forms. All hostas need protection from hot afternoon sun, especially in warm zones; variegated and yellow-leaved cultivars are particularly susceptible to burning. Generally Zones 3–8; some selections may be hardy to Zone 2.

GROWING GUIDELINES: Hostas take several years to reach their mature form and size, especially the large-leaved selections. Be sure to allow ample room when planting to accommodate their ultimate size. New shoots are slow to emerge in spring, so take care not to damage them during spring cleanup. Plant small bulbs such as squills (*Scilla* spp.) around the clumps to mark their location.

Slugs are the bane of hosta fanciers. Set shallow pans of beer in the garden to drown the pests. Slugs may gather under cabbage leaves, fruit rinds, or boards set on the soil; pick up the trap and remove any slugs daily. Cutworms may also attack the foliage, leaving long lacerations; spray with *Bacillus thuringiensis* (BT) according to label directions.

LANDSCAPE USES: Hostas are versatile plants with many uses in the garden. Use the smaller types to edge beds or cover the ground under shrubs and trees. Choose the giants for creating drama in a mixed planting or alone as an accent.

COMPATIBLE COMPANIONS: Combine hostas with wildflowers, ferns, and shade perennials. Contrast the bold, horizontal foliage with the spiky form of Siberian iris (*Iris sibirica*) and daylilies (*Hemerocallis* spp.). Plant bulbs such as giant onion (*Allium giganteum*) among the clumps to add interest as the hosta leaves are emerging. Underplant the large-leaved types with groundcovers such as wild gingers (*Asarum* spp.) and creeping phlox (*Phlox stolonifera*).

Hyacinthoides hispanicus   Liliaceae

SPANISH BLUEBELLS

Spanish bluebells spread quickly to form broad, free-flowering clumps. Use them in mixed plantings with other bulbs, such as tulips, daffodils, and anemones.

DESCRIPTION: Spanish bluebells are spring-flowering bulbs with 1–inch (2.5 cm) wide, strap-like foliage. The slender bloom stalks are lined with nodding, blue, white, or pink, bell-shaped flowers. Formerly known as *Scilla campanulata, S. hispanica,* and *Endymion hispanicus.*

SEASON OF INTEREST: Spring bloom; plants die back to the ground (go dormant) after flowering.

HEIGHT AND SPREAD: Height 15–20 inches (37.5–50 cm) in flower, leaves 6–10 inches (15–25 cm) high; clumps 12–18 inches (30–45 cm) wide.

BEST SITE AND CLIMATE: Plant Spanish bluebells in humus-rich, moist soil in full sun or light shade. Once plants are dormant, they tolerate considerable shade and dryness. Zones 3–8.

GROWING GUIDELINES: Set out fresh, plump bulbs in fall. Space them 3–4 inches (7.5–10 cm) apart and plant them 6 inches (15 cm) deep. Lift and divide overgrown clumps as the foliage turns yellow in early- to mid-summer.

LANDSCAPE USES: Use generous plantings of Spanish bluebells in beds and borders, along woodland walks, or as mass plantings under trees and shrubs.

COMPATIBLE COMPANIONS: In woodland gardens, combine Spanish bluebells with wildflowers such as shooting stars (*Dodecatheon* spp.) and foamflower (*Tiarella cordifolia*). In beds and borders, grow them with spring-blooming perennials.

Hyacinthus orientalis   Liliaceae

HYACINTH

Hyacinths are spring bulbs beloved for their showy blooms and heady fragrance. Flowers come in a rainbow of colors, from white and yellow to pink, blue, and purple.

DESCRIPTION: The flower buds emerge with stiff, strap-like leaves. In full bloom, the flower clusters are packed with tubular flowers that have six reflexed, wavy lobes.

SEASON OF INTEREST: Spring bloom; plants die back to the ground after flowering.

HEIGHT AND SPREAD: Height to 18 inches (45 cm) in flower, leaves 6–12 inches (15–30 cm) high; leaves 10–12 inches (25–30 cm) wide.

BEST SITE AND CLIMATE: Plant in humus-rich, moist but well-drained soil in full sun or light shade. Zones 5–8.

GROWING GUIDELINES: Set bulbs 5–6 inches (12.5–15 cm) deep and 8–12 inches (20–30 cm) apart in fall. Hyacinths need annual fertilization with a balanced organic fertilizer to continue producing quality blooms. Bulbs will multiply after the first season and produce clumps with smaller flower clusters than the original bulb. If having uniformly large flowers—or any flowers, in warmer zones—is important to you, consider growing hyacinths as annuals and discarding them after flowering.

LANDSCAPE USES: Plant hyacinths in beds and borders, as mass plantings, or in containers.

COMPATIBLE COMPANIONS: Combine hyacinths with spring perennials such as primroses. Grow them with ferns and other foliage plants to fill the void left when plants go dormant.

HYSSOP

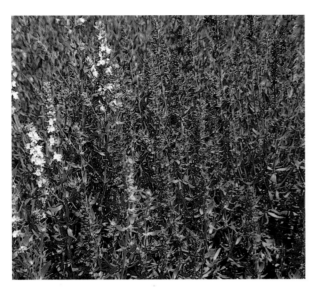

Mature hyssop plants form shrubby clumps that are popular for herb and cottage gardens. The blooms are usually blue, but you may find white- and pink-flowered forms.

DESCRIPTION: Hyssop is an aromatic herb with upright, branched, square stems clothed in opposite, narrow leaves. The terminal flower clusters mingle with the leaves toward the top of the stem. The tubular, two-lobed blue flowers are carried in tight whorls. Plants grow from shallow, fibrous-rooted, creeping rhizomes.

SEASON OF INTEREST: Hyssop blooms throughout the summer. The plants are attractive all season.

HEIGHT AND SPREAD: Height 2–3 feet (60–90 cm); width 1–2 feet (30–60 cm) or wider with time.

BEST SITE AND CLIMATE: Plant hyssop in average to rich, well-drained soil in full sun or light shade. Plants grow well in sandy soils and are somewhat drought-tolerant. Zones 3–9.

GROWING GUIDELINES: Cut stems back by half after flowering to encourage repeat bloom. Propagate by stem cuttings in spring or summer, divide plants in early spring or fall, or sow seed indoors or outside in spring. No serious pests or diseases.

LANDSCAPE USES: Plant hyssop in formal and informal beds and borders, cottage gardens, and seaside areas. For indoor use, cut the stems just before the flowers open. Hang bunches upside down to dry.

COMPATIBLE COMPANIONS: Combine hyssop with yarrows, balloon flower (*Platycodon grandiflorus*), lamb's-ears (*Stachys byzantina*), sages (*Salvia* spp.), and ornamental onions (*Allium* spp.).

CANDYTUFT

Give candytuft well-drained soil, and it will reward you with mounds of white flowers in early spring. The shrubby clumps of evergreen leaves are attractive all year.

DESCRIPTION: Candytuft is a free-flowering, semi-woody subshrub with persistent stems tightly clothed in 1$\frac{1}{2}$-inch (37 mm), narrow, deep-green leaves. The tight, rounded bloom clusters consist of many $\frac{1}{4}$-inch (6 mm), four-petaled flowers. Plants grow from fibrous-rooted crowns.

SEASON OF INTEREST: Early spring bloom.

HEIGHT AND SPREAD: Height 6–12 inches (15–30 cm); width 12–24 inches (30–60 cm).

BEST SITE AND CLIMATE: Plant candytuft in average to rich, well-drained soil in full sun or light shade. Waterlogged soil is sure death to these plants. Zones 3 (with winter protection)–9.

GROWING GUIDELINES: Space plants 1–1$\frac{1}{2}$ feet (30–45 cm) apart in informal plantings or 6 inches (15 cm) apart if edging a bed. Shear plants after flowering to promote compact growth. Mulch plants in winter in Zones 3 and 4 to protect the stems from cold damage. For propagation, take tip cuttings in early summer. No serious pests or diseases.

LANDSCAPE USES: Use candytuft to edge formal plantings, walks, or walls. Set plants in rock gardens and crevices in unmortared walls.

COMPATIBLE COMPANIONS: Grow candytuft with spring bulbs and early-blooming perennials. Combine it with bleeding hearts (*Dicentra* spp.), basket-of-gold (*Aurinia saxatilis*), rock cresses (*Arabis* and *Aubrieta* spp.), and columbines (*Aquilegia* spp.).

Iris bearded hybrids   Iridaceae

BEARDED IRIS

Bearded irises are old-fashioned, cottage garden favorites. Their exceptionally beautiful flowers range in color from white and yellow to blue, violet, and purple.

DESCRIPTION: Bearded irises produce broad fans of wide, flattened leaves and thick, flowering stems from fat, creeping rhizomes. The unique flowers have three segments, called falls, ringing the outside of each bloom. The falls are usually reflexed downward and bear a fringed "beard." The center of the flower boasts three slender segments called standards.

SEASON OF INTEREST: Late spring and early summer flowers; some cultivars rebloom.

HEIGHT AND SPREAD: Height 1–3 feet (30–90 cm); width 1–2 feet (30–60 cm).

BEST SITE AND CLIMATE: Plant bearded iris in evenly moist, average to humus-rich soil in full sun or partial shade. Zones 3–9;

GROWING GUIDELINES: Set out bareroot irises in late summer or container-grown plants in spring, summer, and fall. Divide every 3–4 years in midsummer to late summer. Replant with the top half of the rhizome above the soil line. Cut the foliage back by half. Remove dead foliage in spring and fall.

LANDSCAPE USES: Plant bearded irises in formal or informal gardens with perennials, ornamental grasses, and shrubs.

COMPATIBLE COMPANIONS: Combine the strap-like foliage and lovely flowers with rounded perennials such as peonies, yarrows, pinks (*Dianthus* spp.), and cranesbills (*Geranium* spp.).

Iris cristata   Iridaceae

DWARF CRESTED IRIS

Dwarf crested irises are delicate woodland wildflowers beloved for their diminutive stature, tidy foliage, and exuberant bloom. They form extensive colonies with time.

DESCRIPTION: The flattened, 2-inch (5 cm) flowers are sky blue with a white-and-yellow blaze. Plants grow from a wiry rhizome that creeps on the surface of the soil.

SEASON OF INTEREST: Early spring bloom. The foliage stays neat if moisture is sufficient.

HEIGHT AND SPREAD: Height of bloom to 4 inches (10 cm); leaves 6–8 inches (15–20 cm) high. Each plant is 3–4 inches (7.5–10 cm) wide; clumps spread indefinitely.

BEST SITE AND CLIMATE: Plant dwarf crested iris in moist, humus-rich soil in partial to full shade. Plants bloom more heavily with some direct sun. Zones 3–9.

GROWING GUIDELINES: Clumps may become so congested that plants bloom less. If this happens, lift plants after blooming and tease the rhizomes apart. Replant into amended soil. Slugs and other foliage feeders may damage the leaves.

LANDSCAPE USES: Plant crested iris in shade gardens, along woodland trails, or in rock gardens. Use them as a mass planting under flowering shrubs or among the roots of mature trees.

COMPATIBLE COMPANIONS: Combine dwarf crested iris with spring-blooming wildflowers such as columbines (*Aquilegia* spp.) and creeping phlox (*Phlox stolonifera*). Plant them with masses of ferns and small variegated hostas.

Iris reticulata Iridaceae	*Iris sibirica* Iridaceae
# RETICULATED IRIS	# SIBERIAN IRIS

Choose reticulated irises for the front of beds and borders to add a touch of color before the riot of the season begins. The bulbs increase slowly to form showy clumps.

DESCRIPTION: Reticulated iris is an elfin spring bulb with thick, grass-like leaves. The blue or purple flowers are like miniature Dutch iris, with upright standards and stiff, rounded falls with spotted yellow-and-white blazes.

SEASON OF INTEREST: Late winter and early spring bloom. Plants die back to the ground (go dormant) after flowering.

HEIGHT AND SPREAD: Height 3–5 inches (7.5–12.5 cm) in bloom; foliage may reach 12 inches (30 cm). Each plant is 2–3 inches (5–7.5 cm) wide.

BEST SITE AND CLIMATE: Plant reticulated iris in average to rich, moist but well-drained soil in full sun to partial shade. Soil can become dry once plants are dormant. Zones 4–8.

GROWING GUIDELINES: Set bulbs 5 inches (12.5 cm) deep and 2–3 inches (5–7.5 cm) apart in fall. Lift and divide bulbs in summer as the foliage turns yellow; replant into amended soil.

LANDSCAPE USES: Plant them along open woodland walks, in rock gardens, or in containers.

COMPATIBLE COMPANIONS: Combine reticulated iris with early bulbs such as crocus and snowdrops (*Galanthus* spp.). They are also beautiful with Lenten roses (*Helleborus orientalis*), primroses, and early wildflowers. Use them in mass plantings with spring-flowering shrubs such as forsythia (*Forsythia* spp.) and winter hazels (*Corylopsis* spp.).

Stately Siberian irises are a traditional favorite for both formal and informal gardens. They also look great along ponds and streams with ferns, hostas, and astilbes.

DESCRIPTION: Siberian irises are popular perennials beloved for their handsome flowers whose beauty is comparable to that of orchids. Siberian irises form tight fans of narrow, sword-like leaves from slow-creeping rhizomes.

SEASON OF INTEREST: Early summer flowers; some cultivars rebloom. The foliage is invaluable in the garden all season.

HEIGHT AND SPREAD: Height 1–3 feet (30–90 cm); width 1–2 feet (30–60 cm).

BEST SITE AND CLIMATE: Plant Siberian iris in evenly moist, humus-rich soil in full sun or partial shade. Plants tolerate considerable soil moisture but will not thrive in waterlogged soil. Zones 3–9.

GROWING GUIDELINES: Plant bareroot irises in fall or container-grown plants in spring, summer, and fall. If bloom begins to wane or plants outgrow their position, divide them in late summer. Divide to propagate named cultivars; sow fresh seed outdoors in fall to increase the species.

LANDSCAPE USES: Plant Siberian irises in formal or informal gardens with perennials, ornamental grasses, and ferns. They are perfect for cottage gardens and waterside plantings.

COMPATIBLE COMPANIONS: Combine the strap-like foliage and lovely flowers of Siberian irises with rounded perennials such as peonies, baptisias (*Baptisia* spp.), and cranesbills (*Geranium* spp.).

Lamium maculatum   Labiatae

SPOTTED LAMIUM

Spotted lamium spreads quickly to form broad, ground-hugging clumps that tolerate dry soil and deep shade. White-flowered and yellow-leaved cultivars are available.

DESCRIPTION: Spotted lamium has opposite, rounded leaves streaked or blotched with silver. Inflated, tubular, two-lipped pink flowers are borne in the axils of the smaller leaves at the top of the stem. Plants grow from fibrous roots; stems root at the nodes (leaf joints) as they lay on the soil.

SEASON OF INTEREST: Spring bloom, with periods of flowering throughout the summer. The foliage is a season-long asset.

HEIGHT AND SPREAD: Height 6–12 inches (15–30 cm); width 1–2 feet (30–60 cm).

BEST SITE AND CLIMATE: Plant spotted lamium in average to rich, well-drained soil in partial to full shade. Zones 3–8.

GROWING GUIDELINES: Set plants out at least 2 feet (60 cm) apart. Shear plants after flowering to promote fresh growth. Divide overgrown plants in early spring or fall. Propagate by division or take stem cuttings in spring or summer. Self-sown seedlings may be abundant.

LANDSCAPE USES: Choose spotted lamium as a bright groundcover along walks, in small tight corners, or under shrubs and trees. Use mass plantings on shaded banks and anywhere you need an attractive, fast-growing groundcover.

COMPATIBLE COMPANIONS: Combine spotted lamium with spring-flowering bulbs, hostas, ferns, and astilbes.

Liatris spicata   Compositae

SPIKE GAYFEATHER

Colorful spike gayfeathers are long-lived perennials that offer lots of flowers for little effort. The clumps increase slowly and seldom need division.

DESCRIPTION: Spike gayfeather is a tall perennial with slender flower spikes and erect stems clothed in narrow, grass-like leaves. Plants grow from a fat corm. The red-violet flowers are carried in small heads that are crowded together into dense spikes. The spikes open from the top down.

SEASON OF INTEREST: Midsummer bloom; foliage is attractive all season.

HEIGHT AND SPREAD: Height 2–4 feet (60–120 cm); width 1–2 feet (30–60 cm).

BEST SITE AND CLIMATE: Plant in average to rich, moist soil in full sun. In partial shade, the stems have a tendency to flop. Zones 3–9.

GROWING GUIDELINES: For propagation, divide plants in spring or early fall. Or sow seed outdoors or indoors; place indoor-sown pots in a refrigerator for 4–6 weeks before moving them to a warm, sunny spot. No serious pests or diseases.

LANDSCAPE USES: Plant spike gayfeather in perennial gardens, meadows, and prairie plantings.

COMPATIBLE COMPANIONS: Combine spike gayfeather with garden phlox (*Phlox paniculata*), coreopsis (*Coreopsis* spp.), and ornamental grasses. In meadows and prairies, plant it with culver's root (*Veronicastrum virginicum*) and ironweeds (*Vernonia* spp.). Native grasses such as big bluestem (*Andropogon gerardii*) and Indian grass (*Sorghastrum nutans*) help to support the tall stems.

Ligularia dentata	Compositae

BIG-LEAVED LIGULARIA

Big-leaved ligularias are bold accent plants for moist-soil gardens. Combine them with spiky or rounded plants to contrast or complement their broad leaves.

DESCRIPTION: Big-leaved ligularia has 1–2-foot (30–60 cm), round or kidney-shaped leaves on long stalks. Plants grow from stout crowns with thick, fleshy roots. The 5-inch (7.5 cm), bright orange-yellow flowers are carried in open clusters.

SEASON OF INTEREST: Late summer bloom; most gardeners value the foliage more than the flowers.

HEIGHT AND SPREAD: Height 3–4 feet (90–120 cm); width 3–4 feet (90–120 cm).

BEST SITE AND CLIMATE: Plant big-leaved ligularia in consistently moist, humus-rich soil in light to partial shade. Zones 3–8.

GROWING GUIDELINES: The huge leaves of ligularia lose water rapidly. In hot sun, the plants go into dramatic collapse, but the histrionics are short-lived; plants recover as temperatures moderate in the evening. Ligularias form big clumps but do not need frequent division. To propagate, lift clumps in early spring or fall and cut the crowns apart with a sharp knife. Slugs may devour the foliage; trap them in shallow pans of beer or exclude them with a ring of diatomaceous earth.

LANDSCAPE USES: Use ligularias at pondside, along a stream, or in informal borders. They are particularly attractive next to a fountain.

COMPATIBLE COMPANIONS: Choose ferns, irises, and grasses for contrast or hostas and umbrella plant (*Darmera peltata*) as a daring complement.

Lilium hybrids	Liliaceae

LILIES

Lilies add height and color to beds, borders, woodlands, and cutting gardens. In informal settings, combine them with ferns, grasses, and meadow flowers.

DESCRIPTION: Lilies are grown for their elegant form, beautiful summer flowers, and intoxicating fragrance. The stems rise from a fleshy bulb with thick, overlapping scales. The stems may be stout and densely clothed in leaves or slender with tiered whorls of foliage. The individual leaves may be narrow and grass-like or strap-like. The flowers consist of three showy petals and three similar, petal-like sepals.

SEASON OF INTEREST: Usually early summer bloom.

HEIGHT AND SPREAD: Height 1–6 feet (30–180 cm) but variable; width 1–2 feet (30–60 cm).

BEST SITE AND CLIMATE: Plant most hybrid lilies in humus-rich, near-neutral to slightly acid, moist but well-drained soil in full sun or light shade. Hardiness varies, but usually Zones 4–8.

GROWING GUIDELINES: Plant lily bulbs in fall or spring. A general rule is to set the bulbs 2–3 times as deep as the bulb is tall. Space bulbs 1–2 feet (30–60 cm) apart, depending on their mature size. Remove spent flowers. Propagate by dividing mature clumps in late summer or fall.

LANDSCAPE USES: Grow them in formal borders, in cottage gardens, and along woodland walks. They are perfect for container culture.

COMPATIBLE COMPANIONS: Combine lilies with summer perennials such as shasta daisies (*Chrysanthemum* x *superbum*) and cranesbills (*Geranium* spp.).

Lobelia cardinalis   Campanulaceae

CARDINAL FLOWER

The brilliant scarlet blooms of cardinal flower look like delicate birds in flight. They make an eye-catching addition to any garden with steady soil moisture.

DESCRIPTION: The fiery spikes of cardinal flower top leafy stems that grow from a fibrous-rooted crown. The spatula-shaped to oval leaves form tight rosettes in the fall. The tubular flowers have three lower and two upper petals.

SEASON OF INTEREST: Late summer to fall bloom.

HEIGHT AND SPREAD: Height 2–4 feet (60–120 cm); width 1–2 feet (30–60 cm).

BEST SITE AND CLIMATE: Plant cardinal flower in evenly moist, humus-rich soil in full sun or partial shade. Plants are intolerant of dry soil. Zones 2–9.

GROWING GUIDELINES: Cardinal flowers are shallow-rooted and subject to frost heaving. Where winters are cold, mulch plants to protect the crowns. If the roots have been pushed out of the soil, lift the whole clump in spring and replant it. Individual plants may be short-lived, but self-sown seedlings are numerous. Sow seeds uncovered outdoors in fall or indoors in late winter. Seedlings grow quickly and will bloom the first year from seed.

LANDSCAPE USES: Lobelias need steady soil moisture, so they are normally used around pools, along streams, or in informal plantings.

COMPATIBLE COMPANIONS: Combine with irises, hostas, ligularias (*Ligularia* spp.), and ferns.

OTHER SPECIES:
   L. siphilitica, blue lobelia, has bright blue flowers on 2–3-foot (60–90 cm) plants.

Lupinus polyphyllus   Leguminosae

WASHINGTON LUPINE

Spiky lupine flowers are a cheerful vertical accent in spring and early-summer gardens. Grow them on either side of an arbor or gate to add a welcoming touch.

DESCRIPTION: Washington lupine has conical flower spikes on stout stems with 1-foot (30 cm), palmately divided leaves. Plants grow from thick roots. The $^3/_4$-inch (18 mm), blue, pea-like flowers are crowded into 1–2-foot (30–60 cm) spikes.

SEASON OF INTEREST: Spring and summer bloom.

HEIGHT AND SPREAD: Height 3–5 feet (90–150 cm); width 2–3 feet (60–90 cm).

BEST SITE AND CLIMATE: Plant lupines in moist but well-drained, acid, humus-rich soil in full sun or light shade. Hybrids tolerate near-neutral soil. Lupines are sensitive to high summer nighttime temperatures. Zones 3–7.

GROWING GUIDELINES: Lupines are heavy feeders, so top-dress clumps in spring with a balanced organic fertilizer. They may be short-lived, especially in warmer zones; protect plants from hot, dry winds. Powdery mildew may be a problem. For propagation, remove sideshoots from around the clump in fall or sow seeds outdoors in fall.

LANDSCAPE USES: Use the strong vertical form of lupines to add lift to perennial gardens or to frame attractive views.

COMPATIBLE COMPANIONS: Combine lupines with mounding and rounded border perennials such as columbines (*Aquilegia* spp.), cranesbills (*Geranium* spp.), bellflowers (*Campanula* spp.), irises, peonies, and forget-me-nots (*Myosotis* spp.).

| *Lychnis coronaria*   Caryophyllaceae | *Lysimachia punctata*   Primulaceae |

ROSE CAMPION

YELLOW LOOSESTRIFE

The soft, silvery leaves and shocking magenta flowers of rose campion add excitement to beds, borders, and cottage gardens, especially when combined with softer colors.

Grow yellow loosestrife in informal gardens, where it can spread happily without crowding out less vigorous plants. It thrives in moist to wet soil.

DESCRIPTION: Rose campion is an old-fashioned perennial with elongated oval leaves covered in silver gray felt. The deep rose red, five-petaled flowers are carried in open clusters atop woolly stems. Plants grow from fibrous-rooted crowns.

SEASON OF INTEREST: Late spring bloom; the foliage rosettes are attractive in spring.

HEIGHT AND SPREAD: Height 2–3 feet (60–90 cm); width 1–1¹/₂ feet (30–45 cm).

BEST SITE AND CLIMATE: Plant in average to rich, moist but well-drained soil in full sun or light shade. Zones 4–8.

GROWING GUIDELINES: Divide clumps every 2–3 years in spring or fall to keep them vigorous. Plants may be short-lived, especially in rich soil, but self-sown seedlings are numerous. To propagate, sow seeds outdoors in fall, or remove small crowns from the edge of the clump in spring or fall.

LANDSCAPE USES: Plant rose campion in formal and informal beds and borders or in rock gardens.

COMPATIBLE COMPANIONS: Use the strong-colored flowers to spice up a subdued scheme of blues and pale yellows. Combine them with catmints (*Nepeta* spp), cranesbills (*Geranium* spp.), and blue-leaved grasses such as blue oat grass (*Helictotrichon sempervirens*). Plant them in bright color combinations with marguerites (*Anthemis tinctoria*), yarrows, and sundrops (*Oenothera* spp.).

DESCRIPTION: Yellow loosestrife is a creeping perennial. The wiry stems sport tiered whorls of broadly lance-shaped, felted leaves. The bright yellow, five-petaled flowers are carried in whorls among the leaves on the top one-third of the stem. Plants grow from fibrous-rooted rhizomes.

SEASON OF INTEREST: Summer bloom; the foliage is attractive in the spring and summer.

HEIGHT AND SPREAD: Height 1–2¹/₂ feet (30–75 cm); width 2–3 feet (60–90 cm).

BEST SITE AND CLIMATE: Plant in average to rich, evenly moist soil in full sun to partial shade. It grows well in wet soil. The leaf margins turn crispy if the soil is too dry. Zones 4–8.

GROWING GUIDELINES: Plants need dividing every 2–3 years to keep them from engulfing the garden. Lift clumps in early spring or fall and discard the less vigorous portions; replant remaining divisions. Propagate by division or take cuttings in early summer.

LANDSCAPE USES: Choose yellow loosestrife for cottage gardens and informal plantings. Use large clumps at pondside or along streams.

COMPATIBLE COMPANIONS: Combine yellow loosestrife with Siberian iris (*Iris sibirica*), rose mallow (*Hibiscus* spp.), meadowsweets (*Filipendula* spp.), grasses, ferns, and hostas.

Melissa officinalis   Labiatae

LEMON BALM

Fresh-smelling lemon balm forms attractive clumps in herb gardens and informal plantings. Plant it along paths so you can frequently brush by or pick the foliage.

DESCRIPTION: Lemon balm is a fragrant perennial herb grown for its lemon-scented foliage. The broad, oval leaves are bright glossy green. The loosely branched plants grow from fibrous roots. Small white flowers are produced among the leaves at the tops of the stems.

SEASON OF INTEREST: Season-long interest from the foliage; flowers form in late summer and fall.

HEIGHT AND SPREAD: Height 1¹/₂–2 feet (45–60 cm); width 2 feet (60 cm).

BEST SITE AND CLIMATE: Plant lemon balm in average to rich, well-drained soil in full sun to partial shade. Zones 4–9.

GROWING GUIDELINES: Plants have an open, often rangy appearance, especially in shade. If plants flop, cut them back by two-thirds to encourage fresh growth. Propagate by dividing plants in spring or fall, or take cuttings in early summer.

LANDSCAPE USES: Choose lemon balm for cottage and herb gardens or informal settings such as meadow gardens.

COMPATIBLE COMPANIONS: Combine lemon balm with shasta daisies (*Chrysanthemum* x *superbum*), artemisias, ornamental onions (*Allium* spp.), herbs, and grasses.

CULTIVARS: 'All Gold' has yellow foliage that turns greenish during summer. Shear to 6 inches (15 cm) in midsummer to promote colorful leaves.

Mertensia virginica   Boraginaceae

VIRGINIA BLUEBELL

Bluebells emerge early in spring and go dormant soon after flowering. Grow them where you will not accidentally dig into the roots as you plant annuals or bulbs.

DESCRIPTION: Virginia bluebells are spring wildflowers with sky blue bells that open from pink buds. The arching stems are clothed with blue-green leaves. Plants grow from thick roots.

SEASON OF INTEREST: Spring bloom; plants die back to the ground after flowering.

HEIGHT AND SPREAD: Height 1–2 feet (30–60 cm); width 1–2 feet (30–60 cm).

BEST SITE AND CLIMATE: Plant Virginia bluebells in consistently moist, well-drained, humus-rich soil in sun or shade. Sun is essential when plants are growing, but the spot can become quite shaded after plants are dormant. Zones 3–9.

GROWING GUIDELINES: Divide large clumps after flowering; cut the roots apart, leaving one "eye" (bud) per division. Self-sown seedlings are usually abundant; they will bloom the second or third year. No serious pests or diseases.

LANDSCAPE USES: Plant bluebells along a woodland path, in a shaded garden, or as a mass planting along streams or under shrubs and trees.

COMPATIBLE COMPANIONS: Combine Virginia bluebells with spring bulbs such as daffodils and squills (*Scilla* spp.) as well as with wildflowers such as spring beauty (*Claytonia virginica*) and bloodroot (*Sanguinaria canadensis*). Interplant the clumps with ferns, hostas, and other foliage plants to fill the gaps left as the bluebells go dormant.

Monarda didyma   Labiatae

BEE BALM

The lovely flowers of bee balm add brilliant color to the summer garden and are favored by hummingbirds. The leaves have a pleasant citrusy aroma.

DESCRIPTION: Bee balm, also known as Oswego tea, is a lovely perennial with bright flowers on sturdy stems that grow from fast-creeping runners. Tight heads of tubular, red flowers are surrounded by a whorl of colored, leafy bracts (modified leaves).

SEASON OF INTEREST: Summer bloom; the foliage is attractive in spring and early summer.

HEIGHT AND SPREAD: Height 2–4 feet (60–120 cm); width 2–3 feet (60–90 cm).

BEST SITE AND CLIMATE: Plant bee balm in evenly moist, humus-rich soil in full sun or partial shade. If plants dry out, the lower leaves will drop off. Zones 4–8.

GROWING GUIDELINES: Bee balms spread quickly; divide them every 2–3 years to keep them within bounds. Lift clumps in spring or fall and discard the older, less vigorous portions. Propagate by division or take tip cuttings in late spring or early summer. Powdery mildew causes white blotches on the foliage. To prevent problems, thin the stems to allow good air circulation.

LANDSCAPE USES: Plant bee balms in formal or informal gardens. Site them at the edge of a moist woodland or along a meadow path.

COMPATIBLE COMPANIONS: Combine bee balm with summer flowers such as garden phlox (*Phlox paniculata*), yarrows, ironweeds (*Vernonia* spp.), daylilies, and purple coneflower (*Echinacea purpurea*).

Muscari armeniacum   Liliaceae

GRAPE HYACINTH

After producing masses of spiky spring flower clusters, grape hyacinths retreat underground for the summer. New leaves usually pop up in fall.

DESCRIPTION: Grape hyacinth is a diminutive, delicate spring bulb with curled, grass-like leaves. It bears conical clusters of small, pendulous, jug-shaped flowers in various shades of blue.

SEASON OF INTEREST: Early spring bloom; plants die back to the ground (go dormant) after flowering.

HEIGHT AND SPREAD: Height to 12 inches (30 cm) in flower, leaves 6–10 inches (15–20 cm) high. Plants are 6–10 inches (15–20 cm) wide.

BEST SITE AND CLIMATE: Grow in average to rich, moist but well-drained soil in full sun or partial shade. Bulbs can tolerate dry soil and deep shade while they're summer-dormant. Zones 4–8.

GROWING GUIDELINES: Set out bulbs in fall, 3 inches (7.5 cm) deep and 3–5 inches (7.5–12.5) apart. If flowering wanes or you wish to propagate them, lift and divide the clumps as the foliage yellows in summer.

LANDSCAPE USES: Choose grape hyacinth for early color in beds and borders, around roses and other shrubs, or in drifts under trees. Large plantings are effective in lawns and along woodland walks.

COMPATIBLE COMPANIONS: Combine grape hyacinth with primroses, Lenten rose (*Helleborus orientalis*), lungworts (*Pulmonaria* spp.), and other spring flowers. Use them in mixed plantings with other bulbs or with groundcovers such as common periwinkle (*Vinca major*).

| *Narcissus* hybrids | Amaryllidaceae | *Nepeta* x *faassenii* | Labiatae |

DAFFODILS

CATMINT

Daffodils are cherished as heralds of the end of winter and the start of a new growing season. The many species and hybrids vary widely in size and color.

Catmint offers spikes of dainty violet-blue flowers over mounds of small, gray-green leaves. Good drainage is essential for dense, compact growth.

DESCRIPTION: The narrow, strap-like leaves are fleshy and flattened. The leafless stems bear one to three flowers with three petals and three petal-like sepals that are collectively called the perianth, or corolla. The funnel-shaped segment in the center of the flower is called the corona. Plants grow from a bulb.

SEASON OF INTEREST: Spring bloom; plants die back to the ground (go dormant) after flowering.

HEIGHT AND SPREAD: Height 3–12 inches (7.5–30 cm) in flower, leaves to 18 inches (45 cm) high. Clumps grow 10–12 inches (25–30 cm) wide.

BEST SITE AND CLIMATE: Plant daffodils in average to humus-rich, moist but well-drained soil in full sun or partial shade. The soil can become dry and the site shaded after plants are dormant. Zones 4–8, depending on the species or hybrid.

GROWING GUIDELINES: Set bulbs out in late summer and fall. Plant them one and a half to two times as deep as the bulb is tall. Lift sparse-flowering clumps as the leaves are withering, and air dry the bulbs until they separate easily. Replant immediately or store in a cool, dry place until fall.

LANDSCAPE USES: Plant generous groupings in beds and borders, cottage and rock gardens, and lawns and meadows or along paths in woodland gardens.

COMPATIBLE COMPANIONS: Combine daffodils with spring-blooming perennials, wildflowers, shrubs, and ferns.

DESCRIPTION: Catmint produces terminal flower clusters on wiry stems clothed in soft, hairy, gray-green, oval leaves. The violet-blue flowers are carried in whorls on slender spikes. Plants grow from fibrous-rooted crowns.

SEASON OF INTEREST: Spring through midsummer bloom; may rebloom later in the season.

HEIGHT AND SPREAD: Height 1^1/$_2$–3 feet (45–90 cm); width 2–3 feet (60–90 cm).

BEST SITE AND CLIMATE: Plant catmint in average to rich, moist but well-drained soil in full sun or light shade. Plants thrive in sandy soils and tolerate poor, dry soil. Zones 3–8.

GROWING GUIDELINES: Clumps get quite rangy after bloom; cut plants back by one-half to two-thirds to encourage fresh growth and repeat bloom. Take tip cuttings in early summer or divide plants in spring or fall.

LANDSCAPE USES: Catmints are perfect for edging walks and beds or for planting along rock walls.

COMPATIBLE COMPANIONS: In borders, combine catmint with bellflowers (*Campanula* spp.), cranesbills (*Geranium* spp.), soapworts (*Saponaria* spp.), coreopsis (*Coreopsis* spp.), peonies, and ornamental grasses. In rock gardens, grow them with coral bells (*Heuchera* spp.) and creeping plants such as Missouri evening primrose (*Oenothera macrocarpon*) and bellflowers.

Oenothera tetragona   Onagraceae

COMMON SUNDROPS

Young plants of common sundrops start out small but quickly form large clumps, so leave ample space at planting. Cut them back after flowering to promote rebloom.

DESCRIPTION: Common sundrops are showy perennials with narrow, bright green leaves on upright to slightly sprawling stems. The bright lemon yellow flowers are saucer-shaped and 3–4 inches (7.5–10 cm) wide. Plants grow from fibrous roots and spread by creeping stems to form broad clumps.

SEASON OF INTEREST: Late spring and early summer bloom; may rebloom sporadically throughout the season if cut back.

HEIGHT AND SPREAD: Height 1–2 feet (30–60 cm); width 1–3 feet (30–90 cm).

BEST SITE AND CLIMATE: Plant common sundrops in average to rich, well-drained soil in full sun. Established plants are extremely drought- and heat-tolerant. Zones 3–9.

GROWING GUIDELINES: Divide rosettes in early spring. Take stem cuttings in early summer. No serious pests or diseases.

LANDSCAPE USES: Use common sundrops in the front or middle of borders. They are perfect for cottage gardens, and they also perform well in rock gardens and meadow plantings. Choose them for an open groundcover in a sunny spot.

COMPATIBLE COMPANIONS: Combine common sundrops with wild sweet William (*Phlox maculata*), cranesbills (*Geranium* spp.), catmints (*Nepeta* spp.), yarrows (*Achillea* spp.), and other early-summer perennials.

Paeonia lactiflora   Ranunculaceae

COMMON GARDEN PEONY

The deep red new shoots of garden peony look great with spring bulbs, and the rich green foliage is a lovely foil to later-blooming perennials.

DESCRIPTION: Peonies are showy perennials beloved for their huge, fragrant flowers. The sturdy stalks are clothed in compound, shiny green leaves. Plants grow from thick, fleshy roots.

SEASON OF INTEREST: Late spring to early summer bloom. The foliage is attractive all season.

HEIGHT AND SPREAD: Height 1½–3 feet (45–60 cm); width 3–4 feet (90–120 cm).

BEST SITE AND CLIMATE: Plant in moist, humus-rich soil in full sun or light shade. Good drainage is important to avoid root rot. Zones 2–8.

GROWING GUIDELINES: Plant container-grown peonies in spring or fall. Plant bareroot plants in September and October. Place the "eyes" (buds) 1–1½ inches (2.5–3 cm) below the soil surface. Space plants 3–4 feet (90–120 cm) apart. Apply an annual winter mulch anywhere winter temperatures dip below 0°F (–18°C). Lift sparse-flowering plants in fall, divide the roots—leaving at least one eye per division—and replant into amended soil.

LANDSCAPE USES: Peonies are favorites for cottage gardens, beds, borders, and mass plantings.

COMPATIBLE COMPANIONS: Spring and early-summer perennials such as irises, foxgloves (*Digitalis* spp.), and columbines (*Aquilegia* spp.) are excellent flowering companions.

Papaver orientale   Papaveraceae

ORIENTAL POPPY

Oriental poppies are prized for their colorful, crepe paper-like flowers. Combine them with bushy perennials to fill the gap when the poppies go dormant in summer.

DESCRIPTION: The 3–4-inch (7.5–10 cm) flowers have crinkled petals with black spots at their bases. They surround a raised knob that becomes the seedpod. Plants produce rosettes of coarse, hairy, lobed foliage from a thick taproot.

SEASON OF INTEREST: Early summer bloom; plants usually go dormant and die back to the ground soon after flowering.

HEIGHT AND SPREAD: Height 2–3 feet (60–90 cm); width 2–3 feet (60–90 cm).

BEST SITE AND CLIMATE: Plant oriental poppies in average to rich, well-drained, humus-rich soil in full sun or light shade. Established plants are tough and long-lived. Zones 2–7.

GROWING GUIDELINES: In most areas, the plants go dormant after flowering, leaving a bare spot in the garden. In fall, new foliage rosettes emerge; divide overgrown plants at this time. No serious pests or diseases.

LANDSCAPE USES: Plant poppies with other perennials and ornamental grasses in beds and borders. The showy flowers are favorites of cottage gardeners.

COMPATIBLE COMPANIONS: Combine oriental poppies with bushy plants such as catmints (*Nepeta* spp.), cranesbills (*Geranium* spp.), yarrow, and asters to fill the gap left by the declining foliage.

CULTIVARS: 'Snow Queen' is pure white with large black spots. 'Watermelon' is rosy pink.

Patrinia scabiosifolia   Valerianaceae

PATRINIA

Patrinia's tall-stemmed, bright yellow flower clusters add height and color to late-summer borders. Avoid planting them near paths, though—the flowers have a strong odor.

DESCRIPTION: Patrinia is a tall, airy plant with many stout stems clothed in large, pinnately divided leaves. The stems are topped with open, branched clusters of small yellow flowers. Plants grow from a stout, branched taproot.

SEASON OF INTEREST: Late summer and fall bloom; attractive foliage all season.

HEIGHT AND SPREAD: Height 3–6 feet (90–180 cm); width 3–4 feet (90–120 cm).

BEST SITE AND CLIMATE: Plant patrinia in average to rich, moist but well-drained soil in full sun or light shade. Zones 4–9.

GROWING GUIDELINES: Patrinia is a tough and long-lived plant that seldom needs division. Self-sown seedlings may be plentiful. To reduce seeding, remove heads after flowers fade. Propagate by division in spring or after flowering, or sow seed outdoors in fall. No serious pests or diseases.

LANDSCAPE USES: Choose patrinia for the middle or back of beds and borders, for cottage gardens, and for informal plantings along a woodland edge.

COMPATIBLE COMPANIONS: Combine patrinia with New England asters (*Aster novae-angliae*), butterfly bush (*Buddleia davidii*), sedums, and ornamental grasses. Use the airy flowers as a foil to bold textures such as the leaves of cannas (*Canna* x *generalis*).

Penstemon digitalis   Scrophulariaceae

FOXGLOVE PENSTEMON

Foxglove penstemons are a natural choice for meadow gardens, and they also blend well into formal borders. Enjoy the flowers in late spring and the seed heads in winter.

DESCRIPTION: Foxglove penstemon is a showy plant with upright flower spikes clothed in shiny, broadly lance-shaped leaves. The 1–1¹/₂-inch (2.5–3.5) irregular tubular flowers are white with purple lines. They have two upper and three lower lips. Flowering stems and basal foliage rosettes arise from fibrous-rooted crowns.

SEASON OF INTEREST: Late spring to early summer bloom; the seed heads are attractive in winter.

HEIGHT AND SPREAD: Height 2–4 feet (60–120 cm), occasionally larger; width 1–2 feet (60–90 cm).

BEST SITE AND CLIMATE: Plant penstemons in average to rich, moist but well-drained soil in full sun or light shade. This species of penstemon tolerates wet soil; good drainage is essential for success with most other species. Zones 4–8.

GROWING GUIDELINES: Plants benefit from division every 4–6 years. Plants may need more frequent division if they're growing in rich, moist soil. Sow seed outdoors in fall.

LANDSCAPE USES: Use penstemons in formal borders, informal gardens, and rock gardens. They grow well in low meadows and in light shade at the edge of a woodland.

COMPATIBLE COMPANIONS: Combine the spiky flowers of foxglove penstemon with rounded plants such as cranesbills (*Geranium* spp.), yarrows, and coral bells (*Heuchera* spp.).

Perovskia atriplicifolia   Labiatae

RUSSIAN SAGE

The airy gray buds and soft blue flowers of Russian sage mix well with yellow, pink, deep blue, and purple flowers in borders and cottage gardens.

DESCRIPTION: Russian sage is a shrubby, branching perennial with erect stems clothed in gray-green, deeply lobed leaves. The small, irregularly shaped, blue flowers are carried in slender 12–15-inch (30–37.5 cm) sprays. Plants grow from fibrous-rooted crowns.

SEASON OF INTEREST: Mid- to late-summer bloom; plants are lovely in foliage and in seed.

HEIGHT AND SPREAD: Height 3–5 feet (90–150 cm); width 3–5 feet (90–150 cm).

BEST SITE AND CLIMATE: Plant Russian sage in average to rich, well-drained soil in full sun. Good drainage is essential for success. Established plants are drought-tolerant. Zones 4–9.

GROWING GUIDELINES: The stems of Russian sage become woody with age. After hard frost, cut the stems back to 1 foot (30 cm) above the ground. In Northern gardens, plants die back to the soil line but resprout from the roots. Division is seldom necessary. For propagation, take stem cuttings in early summer. No serious pests or diseases.

LANDSCAPE USES: Plant Russian sages toward the middle or back of the border. They look great in mass plantings, too.

COMPATIBLE COMPANIONS: Combine Russian sage with yarrows, gayfeathers (*Liatris* spp.), balloon flower (*Platycodon grandiflorus*), sedums, phlox, and ornamental grasses.

Phlox paniculata   Polemoniaceae

GARDEN PHLOX

Garden phlox is a beautiful and versatile garden perennial. It forms broad clumps that should be divided every 3 to 4 years in spring or fall to keep them vigorous.

DESCRIPTION: Garden phlox is a popular summer-blooming perennial with domed clusters of fragrant flowers atop stiff, leafy stems. The tubular flowers have flared, five-petaled faces. Flower color varies from magenta to pink and white. Hybrids have a wider color range, including purples, reds, and oranges. The leaves are broadly lance-shaped. Plants grow from fibrous-rooted crowns.

SEASON OF INTEREST: Mid- to late-summer bloom.

HEIGHT AND SPREAD: Height 3–4 feet (90–120 cm); width 2–4 feet (60–120 cm).

BEST SITE AND CLIMATE: Plant garden phlox in moist but well-drained, humus-rich soil in full sun or light shade. Usually Zones 3–8.

GROWING GUIDELINES: For propagation, take stem cuttings in late spring or early summer. Powdery mildew causes white patches on the leaves. To avoid problems, thin by removing every third stem before bloom to increase air circulation. Look for mildew-resistant cultivars.

LANDSCAPE USES: Plant garden phlox in formal and informal beds as well as cottage gardens. It is lovely in meadows and on the edges of lightly shaded woodlands.

COMPATIBLE COMPANIONS: Combine them with summer daisies, bee balms (*Monarda* spp.), daylilies, meadow rues (*Thalictrum* spp.), asters, goldenrods (*Solidago* spp.), and ornamental grasses.

Phlox stolonifera   Polemoniaceae

CREEPING PHLOX

Creeping phlox spreads to form broad clumps of lovely spring flowers. The mats of evergreen foliage make a good groundcover after the bloom stalks have faded.

DESCRIPTION: Creeping phlox is a woodland species with erect flowering stems and creeping leafy stems clothed in evergreen, oval foliage. The pink to lilac-blue flowers bloom in open clusters. Each flower has an orange eye. The flower stalk withers after seed forms. Plants have fibrous white roots.

SEASON OF INTEREST: Spring bloom. Leaves form an attractive evergreen groundcover in warmer zones.

HEIGHT AND SPREAD: Height 6–8 inches (15–20 cm) in flower, leaves 1–2 inches (2.5–5 cm) high. Plants grow 12–24 inches (30–60 cm) wide.

BEST SITE AND CLIMATE: Plant creeping phlox in evenly moist, humus-rich soil in partial sun to full shade. Sun is necessary in spring, but plants can tolerate quite dense shade in summer. Zones 2–8.

GROWING GUIDELINES: Divide the clumps as necessary to control their spread or for propagation. Or take tip cuttings in late spring or early summer from nonblooming stems. Self-sown seedlings usually appear. Powdery mildew may cause white patches on leaves; spray plants with wettable sulfur once or twice a week if you really want to avoid this problem.

LANDSCAPE USES: Use creeping phlox in shaded and wild gardens, along a woodland path, or at the edge of a meadow. It grows well under flowering shrubs and trees as a groundcover.

Physostegia virginiana   Labiatae

OBEDIENT PLANT

Obedient plant gets its name from the tendency of the flowers to stay in position after you shift them to one side or another. This old-fashioned favorite spreads quickly.

DESCRIPTION: The tubular, two-lobed flowers are rose pink to lilac-pink. Plants have toothed, lance-shaped leaves on angled stems. Plants grow from creeping, fibrous-rooted stems.

SEASON OF INTEREST: Late summer bloom.

HEIGHT AND SPREAD: Height 3–4 feet (90–120 cm); width 2–4 feet (60–120 cm).

BEST SITE AND CLIMATE: Grow obedient plant in moist, average to rich soil in full sun or light shade. Plants tolerate wet soil. Zones 3–9.

GROWING GUIDELINES: Unimproved forms of obedient plant tend to flop in rich soil; stake them or choose a compact cultivar to avoid this problem. Divide plants every 2–4 years to control their spread. Propagate by division or take tip cuttings in late spring or early summer.

LANDSCAPE USES: Obedient plant is an old fashioned favorite. Use cultivars in formal beds, borders, and cottage gardens. The wild form is lovely in meadows and informal plantings.

COMPATIBLE COMPANIONS: Combine obedient plant with asters, goldenrods (*Solidago* spp.), garden phlox (*Phlox paniculata*), boltonia (*Boltonia asteroides*), and ornamental grasses.

CULTIVARS: 'Summer Snow' has white flowers on 3-foot (90 cm) stems. 'Variegata' has leaves edged in creamy white with pale pink flowers.

Platycodon grandiflorus   Campanulaceae

BALLOON FLOWER

The rich blue blooms of balloon flower open from curious, inflated buds. Enjoy the flowers with other summer-blooming perennials in both formal and informal gardens.

DESCRIPTION: Balloon flowers are showy plants with saucer-shaped blooms on succulent stems clothed in toothed, triangular leaves. The rich blue flowers have five pointed petals that open from balloon-like buds. Plants grow from thick, fleshy roots.

SEASON OF INTEREST: Summer bloom. Leaves may turn bright yellow in fall.

HEIGHT AND SPREAD: Height 2–3 feet (60–90 cm); width 1–2 feet (30–60 cm).

BEST SITE AND CLIMATE: Plant balloon flower in well-drained, average to humus-rich soil in full sun or light shade. Established plants are drought-tolerant. Zones 3–8.

GROWING GUIDELINES: New shoots are slow to emerge in spring; take care not to damage them by mistake. Remove spent flowers to encourage more bloom. Established clumps seldom need division. To propagate, lift and divide clumps in spring or early fall; dig deeply to avoid root damage. Sow seeds outdoors in fall. Self-sown seedlings may appear. No serious pests or diseases.

LANDSCAPE USES: Plant balloon flower in beds and borders, cottage gardens, and rock gardens. Plants also grow well in containers.

COMPATIBLE COMPANIONS: Combine balloon flowers with summer perennials such as yarrows, sages (*Salvia* spp.), bee balms (*Monarda* spp.), and phlox. They are stunning with ornamental grasses.

| *Polemonium caeruleum* | Polemoniaceae | *Polygonatum odoratum* | Liliaceae |

JACOB'S LADDER

FRAGRANT SOLOMON'S SEAL

Jacob's ladder forms tidy clumps of ferny foliage and leafy stems topped with clusters of saucer-shaped flowers. Sniff the blue blooms to enjoy the grape-like scent.

Greenish flowers dangle from the arching stems of fragrant Solomon's seal in spring. The cream-edged leaves of the variegated form extend the interest through the season.

DESCRIPTION: Jacob's ladder has tall, leafy stems crowned with loose clusters of nodding flowers. The saucer-shaped blue or white flowers have five overlapping petals. The showy leaves are pinnately divided with many narrow leaflets. Plants grow from fibrous-rooted crowns.

SEASON OF INTEREST: Blooms throughout summer.

HEIGHT AND SPREAD: Height 1¹/₂–2¹/₂ feet (45–75 cm); width 1–1¹/₂ feet (30–45 cm).

BEST SITE AND CLIMATE: Grow Jacob's ladder in evenly moist, humus-rich soil in full sun to partial shade. Plants are sensitive to high temperatures. Zones 3–7.

GROWING GUIDELINES: Remove spent flowers to encourage reblooming. Cut stems to the ground after flowering; leave one or two to produce seed, if desired. Plants are carefree and seldom need division. They may be short-lived, but self-sown seedlings can be numerous. No serious pests or diseases.

LANDSCAPE USES: Use Jacob's ladder in formal and cottage gardens as well as along open woodland walks and near streams.

COMPATIBLE COMPANIONS: Combine Jacob's ladder with goat's beard (*Aruncus dioicus*), Russian sage (*Perovskia atriplicifolia*), phlox, and ornamental grasses. Massed plantings are effective in informal gardens with astilbes, irises, and ferns or under flowering trees.

DESCRIPTION: Fragrant Solomon's seal has graceful, arching stems with broadly oval, blue-green leaves arranged like stairsteps up the stem. The tubular, pale-green, fragrant flowers hang in clusters below the leaves from the nodes (leaf joints). Showy blue-black fruits form in late summer. Plants spread from thick, creeping rhizomes to form wide clumps.

SEASON OF INTEREST: Spring bloom; the leafy, arching stems are attractive all season.

HEIGHT AND SPREAD: 1¹/₂–2¹/₂ feet (45–75 cm) tall; 2–4 feet (60–120 cm) wide.

BEST SITE AND CLIMATE: Plant fragrant Solomon's seal in moist, humus-rich soil in partial to full shade. Plants tolerate dry soil. Zones 3–9.

GROWING GUIDELINES: Divide in spring or fall to control the spread or for propagation. Sow fresh seed outdoors in fall. Seedlings may not appear for 2 years and will not bloom for several years.

LANDSCAPE USES: Solomon's seals provide grace and beauty to the shade garden. They also grow well in containers.

COMPATIBLE COMPANIONS: Combine them with hostas, lungworts (*Pulmonaria* spp.), irises, wildflowers, and ferns. Use massed plantings under shrubs or in the dry shade of mature trees.

CULTIVARS: The variety *thunbergii* 'Variegatum' is prized for its broad, oval leaves with creamy white margins.

Polygonum affine   Polygonaceae

HIMALAYAN FLEECEFLOWER

Himalayan fleeceflower produces masses of pink flower spikes in early summer. It makes an excellent fast-spreading groundcover for moist sites.

DESCRIPTION: Himalayan fleeceflower is a fast-spreading perennial with erect flower spikes and pointed, broadly lance-shaped leaves with prominent central veins. The small pink flowers are tightly packed into narrow, erect spikes. Plants grow from creeping stems.

SEASON OF INTEREST: Early summer bloom; the persistent leaves are attractive all year.

HEIGHT AND SPREAD: Height 6–8 inches (15–20 cm) in flower; leaves to about 4 inches (10 cm) high. Clumps 1–3 feet (30–90 cm) wide.

BEST SITE AND CLIMATE: Grow Himalayan fleeceflower in moist, humus-rich soil in full sun or partial shade. Zones 3–8.

GROWING GUIDELINES: Plants spread rapidly to form wide clumps; frequent spring or fall division is necessary to keep them from taking over. To propagate, remove sideshoots from the clump.

LANDSCAPE USES: Plant Himalayan fleeceflower where you need a showy, fast-spreading groundcover. Choose it for the front of the border, along walks, or in rock gardens.

COMPATIBLE COMPANIONS: Combine Himalayan fleeceflower with irises, astilbes, hostas, ferns, and ornamental grasses.

CULTIVARS: 'Border Jewel' has rose-pink flowers. 'Darjeeling Red' has deep crimson-pink flowers. 'Dimity' has light pink flowers.

Primula denticulata   Primulaceae

DRUMSTICK PRIMROSE

Drumstick primroses have distinctive flowers that add a fun touch to the early-spring garden. Combine them with ferns and moisture-loving perennials for all-season interest.

DESCRIPTION: Drumstick primrose has narrowly oval leaves arising in a whorl from a crown of thick, fibrous white roots. The leafless flower stems bear tight, globe-shaped clusters of lavender or pink flowers.

SEASON OF INTEREST: Early spring bloom; the foliage remains attractive all season.

HEIGHT AND SPREAD: Height 6–12 inches (15–30 cm) in flower; leaves 6–8 inches (15–20 cm) tall. Plants 10–12 inches (25–30 cm) wide.

BEST SITE AND CLIMATE: Plant in humus-rich, moist soil in light to partial shade. Zones 3–8.

GROWING GUIDELINES: Drumstick primroses grow slowly to form dense clumps with many flowering stalks. They are heavy feeders, so mulch them with compost or well-rotted manure in early spring or summer to provide extra nutrients. Propagate by dividing plants after flowering, or sow seed outdoors in fall or indoors in early spring.

LANDSCAPE USES: Plant drumstick primroses along a stream, at poolside, or in a moist shade garden. In a low spot, use them in mass plantings with moisture-tolerant shrubs, such as red-osier dogwood (*Cornus sericea*).

COMPATIBLE COMPANIONS: Combine drumstick primroses with astilbe, ferns, wildflowers, and other primroses. In wet soils, plant them with irises, hostas, and rodgersias (*Rodgersia* spp.).

| *Primula vulgaris* | Primulaceae | *Pulmonaria saccharata* | Boraginaceae |

ENGLISH PRIMROSE

BETHLEHEM SAGE

The pale yellow flowers of English primroses are excellent companions for spring-blooming bulbs and wildflowers in woodland gardens and under shrubs and trees.

It's hard to beat the silver-spotted leaves of Bethlehem sage for adding a dramatic touch to shady gardens. The pink buds and blue spring blooms are a bonus!

DESCRIPTION: English primroses have flat, five-petaled, pale yellow flowers. The broad, crinkled leaves rise directly from stout crowns with thick, fibrous roots.

SEASON OF INTEREST: Spring and early summer bloom.

HEIGHT AND SPREAD: Height 6–9 inches (15–22.5 cm); width 12 inches (30 cm).

BEST SITE AND CLIMATE: Plant English primroses in evenly moist, humus-rich soil in light to partial shade. Plants may go dormant if the soil dries out in summer. Zones 4–8.

GROWING GUIDELINES: In Northern zones, mulch plants in winter to minimize the alternate freezing and thawing that can push plants out of the soil. Divide overgrown clumps after flowering. English primroses are easy to grow from fresh seed sown outdoors or indoors in early spring.

LANDSCAPE USES: Grow primroses in light shade in woodland and informal gardens.

COMPATIBLE COMPANIONS: Plant scattered clumps and drifts of primroses with spring bulbs such as daffodils, tulips, and spanish bluebells (*Endymion hispanicus*). Combine them with early-blooming perennials such as hellebores (*Helleborus* spp.), lungworts (*Pulmonaria* spp.), forget-me-nots (*Myosotis* spp.), and cranesbills (*Geranium* spp.). Wildflowers, ferns, and sedges (*Carex* spp.) are other excellent companions.

DESCRIPTION: Bethlehem sage has wide, oval, hairy leaves that are variously spotted and blotched with silver. The nodding, five-petaled flowers vary from pink to medium blue. They are held in tight clusters on short-lived stems. Plants grow from crowns with thick, fibrous roots.

SEASON OF INTEREST: Spring bloom; the spotted foliage is attractive all season.

HEIGHT AND SPREAD: Height 9–18 inches (22.5–45 cm); width 12–24 inches (30–60 cm).

BEST SITE AND CLIMATE: Plant Bethlehem sage in moist, humus-rich soil in partial to full shade. Established plants tolerate drought. Zones 3–8.

GROWING GUIDELINES: The foliage of Bethlehem sage remains attractive all season unless soil remains dry for an extended period. Plants seldom need division. For propagation, lift clumps after flowering or in fall. Slugs may damage leaves; trap these pests in shallow pans of beer. Powdery mildew may turn the leaves white; spray them with wettable sulfur.

LANDSCAPE USES: Plant Bethlehem sage in drifts in shade gardens or along woodland paths. Use the plants as a groundcover under shrubs and trees.

COMPATIBLE COMPANIONS: Plant Bethlehem sage with spring bulbs, primroses, bleeding hearts (*Dicentra* spp.), foamflower (*Tiarella cordifolia*), wildflowers, and ferns.

Rudbeckia fulgida   Compositae

ORANGE CONEFLOWER

Orange coneflowers, also commonly called black-eyed Susans, are tough, long-lived perennials. Grow them in formal borders, casual meadow gardens, or even containers.

DESCRIPTION: Orange coneflowers are cheery summer daisies with yellow-orange rays (petal-like structures) and raised, dark brown centers. The oval to broadly lance-shaped, rough, hairy leaves are alternate on stiff stems. Plants grow from fibrous-rooted crowns.

SEASON OF INTEREST: Mid- to late-summer bloom; the dried seed heads are attractive all winter.

HEIGHT AND SPREAD: Height $1^1/_2$–3 feet (45–90 cm); width 2–4 feet (60–120 cm).

BEST SITE AND CLIMATE: Plant orange coneflowers in average, moist but well-drained soil in full sun or light shade. Extremely heat-tolerant. Zones 3–9.

GROWING GUIDELINES: Orange coneflowers spread outward to form large clumps. Their exuberant growth depletes the soil; the edges of the clumps are the most vigorous. Divide clumps every 2–4 years in spring or fall and replant into amended soil. Sow seed outdoors in fall or indoors in late winter.

LANDSCAPE USES: Plant orange coneflowers in formal and informal beds and borders, cottage gardens, and meadows. Plants grow well in containers.

COMPATIBLE COMPANIONS: Combine orange coneflowers with other daisies, sedums, phlox, bee balms (*Monarda* spp.), and ornamental grasses.

CULTIVARS: The variety *sullivantii* is a stout grower with wide leaves. 'Goldsturm' is a popular compact cultivar of this variety.

Ruta graveolens   Rutaceae

RUE

Rue is a traditional favorite for herb gardens, but its lacy, blue-gray foliage also looks super in ornamental plantings with bold, colorful flowers.

DESCRIPTION: The aromatic, blue-gray leaves are divided into many small, fan-shaped leaflets. Small yellow flowers are carried in open clusters above the foliage. Plants grow from a woody, taprooted crown.

SEASON OF INTEREST: Summer bloom; attractive foliage all season.

HEIGHT AND SPREAD: Height 1–3 feet (30–90 cm); width 2–3 feet (60–90 cm).

BEST SITE AND CLIMATE: Plant in average to rich, well-drained soil in full sun or light shade. Plants tolerate dry, sandy soil. Zones 4–9.

GROWING GUIDELINES: Rue forms broad, dense clumps that seldom need division. Propagate by stem cuttings in summer and fall.

LANDSCAPE USES: Choose rue for herb and knot gardens or for the front or middle of beds and borders. It is also beautiful for edging beds or bordering walks. Think twice about planting rue where people will have to brush by it; it produces an oil that can irritate the skin of some people.

COMPATIBLE COMPANIONS: Combine rue with hyssop (*Hyssopus officinalis*), yarrows, ornamental onions (*Allium* spp.), and ornamental grasses. Contrast the fine-textured foliage with bold flowers such as balloon flower (*Platycodon grandiflorus*), orange coneflowers (*Rudbeckia* spp.), and blanket flowers (*Gaillardia* spp.).

Salvia officinalis   Labiatae   *Salvia* x *superba*   Labiatae

SAGE   # VIOLET SAGE

Sage is an aromatic herb that blends equally well into flower gardens and herb gardens. You can even dry the foliage and enjoy it in cooking and crafts all year.

The spiky blooms of violet sage combine wonderfully with rounded perennials, such as cranesbills (Geranium spp.). Cut back the stems after flowering to promote rebloom.

DESCRIPTION: The broad, lance-shaped, opposite leaves are sea green to purple-green, with a crinkled surface. The pink or purple flowers are less showy than those of other sages but are an added bonus to the leaves. Plants grow from fibrous-rooted crowns.

SEASON OF INTEREST: Summer bloom; the foliage is ornamental through the season.

HEIGHT AND SPREAD: Height 1–2$^1/_2$ feet (30–75 cm); 2–3 feet (60–90 cm) wide.

BEST SITE AND CLIMATE: Plant sage in light, sandy or loamy, well-drained soil in full sun or light shade. Zones 4–9.

GROWING GUIDELINES: Sage grows to form a small shrub, with persistent woody growth in warmer zones. Cut plants back in spring to remove winter-damaged growth and to reshape the plants. Take stem cuttings in summer.

LANDSCAPE USES: Use sage in herb and cottage gardens or for winter structure and foliage interest in formal beds and borders.

COMPATIBLE COMPANIONS: Combine sage with blue-, yellow-, or orange-flowered plants for exciting complements: Consider butterfly weed (*Asclepias tuberosa*), yarrows, ornamental onions (*Allium* spp.), and balloon flower (*Platycodon grandiflorus*). Sage also blends naturally with many other herbs.

DESCRIPTION: Violet sage is a lovely plant covered with colorful flower spikes in summer. The violet-blue flowers are carried in narrow spikes; below each flower is a leaf-like bract. The bushy, well-branched plants have aromatic triangular leaves. They grow from a fibrous-rooted crown.

SEASON OF INTEREST: Early- to mid-summer bloom; often reblooms later in the season.

HEIGHT AND SPREAD: Height 1$^1/_2$–3$^1/_2$ feet (45–105 cm); width 2–3 feet (60–90 cm).

BEST SITE AND CLIMATE: Plant violet sage in average to rich, moist but well-drained soil in full sun or light shade. Plants are drought-tolerant once established. Zones 4–7.

GROWING GUIDELINES: Plants bloom nonstop for a month. After flowering wanes, shear off the spent flowers to promote fresh growth and renewed bloom. Plants seldom need division. Propagate by cuttings in late spring or early summer; remove any flowers that form on unrooted cuttings.

LANDSCAPE USES: Plant violet sages in formal or informal borders or in rock gardens. Use them in cottage gardens or in mass plantings. Plants grow well in containers.

COMPATIBLE COMPANIONS: Combine violet sage with early-summer perennials such as yarrows, lamb's-ears (*Stachys byzantina*), daylilies, coreopsis (*Coreopsis* spp.), and ornamental grasses.

Saponaria ocymoides   Caryophyllaceae

ROCK SOAPWORT

Plant rock soapwort where it can tumble over rocks or walls. After their main flush of early summer bloom, cut the plants back by half to promote compact new growth.

DESCRIPTION: Rock soapwort is a low, creeping plant with thin stems clothed in small, opposite, oval leaves. A profusion of $^1/_4$-inch (6 mm), pink flowers smother the plants for nearly a month.

SEASON OF INTEREST: Early summer bloom with sporadic rebloom.

HEIGHT AND SPREAD: Height 4–6 inches (10–15 cm) tall; width 1–2 feet (30–60 cm).

BEST SITE AND CLIMATE: Grow in average to rich, well-drained soil in full sun or light shade. Plants also grow well in sandy soils. Zones 3–7.

GROWING GUIDELINES: Clumps spread quickly and may die out in the center after a few years. To keep them looking good, divide plants every 2–3 years in spring or fall, especially if you grow them in rich soil. Take cuttings in summer. No serious pests or diseases.

LANDSCAPE USES: Plant rock soapwort as an edging to beds and borders or along the path in a cottage garden. Choose it for rock gardens and unmortared walls as well as for edging walkways.

COMPATIBLE COMPANIONS: Combine rock soapwort with small- and medium-sized plants such as verbenas (*Verbena* spp.), cranesbills (*Geranium* spp.), yarrows, and sages.

CULTIVARS: 'Alba' has white flowers. 'Rubra Compacta' has deep pink flowers on compact plants. 'Splendens' is rosy red.

Scabiosa caucasica   Dipsacaceae

PINCUSHION FLOWER

Pincushion flowers are old-fashioned perennials that are regaining the popularity they had in Victorian gardens. Plant them in groups to increase their visual impact.

DESCRIPTION: The stems are loosely clothed in lance-shaped to three-lobed leaves. The pale blue flowers are packed into flat, 2–3 inch (5–7.5 cm) heads. The flowers increase in size as they near the margins of the heads.

SEASON OF INTEREST: Summer bloom.

HEIGHT AND SPREAD: $1^1/_2$–2 feet (45–60 cm) tall; 1–$1^1/_2$ feet (30–45 cm) wide.

BEST SITE AND CLIMATE: Plant in average to humus-rich, moist but well-drained soil in full sun to light shade. Plants are sensitive to high temperatures. They also will not tolerate wet soils. Zones 3–7.

GROWING GUIDELINES: Plants form good-sized clumps in 1–2 years. Divide in spring if plants become overcrowded. Remove spent flowers to promote continued bloom. Propagate by division in spring, or sow fresh seed outdoors in fall or indoors in late winter. No serious pests or diseases.

LANDSCAPE USES: Choose pincushion flowers for beds and borders as well as for cottage gardens.

COMPATIBLE COMPANIONS: The airy flowers seem to dance above low, mounded plants such as cranesbills (*Geranium* spp.), phlox, pinks (*Dianthus* spp.), and yarrows. They also combine well with bee balms (*Monarda* spp.), daylilies, and columbines (*Aquilegia* spp.).

CULTIVARS: 'Butterfly Blue', of uncertain parentage, is a long-blooming plant with lilac-blue flowers.

Scilla sibirica   Liliaceae

SIBERIAN SQUILL

Siberian squill is among the first plants to bloom in late winter and early spring. The vivid blue, nodding flowers emerge just ahead of the leaves.

DESCRIPTION: The bell-shaped flowers are carried on slender stems. The grassy leaves expand as the flowers fade and disappear by early summer. Plants grow from a true bulb.

SEASON OF INTEREST: Late winter and early spring bloom; plants die back to the ground (go dormant) after flowering.

HEIGHT AND SPREAD: Height 4–6 inches (10–15 cm) tall; width 3–4 inches (7.5–10 cm).

BEST SITE AND CLIMATE: Plant in average to rich, moist but well-drained soil in full sun or light shade. Dormant bulbs can withstand considerable drought and shade. Zones 3–8.

GROWING GUIDELINES: Set bulbs out in fall 2–3 inches (5–7.5 cm) deep and 3–4 inches (7.5–10 cm) apart. To propagate, divide plants after flowering as the foliage withers. Self-sown seedlings are plentiful.

LANDSCAPE USES: Plant squills in beds and borders, cottage gardens, woodlands, and rock gardens. They grow well under trees and shrubs and quickly form a short-lived but stunning groundcover. Squills also look charming seeded throughout the lawn.

COMPATIBLE COMPANIONS: Combine Siberian squill with other spring bulbs such as tulips and daffodils, with wildflowers, and with spring perennials such as hellebores (*Helleborus* spp.).

Sedum spectabile   Crassulaceae

SHOWY STONECROP

Easy-to-grow showy stonecrop is a dependable addition to beds and borders for year-round interest. It also looks great in mass plantings, alone, or with ornamental grasses.

DESCRIPTION: Showy stonecrops are large summer perennials with thick stems clothed in broad, gray-green leaves. Small, bright pink flowers are borne in 4–6-inch (10–15 cm) domed clusters. Plants grow from fibrous-rooted crowns.

SEASON OF INTEREST: Midsummer to late summer bloom. The pale green buds are attractive in summer, and the seed heads hold their shape all winter.

HEIGHT AND SPREAD: Height 1–2 feet (30–60 cm) tall; width 2 feet (60 cm).

BEST SITE AND CLIMATE: Plant showy stonecrop in full sun in average to humus-rich, well-drained soil. Plants are heat-tolerant and extremely drought-tolerant. Zones 3–9.

GROWING GUIDELINES: Clumps get quite full with age and may flop open, leaving a bare center. Divide overgrown plants from spring to midsummer. Division is also an easy propagation method. Or take cuttings of non-flowering shoots in summer, or sow seed in spring or fall.

LANDSCAPE USES: Plant in formal borders, informal gardens, and rock gardens. Stonecrops are also good for mass plantings with shrubs.

COMPATIBLE COMPANIONS: Combine showy stonecrop with yarrows, shasta daisies (*Chrysanthemum* x *superbum*), purple coneflowers (*Echinacea* spp.), cranesbills (*Geranium* spp.), coreopsis (*Coreopsis* spp.), and ornamental grasses.

Sedum spurium   Crassulaceae

TWO-ROW SEDUM

Two-row sedum is an adaptable, low-growing perennial that makes a great edging or groundcover. The leaves age from green to red; the pink flowers bloom in summer.

DESCRIPTION: Two-row sedum is a tough groundcover with succulent, rounded leaves that have toothed edges. The leaves are clustered at the tips of the rubbery stems. Older leaves are deep red while younger growth is bright green. The starry, rose pink flowers are produced in summer. Plants grow from trailing, fibrous-rooted stems.

SEASON OF INTEREST: Summer bloom; year-round groundcover effect.

HEIGHT AND SPREAD: Height 2–6 inches (5–15 cm); width 1–2 feet (30–60 cm).

BEST SITE AND CLIMATE: Plant two-row sedum in average, sandy or loamy, well-drained soil in full sun or partial shade. Zones 3–8.

GROWING GUIDELINES: Divide overgrown plants in spring or fall. Propagate by division or take cuttings in summer.

LANDSCAPE USES: Plant two-row sedum as an edging for beds and borders or in rock gardens. It grows well in the tight crevices of rock walls. Use it as a groundcover on a dry bank or under high-branched trees.

COMPATIBLE COMPANIONS: Combine two-row sedum with evergreen shrubs such as junipers and cotoneaster. Plant it with showy flowers such as yarrows, rock cress (*Arabis* spp.), perennial candytuft (*Iberis sempervirens*), and basket-of-gold (*Aurinia saxatilis*).

Smilacina racemosa   Liliaceae

SOLOMON'S PLUME

Solomon's plume thrives in light to full shade; its leaves may turn brown in full sun. You'll enjoy the flowers in spring, foliage in summer, and berries in fall.

DESCRIPTION: Solomon's plume, also known as false Solomon's seal, is a showy woodland wildflower. The erect arching stems bear broad, glossy green leaves arranged like ascending stairs. Small, starry, creamy white flowers are borne in terminal, plume-like clusters. Red berries ripen in late summer. Plants grow from a thick, creeping rhizome.

SEASON OF INTEREST: Spring bloom. The foliage is attractive all season, and the berries are an asset in fall.

HEIGHT AND SPREAD: Height 2–4 feet (60–120 cm); width 2–3 feet (60–90 cm) or more.

BEST SITE AND CLIMATE: Plant in evenly moist, humus-rich, neutral to acid soil in light to full shade. Zones 3–8.

GROWING GUIDELINES: Divide the tangled rhizomes in spring or fall if plants overgrow their position. Propagate by division or sow fresh seed outdoors in fall. No serious pests or diseases.

LANDSCAPE USES: Use Solomon's plume in woodland gardens, along shaded walks, or as an underplanting for shrubs and flowering trees.

COMPATIBLE COMPANIONS: Combine Solomon's plume with hostas, bleeding hearts (*Dicentra* spp.), lungworts (*Pulmonaria* spp.), columbines (*Aquilegia* spp.), wildflowers, and ferns.

| *Solidago rigida* | Compositae | *Stachys byzantina* | Labiatae |

STIFF GOLDENROD

Don't blame the glorious goldenrods for your fall allergies! The real culprits are ragweeds, which produce the light, airborne pollen that causes hay fever.

DESCRIPTION: Stiff goldenrod is a showy wildflower with flattened clusters of bright yellow, fuzzy flowers on leafy stalks. The basal leaves are oval to lance-shaped and may reach 1 foot (30 cm) in length. The stem leaves are oval and decrease in size near the top of the stem. All the foliage is pale green and has soft hair. Plants grow from a crown with thick, fleshy roots.

SEASON OF INTEREST: Late summer and fall bloom. The foliage is attractive in summer and turns ruby red in fall. The seed heads are silvery.

HEIGHT AND SPREAD: Height 3–5 feet (90–150 cm); width 1–2 feet (30–60 cm).

BEST SITE AND CLIMATE: Plant in average, sandy or loamy, well-drained soil in full sun or light shade. Plants in rich soil produce weak, floppy growth. Zones 3–9.

GROWING GUIDELINES: Propagate by division in spring or after flowering, or take stem cuttings in early summer. Self-sown seedlings may appear.

LANDSCAPE USES: Plant stiff goldenrod in beds and borders, along walls and fences, or in meadows and prairies. The stiff, upright form and showy blooms make them suitable for formal settings as well.

COMPATIBLE COMPANIONS: Combine with fall flowers such as asters, chrysanthemums, anemones (*Anemone* spp.), sneezeweeds (*Helenium autumnale*), and ornamental grasses.

LAMB'S-EARS

Lamb's-ears spread quickly to form dense, broad clumps of tightly packed leaves. They are an excellent edging plant for growing along paths and walkways.

DESCRIPTION: Lamb's-ears are appealing groundcovers with felted, silvery leaves forming dense rosettes from a creeping, fibrous-rooted rhizome. The small, two-lipped, rose pink flowers are carried in whorls on woolly stems; they are secondary to the foliage.

SEASON OF INTEREST: Spring bloom; season-long foliage interest.

HEIGHT AND SPREAD: Height to 15 inches (37.5 cm) in flower, leaves 6–8 inches (15–20 cm) high. Plants 12–24 inches (30–60 cm) high.

BEST SITE AND CLIMATE: Grow in light, sandy or loamy, well-drained soil in full sun or light shade. Hot, humid weather causes leaves to brown, droop, and decay; heavy or soggy soil can lead to the whole plant rotting. Zones 4–8.

GROWING GUIDELINES: Divide in spring or fall to control spread or for propagation. Take cuttings in summer. In wet, humid weather, rot may occur. Cut back plants to remove the affected portions and improve air circulation. Proper siting in well-drained soil is the best defense.

LANDSCAPE USES: Plant lamb's-ears at the front of formal and informal gardens, along paths, in rock gardens, or atop rock walls.

COMPATIBLE COMPANIONS: Combine lamb's-ears with bearded irises, ornamental onions (*Allium* spp.), grasses, yuccas, sedums, and cranesbills (*Geranium* spp.).

CAROLINA LUPINE

Carolina lupine, also called Carolina bush pea or southern lupine, is lovely at the edge of an open woodland or with shrubs in lightly shaded wild gardens.

DESCRIPTION: Carolina lupine produces upright flower spikes atop stout stems clothed in three-parted gray-green leaves. Lemon yellow, pea-shaped flowers are tightly packed into 8–12-inch (20–30 cm) clusters. Plants grow from stout, fibrous-rooted crowns. Also known as *Thermopsis villosa*.

SEASON OF INTEREST: Late spring and early summer bloom. The fuzzy pods are attractive in winter.

HEIGHT AND SPREAD: Height 3–5 feet (90–150 cm); width 2–4 feet (60–120 cm).

BEST SITE AND CLIMATE: Grow in average to humus-rich, moist, acid soil in full sun to light shade. Plants are heat-tolerant. Zones 3–9.

GROWING GUIDELINES: Clumps seldom need division if you allow ample space at planting time. If foliage looks bad after bloom, cut it to the ground. Propagate by seed or by taking cuttings in early summer from sideshoots. Sow seed outdoors in fall, or sow indoors in early spring after soaking the seed in hot water for 12–24 hours.

LANDSCAPE USES: Plant toward the rear of a formal garden or in informal settings such as cottage gardens and meadows.

COMPATIBLE COMPANIONS: Combine Carolina lupine with peonies, willow blue star (*Amsonia tabernaemontana*), bee balm (*Monarda* spp.), garden phlox (*Phlox paniculata*), cranesbills (*Geranium* spp.), and other rounded or mounding plants.

FOAMFLOWER

Foamflowers spread by creeping stems to form broad mats that discourage weeds under shrubs and trees. Combine them with spring bulbs for a colorful spring show.

DESCRIPTION: Foamflowers are elegant woodland wildflowers with fuzzy flowers and rosettes of triangular, three-lobed, hairy leaves. The small, starry white flowers are borne in spike-like clusters. They are often tinged with pink. Plants grow from fibrous-rooted crowns and creeping stems.

SEASON OF INTEREST: Spring bloom. Plants form a dense groundcover that's attractive year-round in mild climates.

HEIGHT AND SPREAD: Height 6–10 inches (15–25 cm); width 12–24 inches (30–60 cm).

BEST SITE AND CLIMATE: Plant foamflowers in partial to full shade in evenly moist, humus-rich, slightly acid soil. Zones 3–8.

GROWING GUIDELINES: Divide plants in spring or fall to control their spread or for propagation. You can also sow seed outdoors in spring (leave it uncovered).

LANDSCAPE USES: Plant them in shade and woodland gardens, in rock gardens, or along paths.

COMPATIBLE COMPANIONS: Combine with bulbs, ferns, and wildflowers like fringed bleeding heart (*Dicentra eximia*) and bloodroot (*Sanguinaria canadensis*) as well as with hostas and irises.

OTHER SPECIES:
T. cordifolia var. *collina* is a clump-former with many pink-tinged flower spikes in each rosette.

Tradescantia x *andersoniana*   Commelinaceae

COMMON SPIDERWORT

Each flower of common spiderwort lasts only a day, but the clumps produce so many buds that you'll enjoy up to 2 months of spring to early-summer bloom.

DESCRIPTION: Spiderworts have 1–1½-inch (2.5–3.5 cm), satiny flowers that open in the morning and fade in the afternoon. They have three blue, purple, or white rounded flowers borne in clusters at the tips of the stems. The thick, succulent stems bear grass-like, light green foliage. Plants grow from thick, spidery roots.

SEASON OF INTEREST: Spring and early summer bloom.

HEIGHT AND SPREAD: Height 1–2 feet (30–60 cm); width 2 feet (60 cm).

BEST SITE AND CLIMATE: Plant spiderworts in moist but well-drained, average to rich soil in full sun or partial shade. Zones 3–9.

GROWING GUIDELINES: After flowering, plants tend to look shabby; cut them to the ground to encourage new growth. Plants in dry situations go dormant in summer. Divide in fall to renew overgrown clumps or to propagate cultivars. Self-sown seedlings often appear. No serious pests or diseases.

LANDSCAPE USES: Plant spiderworts in formal beds, informal gardens, cottage gardens, and meadows. Plants grow well in containers.

COMPATIBLE COMPANIONS: In informal and cottage gardens, combine common spiderwort with bellflowers (*Campanula* spp.), columbines (*Aquilegia* spp.), hostas, and ferns. In formal gardens, try it with tulips and spring-blooming perennials.

Tricyrtis formosana   Liliaceae

FORMOSA TOAD LILY

The creeping stems of toad lilies spread to form handsome clumps that seldom need division. Their curious flowers add interest to the late-summer and fall shade garden.

DESCRIPTION: Toad lilies have 1-inch (2.5 cm), upward-facing, purple-spotted flowers, with three petals and three petal-like sepals around a central column. The flowers are carried in the leaf axils on the upper one-third of the stem. The tall, arching stems are clothed in two-ranked, broadly lance-shaped, hairy leaves with prominent veins. Plants grow from thick, fibrous roots.

SEASON OF INTEREST: Late summer and fall bloom; the foliage is attractive throughout the season.

HEIGHT AND SPREAD: Height 2–3 feet (60–90 cm); width 1–3 feet (30–90 cm).

BEST SITE AND CLIMATE: Plant toad lilies in evenly moist, humus-rich soil in light to partial shade. Full sun will damage the foliage. Zones 4–9.

GROWING GUIDELINES: In Northern gardens, plants may be damaged by frost just as they begin blooming. For propagation, divide clumps in spring or remove shoots from the edge of the clump.

LANDSCAPE USES: Toad lily flowers are subtle and best used where you can appreciate them at close range. Plant them along a lightly shaded path or near the edge of a shade garden.

COMPATIBLE COMPANIONS: The stiff stems make an interesting accent in the garden. Large clumps are effective combined with astilbes, hostas, ferns, and other woodland plants.

Trollius x *cultorum*   Ranunculaceae

HYBRID GLOBEFLOWER

The glorious golden blooms of globeflowers add masses of color to spring gardens. These perennials need steady soil moisture to really look their best.

DESCRIPTION: Globeflowers are showy spring perennials with waxy, cup-shaped flowers. The petals are lacking, but yellow or orange petal-like sepals take their place. The deep green, palmately divided leaves have five to seven ragged leaflets. Plants grow from a fleshy-rooted crown.

SEASON OF INTEREST: Spring bloom. Plants may die back to the ground (go dormant) after flowering.

HEIGHT AND SPREAD: Height 2–3 feet (60–90 cm); basal rosettes 1–2 feet (30–60 cm) wide.

BEST SITE AND CLIMATE: Grow globeflowers in humus-rich, moist soil in full sun or partial shade. Plants are intolerant of dry soil and high night temperatures. Zones 3–6.

GROWING GUIDELINES: The clumps increase from slow-spreading roots to form many crowns. Divide them in early spring or fall for propagation. Or sow fresh seed outside as soon as it ripens; stored seed usually germinates poorly.

LANDSCAPE USES: Plant globeflowers in pond and streamside gardens or in beds and borders where the soil stays evenly moist.

COMPATIBLE COMPANIONS: Combine globeflowers with Siberian iris (*Iris sibirica*), cardinal flower (*Lobelia cardinalis*), lady's-mantle (*Alchemilla mollis*), and primroses. Plants may go dormant after flowering, so plant them with foliage plants such as hostas, ferns, and grasses to fill the void.

Tulipa kaufmanniana   Liliaceae

KAUFMANNIANA TULIP

Kaufmanniana tulips come in a range of colors, including pink, yellow, red, and white; most also have deep-colored blazes on the outside of the petals.

DESCRIPTION: Kaufmanniana tulips have starry flowers composed of three petals and three petal-like sepals. The leaves are broad, with wavy margins and pointed tips. They are sea green with dark brown stripes. Plants grow from true bulbs.

SEASON OF INTEREST: Early spring bloom. Plants die back to the ground (go dormant) after flowering.

HEIGHT AND SPREAD: Height 4–8 inches (10–20 cm); width 4–6 inches (10–15 cm). Established clumps may be 1 foot (30 cm) across.

BEST SITE AND CLIMATE: Plant in rich, moist but well-drained soil in full sun or light shade. Plants go dormant after flowering and can withstand considerable drought and shade. Zones 4–8.

GROWING GUIDELINES: Set bulbs out in fall, 3–5 inches (7.5–12.5 cm) deep and 5–6 inches (12.5–15 cm) apart. For propagation, lift and divide bulbs as the foliage withers; replant immediately.

LANDSCAPE USES: Choose Kaufmanniana tulips for the front of the garden, along a woodland path, or in a rock garden. They also grow well in pots.

COMPATIBLE COMPANIONS: Combine Kaufmanniana tulips with primroses, shooting stars (*Dodecatheon* spp.), lungworts (*Pulmonaria* spp.), sweet woodruff (*Galium odoratum*), and ferns. In beds and borders, plant them with columbines (*Aquilegia* spp.), rock cress (*Arabis* spp.), and candytuft (*Iberis* spp.), as well as with other bulbs.

| *Uvularia grandiflora* | Liliaceae | *Verbascum chaixii* | Scrophulariaceae |

GREAT MERRYBELLS

NETTLE-LEAVED MULLEIN

The nodding flowers of great merrybells look wonderful with other spring wildflowers and bulbs. The leaves are attractive in summer and turn bright yellow in fall.

DESCRIPTION: Great merrybells is a graceful wildflower with nodding, bell-shaped, lemon-yellow flowers. Each flower has three petals and three petal-like sepals that twist in the middle. The main stalk pierces the blade of the gray-green leaves. Plants grow from rhizomes with brittle white roots.

SEASON OF INTEREST: Spring bloom; the foliage makes an attractive season-long groundcover.

HEIGHT AND SPREAD: Height 1–1½ (30–45 cm) feet; width 1–2 feet (30–60 cm).

BEST SITE AND CLIMATE: Plant great merrybells in moist, humus-rich soil in partial to full shade. Spring sun is important for bloom, but summer shade is mandatory. Zones 3–8.

GROWING GUIDELINES: Merrybells spread to form tight, attractive clumps. When flowers fade, the gray-green foliage expands to form a leafy groundcover. Divide plants in early spring or fall. No serious pests or diseases.

LANDSCAPE USES: Plant merrybells in woodland gardens and shaded rock gardens or as a groundcover under shrubs and trees.

COMPATIBLE COMPANIONS: Combine great merrybells with wildflowers such as bloodroot (*Sanguinaria canadensis*), wild bleeding heart (*Dicentra eximia*), and wild gingers (*Asarum* spp.). Ferns and hostas are also good companions.

Nettle-leaved mullein produces clumps of crinkled green leaves and tall stems topped with spikes of yellow flowers. They are an excellent contrast to mounded perennials.

DESCRIPTION: Nettle-leaved mullein has thick flower spikes and stout stems clothed in broadly oval, pointed leaves. The small, five-petaled, yellow flowers are tightly packed into dense clusters. Plants form tight rosettes from fibrous-rooted crowns that overwinter and form next year's bloom stalk.

SEASON OF INTEREST: Summer bloom; the foliage is attractive in spring and summer.

HEIGHT AND SPREAD: Height 2–3 feet (60–90 cm); width 1–2 feet (30–60 cm).

BEST SITE AND CLIMATE: Plant in average, well-drained soil in full sun or light shade. Zones 4–8.

GROWING GUIDELINES: Established plants spread slowly and seldom need division. For propagation, take root cuttings in early spring or dig and move young self-sown seedlings.

LANDSCAPE USES: Grow in the front or middle of formal borders, in rock gardens, or in meadow plantings. They also grow well in containers.

COMPATIBLE COMPANIONS: In borders, combine nettle-leaved mullein with fine-textured perennials such as thread-leaved coreopsis (*Coreopsis verticillata*), cranesbills (*Geranium* spp.), and meadow rues (*Thalictrum* spp.). In informal gardens, grow them with mounded plants such as catmints (*Nepeta* spp.) and ornamental grasses.

CULTIVARS: The variety *album* has white flowers with purple centers.

| *Veronica spicata* | Scrophulariaceae | *Yucca filamentosa* | Liliaceae |

SPIKE SPEEDWELL

Spike speedwell grows slowly to form neat clumps. It is an excellent companion for ornamental grasses and a wide variety of other summer-blooming perennials.

DESCRIPTION: Spike speedwell has pointed flower clusters atop leafy stems. The small, two-lipped, pink, blue, or white flowers are tightly packed into erect spikes. The opposite leaves are oval to oblong and clothed in soft hairs. Plants grow from fibrous-rooted crowns.

SEASON OF INTEREST: Summer bloom; the foliage is attractive all season.

HEIGHT AND SPREAD: Height 1–3 feet (30–90 cm); width 1½–2½ feet (45–75 cm).

BEST SITE AND CLIMATE: Plant spike speedwell in average to rich, moist but well-drained soil in full sun or light shade. Zones 3–8.

GROWING GUIDELINES: To encourage continued bloom or control rangy growth, cut stems back after flowering; plants will produce fresh growth. Divide overgrown plants in spring or fall. Propagate by division, or take stem cuttings in late spring or early summer; remove the flower buds.

LANDSCAPE USES: Choose spike speedwell for formal and cottage gardens where the upright spikes add lift to flat plantings. Use them in rock gardens, meadows, and other informal settings, or grow them in containers.

COMPATIBLE COMPANIONS: Combine speedwells with other summer-blooming perennials that need good drainage, including yarrows, catmints (*Nepeta* spp.), and sundrops (*Oenothera* spp.).

ADAM'S-NEEDLE

The spiky, evergreen clumps of Adam's-needles add a dramatic accent to any planting. The showy clusters of white summer blooms are a bonus!

DESCRIPTION: Adam's-needles produce rosettes of sword-shaped, blue-green leaves. The nodding, creamy white flowers have three petals and three petal-like sepals that form a bell. They grow from a woody crown with fleshy roots.

SEASON OF INTEREST: Summer bloom; the evergreen foliage rosettes provide year-round interest.

HEIGHT AND SPREAD: Height up to 15 feet (4.5 m) in flower, although 5 feet (1.5 m) is more usual. Leaves can be 1–3 feet (30–90 cm) long; clumps are 3–6 feet (90–180 cm) wide.

BEST SITE AND CLIMATE: Plant Adam's-needles in average to rich, well-drained soil in full sun or light shade. Zones 3–10.

GROWING GUIDELINES: After flowering, the main crown dies, but new sideshoots keep the plants growing. For propagation, remove young, rooted sideshoots from the clump in spring or fall.

LANDSCAPE USES: Grow as accent plantings in dry borders, rock gardens, or seaside gardens. These plants also grow well in pots and raised planters.

COMPATIBLE COMPANIONS: Contrast the stiff foliage with soft or delicate plants such as lamb's-ears (*Stachys byzantina*), sedums, sundrops (*Oenothera* spp.), and verbenas (*Verbena* spp.). Plant them with other drought-tolerant plants such as yarrows, pinks (*Dianthus* spp.), catmints (*Nepeta* spp.), and sages (*Salvia* spp.).

USDA Plant

Hardiness Zone Map

The map that follows shows the United States and Canada divided into 10 zones. Each zone is based on a 10°F (5.6°C) difference in average annual minimum temperature. Some areas are considered too high in elevation for plant cultivation and so are not assigned to any zone. There are also island zones that are warmer or cooler than surrounding areas because of differences in elevation; they have been given a zone different from the surrounding areas. Many large urban areas are in a warmer zone than the surrounding land.

Plants grow best within an optimum range of temperatures. The range may be wide for some species and narrow for others. Plants also differ in their ability to survive frost and in their sun or shade requirements.

The zone ratings indicate conditions where designated plants will grow well and not merely survive. Refer to the map to find out which zone you are in. In "Perennials for Every Purpose," starting on page 86, you'll find recommendations for the plants that grow best in your zone.

Many plants may survive in zones warmer or colder than their recommended zone range. Remember that other factors, including wind, soil type, soil moisture and drainage capability, humidity, snow, and winter sunshine, may have a great effect on growth.

Average annual minimum temperature (°F/°C)

Zone 1	Below -50°F/-45°C	Zone 6	0° to -10°F/-18° to -23°C
Zone 2	-40° to -50°F/-40° to -45°C	Zone 7	10° to 0°F/-12° to -18°C
Zone 3	-30° to -40°F/-34° to -40°C	Zone 8	20° to 10°F/-7° to -12°C
Zone 4	-20° to -30°F/-29° to -34°C	Zone 9	30° to 20°F/-1° to -7°C
Zone 5	-10° to -20°F/-23° to -29°C	Zone 10	40° to 30°F/4° to -1°C

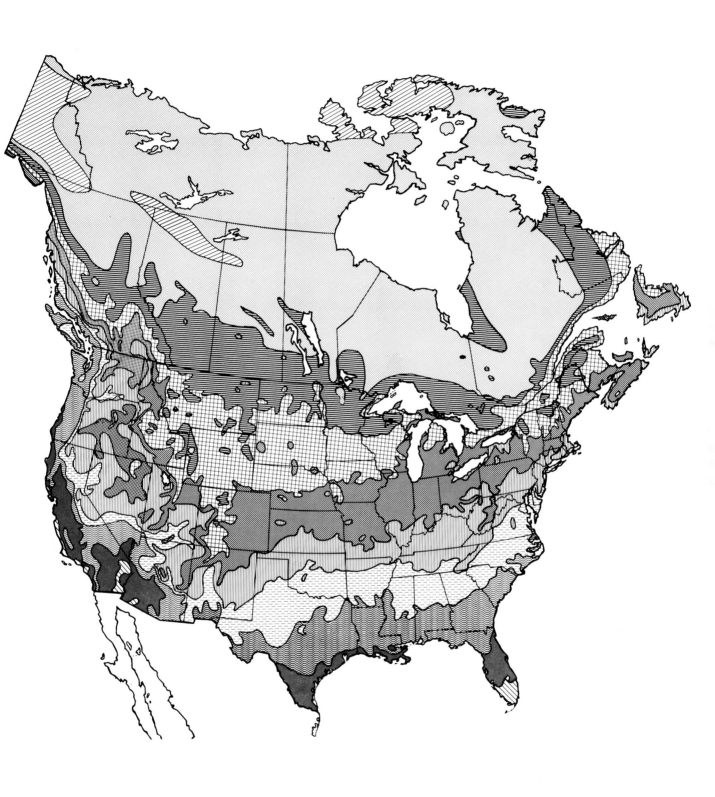

The numbers in bold indicate main entries, and the numbers in italic indicate illustrations.

ACKNOWLEDGMENTS

Photo Credits

Heather Angel: page 94 (right).

Ardea London: photographer A. P. Paterson: page 136 (right).

A–Z Botanical Collection: page 100 (right); photographer Anthony Cooper: page 116 (left); photographer Derek Gould: pages 107 (left) and 111 (left); photographer Peter Jousiffe: page 120 (right); photographer Geoff Kidd: page 143 (right); photographer Malcolm Richards: page 130 (left).

Gillian Beckett: pages 74 (left), 94 (left), 95 (left), 96 (left), 99 (right), 102 (right), 111 (right), 115 (right), 118 (left), 119 (left), 134 (right), 137 (right), 142 (left), 142 (right), 150 (right), 151 (right), and 152 (right).

Bruce Coleman: photographer Jules Cowan: page 48 (bottom left); photographer Eric Crichton: page 45 (top).

Thomas Eltzroth: pages 73 (bottom), 93 (right), 95 (right), 106 (right), 119 (right), 125 (left), 128 (right), 131 (left), 131 (right), 132 (right), 145 (left), 146 (right), 150 (left), 153 (left), and 153 (right).

EWA Photo Library: page 66 (bottom).

Derek Fell: pages 50, 59, 62 (right), 66 (top), 72 (bottom right), 89 (right), 93 (left), 101 (right), and 138 right.

Garden Picture Library: photographer Lynne Brotchie: page 44 (top); photographer Linda Burgess: page 46 (bottom); photographer John Glover: page 57; photographer Michael Howes: pages 53 (top) and 84; photographer Roger Hyam: page 115 (left); photographer Michelle Lamontagne: page 78 (top left); photographer Marianne Majerus: page 70 (left); photographer Clive Nichols: page 52 (bottom); photographer Howard Rice: page 82 (right); photographer Stephen Robson: page 82 (left); photographer Gary Rogers: back cover (center); photographer J. S. Sira: page 113 (left); photographer Brigitte Thomas: pages 43 and 65; photographer Mel Watson: page 52 (top); photographer Steven Wooster: page 73 (top).

Holt Studios International: photographer Nigel Cattlin: pages 15 (bottom center), 15 (bottom right), 48 (top) 48 (bottom right), and 72 (top right); photographer Jorgen Dielenschneider: page 15 (bottom left); page 49 (top); photographer Rosemary Mayer: pages 20 (top right) and 136 (left); photographer Primrose Peacock: pages 49 (bottom right), 90 (left), and 126 (left).

Andrew Lawson: pages 6, 31 (top left), 63 (bottom), and 118 (right).

S & O Mathews: pages 8, 11 (right), 46 (top), 61 (bottom), 64 (right), 67 (bottom), 74 (bottom right), 74 (top right), 78 (top right), 78 (bottom left), 78 (bottom right), 80 (bottom), 88 (left), 98 (left), 105 (left), 108 (right), 110 (left), 116 (right), 121 (left), 121 (right), 123 (left), 124 (left), 124 (right), 125 (right), 129 (right), 133 (left), 133 (right), 138 (left), 140 (right), 141 (right), 146 (left), 147 (left), 147 (right), 151 (left), and 152 (left).

Clive Nichols: back cover (top), pages 1, 2, 3, 4–5, 7 (top left), 11 (left), 12, 14, 16 (bottom left), 16 (top right), 17 (top left), 17 (bottom left), 19 (top), 20 (bottom left), 20 (bottom right), 22, 24, 25, 26 (top), 26 (bottom), 27, 28, 29 (top), 29 (bottom), 30 (top), 30 (bottom), 31 (top center), 31 (top right), 31 (bottom left), 32 (top), 33, 34 (bottom left), 34 (bottom right), 34 (top), 36, 38, 39, 40, 41 (top), 41 (bottom), 42 (top left), 42 (bottom right), 44 (bottom), 45 (bottom), 47 (top), 53 (bottom), 54, 56 (left), 56 (right), 58, 61 (top), 64 (left), 67 (top), 68, 70 (right), 71 (left), 72 (left), 76, 77 (top), 77 (bottom), 80 (top), 81 (top), 83 (right), 85, 86, 90 (right), 98 (right), 108 (left), 127 (left), 128 (left), 141 (left), 143 (left), 144 (left), 148 (left), and 148 (right).

Jerry Pavia: endpapers, pages 62 (left), 83 (left), 101 (left), 102 (left), 103 (right), 106 (left), 109 (right), 112 (left), 113 (right), 117 (right), 120 (left), 127 (right), 134 (left), 135 (right), 139 (left), and 110 (right).

Joanne Pavia: pages 122 (right) and 132 (left).

Philippe Perdereau: pages 35, 71 (right) and 109 (left).

Photos Horticultural: front cover, back cover (bottom), pages 7 (right), 17 (bottom right), 18, 19 (bottom), 32 (bottom), 51 (left), 51 (right), 60, 63 (top), 75, 81 (bottom), 89 (left), 91 (left), 91 (right), 92 (left), 96 (right), 105 (right), 112 (right), 114 (left), and 130 (right).

Harry Smith Collection: pages 88 (right), 92 (right), 97 (left), 97 (right), 100 (left), 103 (left), 104 (left), 104 (right), 107 (right), 114 (right), 117 (left), 123 (right), 126 (right), 129 (left), 135 (left), 137 (left), 139 (right), 144 (right), 145 (right), 149 (left), and 149 (right).

Weldon Russell: pages 7 (bottom left), 16 (center), 42 (top right), 49 (bottom left), 99 (left), 122 (left), and 140 (left).